Patterns of the Western Mind

A Reformed Christian Perspective

Patterns of the Western Mind

A Reformed Christian Perspective

Second Revised Edition

by John H. Kok

Dordt College Press

Sioux Center, Iowa

Printed in the United Sates of America.

Dordt College Press
498 Fourth Avenue NE
Sioux Center, IA 51250

ISBN: 0-932914-41-1

Cover design by Monique Sliedrecht

The first edition of this book was published under the same title in South Africa by the Potchefstroom University for Christian Higher Education in 1996.

Portraits on pages 180, 182, 183, and 184 are reproduced from Jacob Klapwijk's *Kijken naar kopstukken* (Amsterdam: Buijten & Schipperheijn, 1987).

In recognition of their quiet but firm support
of Christians, both free and persecuted,
who with them seek to serve the cause of Christ,
this book is gratefully dedicated to
Jan and Greetje Breukelaar,
living today in The Netherlands.

TABLE OF CONTENTS

PREFACE

In order to get the reality of time into perspective, I sometimes remind myself that centuries have gone by with, relatively
speaking, nothing much happening. For example, the children
of Jacob in Egypt did not hear from their God much worth writing about for four centuries. Prior to Christ's birth, things once
again had been "just sort of normal" for hundreds of years. And
so when God finally spoke and moved in a mighty way, it was
clearly time to listen: to hear and to do the will of God. But the
same is true today, even though many things are happening
quickly and time just keeps ticking away. This little book seeks
to take a gander at the whole, while taking God at his word and
keying in on the thoughtful responses of people from Thales the
Greek to Rorty the American concerning foundational matters.

When reflecting on "the western mind," I am often
reminded of drops in a bucket. My thoughts about that reality
are obviously not much more than just one of those drops. Some
today want to make the case that all drops are created equal, but
that is definitely not the case when it comes to reflecting on the
western mind and what it is about. In the pages that follow I
articulate first a general approach to the nature of things in the
light of God's word and his mighty acts in history. Then I sketch
some heartfelt, history-making, theory-laden responses in the
West to the Word and works of God over the course of time.
And finally, standing on some of the shoulders of those who
have gone before in the name of Christ, I explain the sense of
some basic thought patterns that are in line with Scripture and
only in that sense deserve the name "christian." What the name
"reformed" means in this context, I invite the reader to discover.

Scripture is useful for refuting error, for guiding people's
lives, and for teaching them to be upright—for the Way, the
Truth, and the Life it reveals is the only way to the Father. But
Scripture is not philosophical. It does not provide instant access
to philosophic truth nor supply its readers with philosophic

answers to philosophic questions. All the same, the truth it does reveal and record is other than and a cut above any other "revelation" that has the last word in people's lives and that defines and informs the framework of basic beliefs about things that has become second nature to them. Philosophies are philosophical and are expressive of a person's worldview, of a *Weltanschauung*, many of which are not in line with Scripture. Ill-founded convictions will usually define an ill-fated course; however many right turns and respectable insights are had along the way. When ideas and beliefs inconsistent with the biblical witness are uncritically incorporated in the life of the christian community, problems are inevitable, also when it comes to doing philosophy. But don't assume that biblical insights about the world will automatically reverberate with coherence throughout the edifice of one's thought. There is no shortcut for those who know the God of Scripture around the work it takes to bring biblical insight to bear simply and profoundly upon the most basic of problems and intuitions. The theoretical solutions and covenantly consistent alternatives that result from the effort may well be different from those arising from an unregenerate heart, but one's philosophizing, if it is going to be that, will be an investigation and account of the diversity, dimensions, and interrelatedness of the cosmos; a response to foundational questions raised in the course of living. Deductions and derivations from Scripture just won't do.

This book originated a number of times. Most recently it was written and revised for an undergraduate, college-level, general education course in foundational perspectives that I have been teaching since 1983 at Dordt College. This most recent edition includes a number of revisions, among which is an expanded section on recent "postmodern" developments. A critical reading by Calvin College philosopher Lee Hardy helped and challenged me to hone numerous passages. Some students over the years also have not hesitated to indicate some of the rough places that needed to be made plain, and I have tried to do that. The text, on that score, is my own and I take full responsibility for it. At the same time, the readers should know that the second unit is a revision of an earlier syllabus prepared in the late 1960s by John Van Dyk, also of Dordt College, who most graciously allowed me to edit, revise, or expand it with a free hand. His work, in turn, was loosely based on a Dutch manuscript of a syllabus most recently revised in 1956 by a professor of philosophy at the Free University in The Netherlands, Dirk Vollenhoven, and a book published around that time, also in Dutch, by J. M. Spier, *Van Thales tot Sartre*. I will mention the name of Vollenhoven again, because much of what I am discussing in the first and third units leans heavily on another syllabus written by him, the first drafts of which go back to the late 1920s! In other words, between these covers are some vintage reformed reflections in renewed guise.

Sioux Center, Iowa USA
Christmas 1997

INTRODUCTION

I. A.
Western Thought:
What is that?

For a beginning student there is something abundantly vague about thinking about thought, let alone about Western thought. What do you study when you study thoughts? What is "the Western mind"? Other subjects, such as grammar or biology, seem to point to a clear and distinct area of inquiry. After all, everybody knows that languages have rules for correct grammar or that there are such things as plants and animals. But what is "Western thought" all about? Of what is the history of Western thought a history?

If we were to survey a randomly selected group of scholars who call themselves "philosophers," we would find that opinions differ widely. Interestingly, they would also differ as to what they were about, about what philosophy is. My hunch is that most nonphilosophizing types would not be surprised to hear that philosophers disagree on what it's all about. After all, what good are the convoluted arguments and hyper-abstractions of philosophers anyway? And yet the self-reflective comments of many philosophers and most "thinkers" are revealing and sometimes even make some sense.

For some the main concern of philosophy is "to question and understand very common ideas that all of us use every day without thinking about them" (Thomas Nagel); for others the most important problem of philosophy is "to give a general description of the whole Universe" (G. E. Moore). For the famous British philosopher Bertrand Russell, philosophy is a "no man's land" somewhere in between theology and science. Russell explains:

Like theology, it consists of speculations on matters as to which definite knowledge has, so far, been unascertainable; but like science, it appeals to human reason rather than to authority, whether that of tradition or that of revelation. All *definite* knowledge—so I should contend—belongs to science; all *dogma* as to what surpasses definite knowledge belongs to theology. But between theology and science there is a No Man's Land, exposed to attack from both sides; this No Man's Land is philosophy. (xiii)

And for the Roman Catholic Jacques Maritain, philosophy is "essentially a disinterested activity, directed toward truth [that is] loved for its own sake, not a utilitarian activity for the sake of power over things." No wonder an introductory course in philosophy at one university can differ radically from a similarly titled course at another institution. While at times and in places there may be a majority opinion, there is no general agreement among philosophers about philosophy's place and task. The spectrum ranges all the way from those who see its task as little more than solving logical puzzles to those who attempt to construct grand systems of thought that will explain everything there is to explain.

That there are different views about what philosophy is and about what philosophers ought to be doing is as such no reason for being discouraged. This labyrinth of definitions reflects a deeper problem. To a certain extent these differences are rooted in historical development and traditions. Hence one answer to the question "What do historians of thought do?" is this: they try to trace historical developments in order to discover why people differ about so many things, including the nature of thought or of philosophy. This, indeed, is one task that this survey sets before itself (see Unit II). But this lack of consensus is due to more than the historical influence of bygone philosophers. People's basic beliefs are just as much an influence. The place and task that philosophy is said to have is in many ways determined by beliefs that are neither philosophic nor even scientific.

Bertrand Russell's definition of philosophy is a case in point. Inherent to his circumscription of philosophy is the contestable belief that theology consists of speculations and lacks a knowledge of what is certain. He also is assuming that the only authority that science listens to is human reason—an assumption that few today, christian or not, would be willing to grant. And, of course, some Christians would want to differ with his dismissing what one knows from Scripture when one turns to pursue scientific activity. Russell also claims that all definite knowledge belongs to science. If that were the case, then either knowing we belong in life and in death to Jesus Christ is scientific knowledge—which it is not—or, because some of the things we know most definitely are matters of faith, Russell is confused on this point. That Jesus Christ has fully paid for our sins and set us free from the tyranny of the devil is definite for Christians, but not something you have to go to seminary to come to know. So, what are we left with if we disagree with Russell's understanding of theology, science, definite knowledge, and the place of human reason?

Someone with a marxist worldview is going to define what philosophy should concern itself with in a way that is different from someone whose basic beliefs about things are rooted in the capitalistic religion of the survival of the fittest. Worldviews contribute to different perspectives on facts, values, and events. That is one reason why we will also briefly discuss the nature of worldviews and the content of a biblical worldview in particular. The ultimate criterion, however, will prove to be whether or not people in their thinking and theoretical activities reckon and are in line with what God has revealed in Scripture (see Unit III).

The pages that follow build on the insights and contours of a scriptural tradition of everyday living and theorizing that has been articulated during the last hundred years or so and the biblically informed worldview in which it is rooted. In doing so, this book also takes a stand with respect to the history of Western thought that is different from most. I will be using Western "thought" and "philosophy" synonymously. We will tentatively define the reality to which they refer as the theoretical investigation and account of the diversity, dimensions, and interrelatedness of the cosmos. To show how and why this is a worthy definition is also the task of this survey.

I. B.
Ontology, Anthropology, and Epistemology: It's all Greek to me!

Although the stated definition and task of theoretical thought generally, and philosophy in particular, will become more understandable as we proceed, some general observations at the outset will not be out of place. Let's begin with an analogy.

Scholars, thinkers, and scientists such as theologians, philosophers, aestheticians, economists, linguists, sociologists, psychologists, physicists, mathematicians, and so on can be compared to a group of geographers. Let's say, for example, that theologians are the geographers studying Michigan, linguists are the geographers studying New York, physicists are the geographers studying Wyoming, and so on. Each one of the various sciences concentrates on a particular area. Now we ask, what kind of geographer would the philosopher be? The answer is that philosophers differ from the others in that their field of investigation would not be any one single area, but the whole picture of how all the states are positioned in relation to each other. The philosopher has the task of drawing the map of the entire country. The focus is not so much on this or that detail, but on the way the details constitute an interrelated and interconnected whole. Pervasive and recurrent realities also fall under the philosopher's purview. We can begin to grasp this interest in wholeness, contexts, and relationships by looking at three basic problem areas: ontology, anthropology, and epistemology.

The term "ontology" derives from Greek words that mean "the study of being" or "the study of that which is." Ontology investigates the structure of reality as a whole. For example, if we ask a philosopher, "What is reality?" and he answers, "It is a composite of mind and matter," then we have asked an ontological question and received an ontological answer. Other kinds of ontological questions: Did the cosmos, the world as a whole, come into being or has it always been? Is reality essentially orderly or chaotic? Is it basically one or is it a collection of minute parts? Is there one fundamental element in the universe of which all others are manifestations? Or are there two? What counts as real? Are numbers and concepts real, or are only physical things real? What is the difference between appearance and reality? What is reality, ultimately?

Ontological questions are commonly called metaphysical questions. We prefer the term "ontology" to "metaphysics" largely because metaphysics as it is practiced today is still deeply entrenched in an aristotelian tradition, which itself requires critical examination. Aristotle, one of the greatest of the ancient Greek philosophers, wrote an untitled book on "being," "substance," and similar concepts of dubious merit. After his death, the writings of Aristotle were collected in a book. His writings about tangible reality were placed in a chapter called *Physics*, and the chapter on "being" and "substance" was placed *after* the one on physics. Hence the name "*meta*physics," which means "that which comes after the physics" (*ta meta ta physika*). Thereafter, the word "metaphysics" has come to refer to the study of the basic constituency of reality.

The term "anthropology" is also derived from the Greek language. Literally it means "the study of man." There are, of course, many branches of inquiry that study human beings. For example, a psychology that knows its limits studies the sensitive and emotional aspects of man. Medicine deals with health and man's biotic and physical structure. Aesthetics will deal with other facets crucial to being human, like play and imagination. Philosophical anthropology, however, like ontology, is interested in totality and wholeness and, therefore, examines being human as a whole. Various anthropological questions are these: What is the relationship between body and soul? Is a person basically a composite of mind and matter, or can we better be described as a bundle of chemical and physical elements and properties? What is the relation between man's artistic and emotional dimensions? When it comes right down to it, are human beings simply highly developed animals?

We must be careful to distinguish philosophical anthropology from cultural anthropology, which is usually included as a branch of sociology and investigates cultural development of human beings. The late Margaret Mead, for example, was a famous American anthropologist who with her studies of Polynesian peoples did much to popularize cultural anthropology.

The third of our three terms, "epistemology," is derived from Greek words meaning "the study of knowledge." Epistemology examines the nature of knowledge and the ways in which we obtain it. Simply translated, Plato's epistemology is his theory of knowledge, his perspective on the nature of knowing. Examples of epistemological questions are these: How do we come to know? What is knowledge? Is there a difference

between knowing and believing? If so, what is it? Is scientific
knowledge a special kind of knowledge or a better kind of
knowledge? What is the structure of logical reasoning as compared with intuition? How can we be sure of our knowledge?
What determines truth and falsity? And so on.

These three problem areas are interrelated. Plato's view of
what it means to be real influences his view of what it means to
be human. What being human means to you will affect your
understanding of what it means to know and to believe. Likewise, what one knows and believes in, as well as one's sense of
what knowledge and belief are, will influence the convictions
one holds about what it means to be. In other words, these problems areas can be distinguished, but they are never separately
operative. Life remains of one piece even though we cannot
grasp all of it in one glance.

For Christians this interrelationship is not as scary as it may
first appear. Christians all have a starting point they can count
on—a *pou sto*, a "Here I stand, I can do no otherwise"—a firm
place from which to begin. By having the same starting point I
do not mean to suggest that every Christian comes to wonder or
theorize about the same things for the same reasons. Nor will it
be that they come to embrace the same theories. Some may
come to ask these kinds of basic questions after being moved
initially by social injustice or personal suffering or changing
times. Maybe the need to deal with foundational issues was
sparked by a moving lecture or interesting class in high school,
or possibly by the awe that a pristine landscape or a modern ma-
chine can inspire. Nor does their similar starting point in the
covenantal faithfulness of the creator God to whom we and our
world belong require Christians to try to begin or end their
theorizing by seeing things from God's point of view. Wanting
to know as God knows was Satan's lure and the downfall of
Adam and Eve. Hope can only be had in Jesus Christ, the image
of the invisible God, who in his birth, in his teachings, in his
death, and in his resurrection set things straight again.

All Christians who confess that the God of Scripture is the
beginning and the end, the alpha and the omega, know that he is
faithful, that his love is steadfast, and that everything is subject
to his laws and therefore owes obedience to him. It's the fear of
the Lord that is the beginning of wisdom and the reality of the

covenant that allows Christians, at least in principle, to see reality as it really is.

At the same time, boasting in God all day long (Psalm 44:8) is one thing; to boast forever about one's theory is another. There is not a one to one connection between divine witness and human theorizing. Christians cannot simply read off a christian philosophy or psychology from the pages of Scripture. There are a number of theoretical options possibly compatible with what Christians in faith know to be the case that we need to explore and assess. It would be inappropriate, given our finite and fallible state, to pull rank and claim that one of these options obviously flows directly from Scripture. What is clear is that we must "See to it that no one takes [us] captive through hollow and deceptive philosophy, which depends on human tradition and the basic principles of this world rather than on Christ" (Colossians 2:8). Nor should we be fooled into despair: "Christian" (philosophy) does not spell "perfect" (theorizing). When it comes to christian art and christian songs and christian journalism and christian philosophy, as Calvin Seerveld writes in *Rainbows for the Fallen World*:

> "Christian" does not spell "sinless." "Christian" means that "the lordship of Jesus Christ as revealed in the Bible leads the way and marks the act or product with the holy spirit of compassionate judgment." Human cultivating ... that ranges as far and wide as creaturely diversity and has a cohering center to it that holds together and enriches with saving grace whatever comes under its influence is "christian culture." (182)

"Christian philosophy," then, is not a contradiction in terms. The word "philosophy," feared by too many, comes from two simple Greek words: *sophia*, ordinarily translated as "wisdom," and *philo*, having to do with "love or yearning for." Hence, the term literally means "love of wisdom." It was probably first coined by the Greek thinker Pythagoras (c. 582-507 B.C.). But the *sophos* that he knew and yearned for was of a particular stripe and not the wisdom of which the psalmist speaks.

For the Greek mind, wherever human intelligence can be exercised, there is room for *sophia*. The skilled carpenter, knowing how everything fits together, was said to have *sophos*. Poets, too, like Homer and his predecessors, claiming to know what the gods knew, were said to have it as well. What Pythagoras

wanted was to know how *it all* fit together. He was convinced
that intellectual knowledge based on disciplined human contemplation (the eating of beans, for example, was prohibited at
his school) would give him and his disciples a god's eye view of
the world. Starting with the hypotenuse of a right triangle, he
was convinced that everything can quite literally be *figured out*,
for everything *is* number and its orderliness is *rational*. Mathematics, and not the fear of the Lord, is here the beginning of
what Pythagoras, and many in his stead, took to be "wisdom."
And because numbers and ratios are certain, eternally ordered,
and unchanging, he even thought this wisdom to be divine.

As we embark on this survey it is important to keep in
mind that the very best that philosophy can offer is human wisdom. For the Christian, the activity and results of human
thinking may never have the last word. The most they may have
to contribute is just a word. It is God and his word that has the
last word in everything. To honor that fact is indeed the beginning of wisdom.

I. C.
A Thetical-Critical Method

If you would consult the dictionary, it would tell you that
"method" comes from the Greek word *methodus*, which means a
going after, pursuit, investigation (from *meta* "after" + *hodos* "a
way"). If someone asks you about your method, she is wondering, "How are you going to proceed?" given some problem or
question.

Assuming for the moment that philosophy involves a theoretical investigation and account of the diversity, dimensions,
and inter-relatedness of the cosmos, one might well ask how are
Christians to proceed in investigating this cosmos. Interestingly
enough, asking this question shows that we are already "on the
way." By accepting the word "cosmos" we assume that the universe is a harmonious and ordered whole. That understanding,
as opposed to "chaos," is what "cosmos" means. And many people, though not everyone, will agree: our world is an ordered
whole; there is some rhyme or reason for everything. But anyone who claims something is ordered must also have some notion as to where that order came from, that is, as to who or what
is responsible for this ordering. One thing that distinguishes

Christians from non-Christians is their answer to this question. People who believe the Bible know that the cosmos is creation, the result of God's creating activity. It is God who orders the cosmos. But that leads to another question: How are these two related? What is the relationship between God and the cosmos? We should pause here a moment to note two things. First of all, answering one question often involves asking and answering other questions. In order to answer the question about our method of doing philosophy, we may well have to make an initial "detour," via other questions and answers, in order to clarify a number of contextual issues before we can answer our original question in a clear and succinct manner. Second, no one can ask questions without making some fundamental assumptions. Any question presupposes, that is, takes for granted, many things that remain, at least for the moment, unquestioned. Remember Russell's description of philosophy as a no man's land. In fact, when listening to other people's questions, it is very important to have at least some understanding of those unstated and unquestioned *presuppositions* which lie at the basis of those questions—so to speak, some knowledge of what, for them, "goes without saying."

But now, how do we go about answering our own questions? How can a Christian best proceed when trying to define his or her position on some issue? Standard operating procedure often finds us proceeding by defining our position, who we are and what we are about, in terms of what we reject. That is to say, we often define our position *negatively*. For example, "I disagree with this..., I can't accept that..., I am not comfortable with that suggestion." Or, "To be a Reformed Christian means you don't..., you keep away from..., and you try not to...." Sometimes you just might not know any better way of identifying your position than to distance yourself from what is not yours. But sooner or later what you will need is a *positive* articulation of your position. A more specific example may clarify what I mean by "proceeding negatively."

A very common way for Christians to answer the question, "What is the relationship between God and cosmos?" is as follows. If you believe the Bible, you know that God is *transcendent*, that is, he is above and beyond the limits of creation. God transcends the cosmos and rules as sovereign in majesty and might.

But you also know that God is *immanent*, that is, he works and is active within creation. If he wasn't, providence would be mechanical and our prayers of petition, for example, would, by definition, be to no avail. God loves the world and cares for it; he lives within us and among us.

But now, if you have to come to some conclusion on this matter, if you want to describe Christianity's position with respect to this question—that God is both transcendent and immanent—what then? Reformed Christians are obviously not deists. Deists acknowledge God's transcendence, but reject any notion of his immanence. They maintain that God, in the beginning, created this most beautiful and rationally ordered world and set everything in motion. But he then stepped back to let the world "run its course" according to the unchanging laws of nature and without further divine interference. This is obviously not in line with Scripture. At the same time, we are not pantheists. Pantheists believe that God is everything or that everything is god; that God and the world are so entwined that god has no separate existence or personality. This can't be right either. Where does that leave us but suspended in the "middle" between these two "extremes"? (For more on this "golden mean" approach, see the second quotation from Aristotle on page 58.) Each pole emphasizes, one-sidedly, an important truth. Pantheism makes an absolute out of God's immanence; deism, an absolute out of God's transcendence. And so, many Christians, in their attempt to ride the line between deism and pantheism, come to describe their position as "theism": God is greater than his creation and may not be identified with what he has made, and yet he constantly works within it.

Don't get me wrong. I think all Bible-believing Christians acknowledge that God is both sovereign and personal, both present and majestic. But when Christians define their position as "theistic," in opposition to both deism and pantheism, they in effect define their position in terms of the op-position. That is, they are portraying their stance in terms of what they reject: I am not-this, I am not-that. And for all this positioning, more often than not we will be able to say little more than we knew all along. Actually things might even get a bit more complicated —in this case, for example, Judaism and Islam prove to be just as theistic as Christianity.

Is there a viable alternative for Christians seeking to proceed methodically in the realm of theory, to work with a sense of orientation in the diverse field of human thought? Must we proceed by leaning on conceptions that we reject? The American thinker Alvin Plantinga, for one, has urged christian philosophers to take a different route. In his "Advice to Christian Philosophers," this professor of philosophy at the University of Notre Dame presents a three-point challenge to "theists" busy in the area of philosophy.

a. Plantinga, first of all, urges Christians that, rather than being defined by the projects and concerns of the nontheistic philosophic world, they ought to be more independent from mainline establishment philosophy. Its fundamental commitments and projects must be seen as wholly different from and even antithetical to those of the christian community. He warns that the result of attempting to graft christian thought onto some presently prevailing view of the world would at best be an unintegrated hodgepodge and, at worst, seriously compromise, distort, or trivialize the claims of christian theism. Rather than adopting principles and procedures that do not agree with christian beliefs, we have to realize, says Plantinga, that Christians have their own topics and projects to think about; that they also have a right to think about topics of current concern in their own, possibly different, way; and that they may have to reject some fashionable philosophic assumptions, such as those concerning proper starting points and appropriate procedures for the philosophic endeavor.

b. Second, christian philosophers must display soundness, in the sense of unity and integral wholeness, such that they and their work are of one piece. Philosophy is in large part a clarification, systematization, and articulation, a relating and deepening of pre-philosophic opinion. Therefore Christians, according to Plantinga, not only have as much right, in philosophy, to start from what they believe as do others; they also have a fundamental responsibility or duty to the christian community to get on with the philosophic questions of importance to them. As Plantinga sees things, it is simply a matter of intellectual propriety to start from basic beliefs and, taking these for granted, to go on from there in theoretical and philosophic work. The Christian has his own questions to answer, his own projects, his own starting point in investigating these questions; all are essential parts of his task as a christian thinker.

c. Plantinga's third point is that christian philosophers, shunning accommodation, should be courageous, bold, and strong—not in themselves, but with a christian self-confidence: "We Christian philosophers must display more faith, more trust in the Lord; we must put on the whole armor of God" (254). The christian philosopher must of course listen, to understand and learn from the broader philosophic community, but his work may not be circumscribed by what either the skeptic or the rest of the philosophic world thinks of theism. Responsible for much of what we do, we also have a right and duty to take as knowledge what we believe and proceed in confidence, also philosophically, on that basis.

I think that Plantinga's intention with respect to how Christians ought to proceed philosophically can best be summarized in terms of what Dirk Vollenhoven (1892-1978), professor of philosophy at the Free University in Amsterdam, referred to as a "thetical-critical method."

Rather than cursing the darkness, Christians should seek with the power and insight of the Holy Spirit to light a candle. In other words, rather than defining one's position in terms of what one rejects, Vollenhoven suggests that Christians proceed *thetically*. (According to the *Oxford English Dictionary* "thetical" means "Of the nature of or involving direct or positive statement; laid down or stated positively or absolutely.") That is to say, Christians should approach the (philosophic) problems and questions they are confronted with from their own positively stated point of view. Christians should be uneasy, for example, to describe the methodological route of the social sciences as one that rides the line between positivism (i.e., we can know, quantify, and scientifically control all natural phenomena) and skepticism (i.e., we can know little or nothing with certainty). People who acknowledge that God is both sovereign and personal should not be satisfied with a standpoint described in terms of a conceptual mean somewhere in between the extremes of pantheism and deism. Priority number one should be to work out a basic conception, in line with Scripture, that affirms and articulates as clearly and succinctly as possible one's perspective on the matter in question. In other words, we should proceed boldly, articulating, clarifying, and honing the coherence of the comprehensive framework of basic beliefs that Christians hold dear.

This thetical procedure—to deal with situations and questions new and old from one's own (communal, christian) point of view—presupposes an increasingly specific and consciously delineated basic conception such that one can say in confidence, "Here I stand." But in confidently living out a biblically informed and religiously grounded framework, Christians should definitely avoid the temptation to pontificate: "This is the way I see it and, therefore, that's the way it is." Brazen oracular pronouncements help no one. A related disease is what some call "ethnocentrism": thinking that there is nothing more to the world than lies within one's own purview, with its well-entrenched beliefs, attitudes, standards, methods, and procedures. No, in addition to proceeding thetically, Christians also need to work critically.

In this context, to proceed *critically* means to investigate seriously and, when necessary, meticulously, that is, to get to know, question, analyze, size up, and re-evaluate with an eye to determining both merits and faults (as in "a critical review"), specifically: (1) the ethos that shapes the culture in which God calls us (to live as his people); (2) what others, for example, non-Christians, are saying and have said; (3) what those within the christian tradition have said; as well as (4) what we ourselves communally or individually have held to date to be the case. There is no knowledge without preconceptions and prejudices. Our task is not to remove all such presuppositions, but to listen for, test, and evaluate them critically in the course of our inquiries.

Taking distance from the present is always a difficult task, but Christians must take time to assess the times in which they live, to test the spirits and challenges of their age. What must we make of the debate between modernism and postmodernism? Have Christians in North America slowly but surely capitulated to the values and structures of modernity? Does multiculturalism deserve our support? Have we become enamored of advanced management and marketing techniques? Does God rest too inconsequentially upon the church? David Wells (in *God in the Wasteland*) claims that God's truth is too distant, his grace is too ordinary, his judgment is too gentle, his gospel is too easy, and his Christ is too common.

> We have turned to a God that we can use rather than to a God we must obey; we have turned to a God who will fulfill our needs rather than to a God before whom we must surrender our rights to ourselves. He is a God *for* us, for our satisfaction—not because we have learned to think of him in this way through Christ but because we have learned to think of him this way through the marketplace. In the marketplace, everything is for us, for our pleasure, for our satisfaction, and we have come to assume that it must be so in the church as well. And so we transform the God of mercy into a God who is at our mercy. We imagine that he is benign, that he will acquiesce as we toy with his reality and co-opt him in the promotion of our ventures and careers. (114)

Is Wells on to something? Are we party to smoothing out God's angularity and the sharp edges that truth so often has? And, more broadly, do we sense the emptiness of our age? Do we have too much to live with and too little to live for? It seems that anything goes and nothing is important. Is Os Guinness on target when he writes (in *The American Hour*) about "a time of reckoning"? Is American secular liberalism really in danger of pulling its own house down on itself (and some Christians with it)? Guinness writes:

> Modern cities make people closer yet stranger at once; modern weapons bring their users to the point of genocide and impotence simultaneously; the modern media promise facts but deliver fantasies; modern education introduces mass schooling but fosters subliteracy; modern technologies of communication encourage people to speak more and say less, as on the telephone, and to hear more and listen less, as on the television; modern life-styles offer do-it-yourself freedom but slavishly follow fads; modern self-expression has been crowned as the winner in the all-American value contest just as the notion of the self has all but disappeared; modern rejection of restraints has ended in addictions; modern styles of relationships make people hungry for intimacy and authenticity but more fearful than ever of phoniness, manipulation, and power games; modern therapies multiply the promise of cures but make people ill with the frantic pursuit of health; modern control of the planet leads directly to the sense of the world out of control; modern humanization of life deepens a spreading feeling of existential despair. And so on and so on. (398-9)

Christians cannot afford to procrastinate when it comes to the air they breathe. Complacency is not going to cut through to the underlying currents. Professors and students in college classrooms can talk casually of worldviews in static, abstract, and philosophic terms, but in the "real world," in the living, breathing universe where the rubber hits the road (for believers and unbelievers), worldviews that move the good, the bad, and the ugly are shaping aims and aspirations as well as answers, few of which are reliable. And so we all have to test the spirits and discern the ethos that shapes the culture in which God calls us to be different (= holy). As Paul writes: "Don't you know that when you offer yourselves to someone to obey him as slaves, you are slaves to the one whom you obey—whether you are slaves to sin, which leads to death, or to obedience, which leads to righteousness? [You] used to offer parts of your body in slavery to impurity and to ever-increasing wickedness, so now offer them in slavery to righteousness leading to holiness" (Romans 6:16, 19).

As for getting a bead on what non-Christians are saying and have said, Christians cannot afford to be ignorant of pacesetters and historically influential figures, particularly in those areas that come closest to home; whether that be Dr. Spock when it comes to raising children, to Darwin for people in biology, to Marx for those pursuing interests in sociology or business, to the Federalist Papers for those working politically, to what's written between the lines of the scripts we call entertainment.

One good procedure for bringing out what is distinctive in other authors, movements, or cultures is the skillful use of comparison and contrast. It is not very difficult to come to an understanding of what is distinctive about B. F. Skinner in psychology, or John Rutter in music, or Aldo Leopold in environmental ethics. Neither jumping out of one's own skin nor transforming oneself by some sort of mystical intuition or empathy is necessary. Critical analysis proceeds by a careful attention to detail, to the various components and dimensions, working back and forth in order to highlight similarities with and differences from one's own position and that of others. It works to arrive at an outline of the underlying worldview, including a sense if not an account of the way in which this worldview influences perception, thought, argument, and action.

This kind of critical appraisal will also help the christian community to acknowledge the value and nature of authority and tradition. Almost everyone belongs to a tradition before it belongs to them. Traditions have a power that in many ways defines what we are in the process of becoming. Going with the (traditional) flow is often the easy way and may indeed keep one from upsetting anyone's applecart. But what good is an unexamined tradition, even if it is an orthodox one? We ought not to do to orthodoxy what we do to hot dogs and pickles; when vacuum packed and preserved under glass even right teachings quickly age into dead orthodoxy. Healthy traditions remain that way by being engaged and celebrated, but never uncritically. We can learn from critical activity as we come to a more sensitive and accurate understanding of our tradition and its strengths and weaknesses.

However much our age celebrates individualism and personal space, no one is truly a soloist; no one ever really acts or thinks or writes in isolation. A person should also not act as though his predecessors and contemporaries lacked any insight. On the contrary, one must seriously consider what they are doing or have said or written. Nor may one swear by the words of a teacher or patriarch or seek a solution in an eclectic patchwork of insights. Randomly selecting and then seeking to amalgamate elements from different views of the world or systems of thought only fosters confusion. We have to ask ourselves the question, "What is the spirit that moves them?" "What am I doing when I repeat what they say?" "Did those we respect sufficiently appreciate the difficulties that have become apparent in our age? Did they pose the problem or alternatives correctly?" When the Bible instructs us to test the spirits to see whether they are of God, it does not mean to exempt the thinking of fellow Christians. We also have to repeatedly ask the same question of the results that we ourselves have arrived at.

While one can indeed come to a deeper understanding of oneself precisely in and through the study of others, it is also good to take real time for self-critique along the way. Reassessing and confirming previous choices pro and con helps one mature and take ownership of the line one's life marks out.

Freshly considering answers and questions old and new can lead to two kinds of results: the solution being examined will be found to be satisfactory or to be unsatisfactory—either because it answers wrongly a correctly formulated question or because it proceeded from a wrong formulation of the problem. In both cases we will be moving toward greater understanding and insight. Likewise, our attitude toward living and learning will become anticipatory and open. We come to understand what is "other" than us, but also better understand ourselves. The truth of one's experience and tradition will nurture an orientation toward new experiences and challenges, helping us to acknowledge the possibility of "learning from" what is different and alien. Doing so will help us even more to grasp an understanding of what it means to be finite historical beings who are "on the way," who must assume personal responsibility for our decisions and choices, and who also must always be ready to give account of the hope that lives within us.

Criticism does not imply that answers found earlier, and now subjected to re-evaluation, must be found wanting: critical examination can just as well result in a cordial recommendation of claims or a plan of action advanced by others, or that one maintains a thesis of one's own that others have contested. Criticism is therefore certainly not equivalent to "negation," to "hypercritically" just finding faults or pointing out shortcomings. To be sure, criticism can lead to a negative result: "I disagree with this, that, and the next thing, for these reasons...." But such a negative result has great value: tenaciously maintaining thoughts, words, and deeds that constantly or implicitly clash with the main lines of one's framework of beliefs undermines its power and prevents one from asking good questions and acquiring results that speak more profoundly to the challenge of our age.

The bounce of Baptists and the legal theories of Lutherans deserve as much curiosity from the Reformed remnant—and vice versa—as the centerpieces of their lives and living rooms deserve their scrutiny. Life in all of its dimensions, from the breakfast table to the nightstand, is permeated by a diversity of spirits, only one of which is holy. If Christians allow the unholy permutations that result to hold sway, they will find themselves blind to a biblical glimpse of the whole and moved, as is the majority, by answers blowing back and forth in the wind.

One final point: these thetical and critical approaches are not isolated from one another, but related. Zeal in one without the other spells BIG trouble. Their relationship is as follows: on the one hand, every critical activity implies that one takes a thetical stance; and, in turn, a christian thetical stance that leaves no room for listening to, thinking about, and communicating with others will result in uncritical parochial dogmatism. It is quite possible that something in one's stance will later prove to be untenable, but all that means is that one has modified one's position somewhat: one has drawn back a bit or has adopted a thesis that one thought earlier had to be opposed. But whatever the case may be, all criticism presupposes, if it is worthy of the name, that one is confident in maintaining and engaging one's present view of the world and human living. Although all our claims are fallible and open to critique, they still require validation. That can be realized both through "walking our talk" as well as through offering the best reasons and arguments that can be given in support of them, arguments which are themselves usually embedded in the practice of those who have gone before us. By boldly embracing what is living in one's tradition and honestly rejecting what no longer can be warranted, Christians will seek to meet the new challenges of their age.

Christians know they are called to be holy, which, among other things, means that they are to be different, literally "marked off" from others. When the relationship between being thetical and being critical is forgotten, Christians lose a real sense of what that being different means practically. When the rubber hits the road of business, politics, home life, and entertainment, Christians often lack a sense of direction and discretion. A tempting alternative is to become a mindless eclectic, picking and choosing with random abandon what appears to be the best among a variety of doctrines or styles. But the undertow of intentional (postmodern) eclecticism is no more gentle. Christians who know their Bible and live by the power that only God's spirit can give should be able to arrive at solutions and covenantally consistent alternatives that are different from those arising from an unregenerate heart. And yet, millions of "born again" Christians show little or no sign of having a perspective on the everyday issues different from their nonchristian compatriots. Unequipped to discern the spirits of their time, to penetrate as far as the underlying questions that are at issue, they simply support thoughts and fashions from here or there, without even bothering to inquire whether they are compatible.

In conclusion: A conglomerate of people, places, and events indelibly marks the lives of Christians. Aided by the power of the Holy Spirit, Christians are called to bring all of these, every thought and action, into obedience to Christ. *The Life* he gives us is not just for by-and-by. Rather than using one's human nature as an excuse for past indiscretions, we can better, in light of *The Truth*, admit our frailty and the fact that we have so much to learn as we walk *The Way* of christian discipleship. We can maintain what is viable in our own position by critically investigating the results reached previously not only by others, but also in the course of one's own life, and by daring to draw conclusions. Christians working communally and methodically can make progress through struggle and attain a double profit: a reinforced *position*, articulated in deed and word, and a more definite and accountable *rejection* of that which is inconsistent with it. When our basic beliefs about things can cut both ways, they will help "straighten us out," the psalmists would say, and lead to a prophetic integration of how we do things in the shop, at home, in our neighborhood, as parents, students, citizens, or whatever.

I.
Guide Questions

1. Why do opinions about the nature of philosophy differ?
2. How does the task of philosophy differ from that of the other sciences and disciplines?
3. What do the terms "ontology," "anthropology," and "epistemology" mean?
4. Why might some people find the relationship between one's view of reality, of being human, and of knowledge scary?
5. What are presuppositions?
6. What do deists and pantheists have to say about the transcendence and immanence of God?
7. How are the thetical and critical tracks related?
8. Of what value is a thetical-critical method?
9. What does it mean to be an eclectic?

A HISTORICAL SURVEY
OF WESTERN THOUGHT

II. A.
Introduction

Part Two surveys some of the great ontological, anthropological, and epistemological issues of the past, but cannot touch on everything. Other factors, including political, aesthetic, and scientific thought of the past, are obviously important and would need to be incorporated in a more broadly defined intellectual history. The three problem areas outlined above will define our focus. From time to time we will refer to other aspects of human activity.

1. HISTORY

In Part One we concentrated on the content of the term "philosophy." In this unit we are interested not so much in philosophy as in the history of philosophy: not so much in philosophizing, in actual philosophic activity, as in the body of judgments that philosophers have articulated in the past as a result of their philosophic activity. And many of their ideas are not just ideas; a good deal of them prove to have legs! They have gone and still go places, carrying people and cultures to peculiar and precarious conclusions.

Before turning to this history we should briefly consider the term "history." The Greeks had a word just like it and used it to mean "search," "inquiry," or "investigation." Later on the word came to refer to "inquiry into the past." Note that the term "history" is ambiguous on that score, for it has two distinct meanings: (a) the actual events of the past; for example, when Brutus stabbed Caesar, something indeed happened, in this case

with devastating consequences for Caesar. This first meaning is
what we refer to when we say, "The Berlin Wall is history now";
that is, these are the facts, values, and events that now belong to
the past and can no longer be undone. And (b) is the discipline
of determining with a degree of systematic exactitude what was
"historical" about certain events in the unfolding of creation and
culture. The focus is on significant change and interlinking formative alterations. We refer to this second sense of "history"
when one student asks another, "Have you studied your history
already?" To study a history textbook is to study another's selection, interpretation, and account of what are significant events in
the past. Such an investigation or account is clearly different
from all the events themselves. An actual event is not the same
thing as someone's (always limited) view and analysis of the
event, just as surely as there is a difference between, for example,
the Battle of the Bulge and a book on the history of World War II
lying on your desk, in which that battle is described and
assessed.

It should be immediately clear that the expression "history
of Western thought" uses the term "history" in its second sense.
The actual events—many people thinking about foundational
questions—have long since passed. And however much we will
seek to investigate and describe how philosophers once engaged
in questions of ontology, anthropology, and epistemology, the
reader must realize that what follows is an interpretation, a
focused and selective reading of the patterns of the Western
mind.

Much is to be gained, first of all for Christians, when this
investigation focuses on factors that are of primary significance
(for Christians). For that reason anyone engaging in an initial
study ought not simply select any text on the history of philosophy and then proceed with their study. Pick up any textbook
and the discerning reader will soon discover that the author's
perspective is colored by certain prejudices, by underlying sup-
positions. Some textbooks, for example, will present the history
of philosophy in a rationalistic light; that is, the various philosophic conceptions of various thinkers are described and eval-
uated by rationalistic standards. Roman Catholic authors will
tend to write from a perspective oriented to the great medieval
philosopher Thomas Aquinas. In sum, historians of Western

thought, like all other historians, interpret the past on the basis of a set of prior beliefs and presuppositions. A set of resolute commitments and assumptions precede the historian's analysis, define his focus, and govern his evaluations and judgments. These prior assumptions bear ultimately a confessional and even religious character.

An example will make this situation clear. A christian historian will begin her analysis of the Greek philosophers, for instance, acknowledging that they too lived in God's world, our home, and achieved a good deal of insight to that world. But she will also recognize that Greek culture continued the pagan tradition of suppressing the truth in unrighteousness. This judgment does not mean that Greek historians didn't get any of the facts about the Peloponnesian Wars right, or that Plato's argument against moral relativism in the *Gorgias* is wholly uninstructive. But in the light of Scripture and her biblically informed sense of the nature of things, the christian historian will see a good deal of distortion in Greek philosophy. The rationalistic historian, on the other hand, will approach these same Greek philosophers in an entirely different way. His analysis will be determined by the belief that humans are essentially rational, autonomous (self-regulating) beings, in need of neither God nor redemption. For the rationalist, therefore, the pagan Greek emphasis on autonomous rationality is not a suppression and distortion of the truth, but a praiseworthy emergence and liberation from religious and mythological slavery.

Observe that the assumptions of neither the Christian nor the rationalist are the result of analysis. It is the other way around: analysis follows the assumptions and confessions. The Christian confesses the sovereignty of God and the fallen state of creation as well as the radical redemption in Jesus Christ, whereas the rationalist confesses the autonomy and rationality of humankind. Analysis and evaluation follow these prior commitments.

These examples should make it clear that there cannot be an "objective"—fact neutral—description of the history of philosophy (or of psychology or of physics). Every historian carries his beliefs and assumptions into the task of investigating, interpreting, and assessing the past. Even those who believe in objectivity and in a presumably neutral and unbiased evaluation of supposed "facts" cannot escape the very same situation. For they, too, begin with a belief in neutrality and objectivity and must make choices at every turn.

2. OUR APPROACH

With Scripture as a light to one's path, how ought Christians to approach the history of Western thought? All too often Christians have taken what we might call a compartmentalized approach. Such an approach sees little connection between one's christian faith and one's task as a historian of philosophy. The christian faith is tucked away in one compartment, the task as historian in another, and the door between them securely locked, perhaps even the key thrown away. In many other areas of life Christians compartmentalize. Take politics, for example. Many christian politicians publicly and emphatically state that they will do their utmost to keep their religion out of politics. But doing politics is no more neutral or objective an activity than the writing of a history of art. The compartmentalization of religion from the rest of life is the result of a medieval nature/grace thought pattern that we will have occasion to examine more closely later on in this unit. Rather than advocating a nature/ grace approach, we will want to let the light of Scripture fall squarely on the philosophies of the past. We will want to describe and evaluate philosophic conceptions in terms of christian, biblical assumptions and presuppositions. David Moberg of Marquette University makes the same case in more general terms:

> Christians in higher education are strongly, though subtly, tempted to compartmentalize our faith. We are inclined to consider it relevant under special circumstances, such as when attending church or campus religious activities, when counseling students or friends about personal problems, when engaging in personal or family devotions, or when sharing the relevance of the Bible to political or social issues. But when we are teaching and doing our research, we usually center our attention upon the theories, concepts, and other subject matter that are conventional to our respective disciplines.
>
> Yet Jesus Christ calls us to "Love the Lord your God with all your heart and with all your soul and with all your mind and with

all your strength," as well as to "Love your neighbor as yourself" (Mark 12:30-31, NIV). In our most rational moments we acknowledge that this means having a genuinely holistic faith, being so permeated with God's love that every thought and activity is captivated to make it obedient to Christ (2 Cor. 10:5). Surely this means that every nook and cranny of our professional, as well as personal, life must be saturated with and purified by our knowledge of and love for the Lord. (147)

If we are to assess properly the ontologies, anthropologies, and epistemologies of the past, we will need a set of articulated criteria. After all, judgments require criteria. One cannot distinguish between good and bad or between correct and incorrect unless one applies some standard, some kind of norm for goodness and correctness. The same holds for historical analysis. What will count as significant and insignificant? What as crucial or coincidental? Many philosophy textbooks restrict themselves to the standard of logic. They will describe, for example, Greek philosophy in terms of its logical consistency and coherence. Wherever the Greek thinkers follow the laws of logic, their philosophy is judged acceptable; whenever they commit logical fallacies, their work is judged to be unacceptable. While the role of logic in philosophic thought is undoubtedly a very important one, I believe that it does not constitute the sole criterion for historical evaluation. Along with the Dutch philosopher Dirk Vollenhoven, I would suggest the breadth of God's word-revelation as a broader, but also more reliable horizon against which to measure the human thought products we call ontologies, anthropologies, and epistemologies.

To recognize a good used car when you see one, you have to know what to look for. So also Christians reviewing perspectives on reality, humanity, and knowledge stand in need of an articulated biblical ontology, anthropology, and epistemology. While these topics will be dealt with in our final unit, a few remarks at this point already will not be out of place.

The Scriptures reveal to us contours of a biblical ontology. They tell us about God, about God's laws, and about the created world. God, the sovereign Law-giver, created the cosmos by his Word and his word is law. Moment by moment the universe is upheld and sustained by his faithfulness through Jesus Christ, the Word, in whom all things hold together. There is nothing more than Creator and creature, and every creature, be it heavenly or earthly, is subject to God and his law.

The Scriptures, furthermore, provide us with insight into anthropology: human beings are not the accidental product of a blind evolutionary process, but God's special creation, wondrously and integrally knit together, called to serve their Creator from the inside out in loving obedience. Finally, with regard to epistemology, Scripture helps us understand that human knowledge is primarily a personal and tacit knowing of what we can count on from day to day. True knowledge, therefore, is rooted in intimate acquaintance with and basic beliefs informed by God's revelation of words and works, to which we are called to respond with love, obedience, and responsibility.

The sketch of a biblical ontology, anthropology, and epistemology provides us with the key to a christian method of analysis. Since the philosophers of the past, like all of God's creatures, found themselves within created reality, they constantly bumped into, as it were, the laws and ordinances of the Lord. Consequently, we may say that in their philosophizing they attempted to account for the order and regularity around them, all of which existed by virtue of God's upholding hand. But in their inability or unwillingness to recognize the true nature of God's laws, their paganism and unbelief brought about a good deal of distortion. Our method of analysis, then, is designed to sort out the various ways in which philosophers, as they wrestled with issues of ontology, anthropology, and epistemology, have responded to the order manifest in creation. What emerge are patterns of the Western mind.

3. SCOPE AND ORGANIZATION

One should not infer from our focusing on the Western mind that non-western philosophy is insignificant. On the contrary, in our steadily shrinking world a knowledge of Eastern philosophies is increasingly important. Their influence is growing, particularly as the promises of the Enlightenment and the bells and whistles of technology ring true less and less. Limitations of competence and space, however, simply do not allow me to include a survey of non-western thought.

The vast majority of textbooks divide the history of Western thought into four chronological periods: ancient, medieval, modern, and contemporary. While this is a useful convention, Christians might want to consider if there are more important criteria than "really old," "really recent," and "somewhere in between." A more radical and I would suggest more biblical criterion would be to group chronological differences on the basis of when and how the Gospel has affected human thought. That is for the Christian what history is all about: the mighty acts of God and how humankind have responded to these words and deeds. After all, using the yardstick of old, older, oldest, can only lead to the apparent conclusion that Jesus Christ is ancient history!

In the centuries after Cain and before Christ the spoken word of God was restricted to Israel. Greek and hellenistic philosophies, therefore, were the result of wondering and wandering in the world without an indispensable light. About A.D. 40, when the Gospel through Paul and others became known outside the Hebrew community, Western thought was confronted by the liberating message of the early Christians. Very soon, however, an era of "synthesis philosophy" began, a period characterized by the attempted reconciliation and union of biblical themes with pagan thought patterns. Synthesis philosophy played a predominant role until approximately 1500, when the rise of humanism began to destroy the medieval synthesis and opened the way for the development of secularistic patterns of thought. In view of these major turning points, we may divide the history of Western thought into three main periods: the *pre-synthesis* mind, *synthesis* philosophy, and *anti-synthesis* thought patterns. We will consider each in chronological order.

As we review these three major periods in the history of philosophy from our late twentieth century vantage point, we will see different thinkers tackle fundamental questions about reality from different perspectives. Not only are there a good number of perennial problems that hold sway throughout the history of Western thought, there are also recurring answers to these questions that give rise to what we can call the types or patterns of the Western mind. As a result, we are able to develop a typology, that is, we can describe a set of foundational thought patterns that reflect attempts of various thinkers to give answers to fundamental questions of ontology, anthropology, and epistemology.

A simple illustration from the area of epistemology may help to make this clear. Throughout history the question has been asked, "How do we come by our knowledge?" A good number have replied to this question by saying that everything we know is the result of sense perception. All knowledge, they answer, comes from the senses. We call this position "empiricism." Empiricism, therefore, is a type, a thought pattern, a recurring answer to a standing epistemological question.

While the fundamental questions and their various answers recur and remain therefore more or less constant, the times in which the questions are asked change. There is a vast difference between the historical context of, let's say, ancient Greece and that of the Middle Ages. Consequently we can describe the history of thought not only in terms of type but also in terms of the time current, that is, as reflecting the spirit of the time or the intellectual climate during a given period. In the history of the West a number of time currents have succeeded one another. Sometimes a current begins or ends suddenly, sometimes they emerge or decline gradually, sometimes they overlap, or sometimes they blend together.

Types and time currents constitute the basic ingredients of the so-called "problem-historic method." This method was used extensively and with interesting and useful results by the Vollenhoven, for many years professor of philosophy at the Free University of Amsterdam. Although this survey differs markedly, and at times totally, from the understanding, categorizing, and formulation of the types and time currents Vollenhoven suggested, the inspiration of the original versions will be evident to anyone familiar with his work.

II. A.

Guide Questions

10. What is the relationship between historical inquiry and one's basic beliefs (i.e., presuppositions, assumptions, confessions)?

11. What does a "compartmentalized approach" to the history of philosophy assume?

12. Do you agree with Moberg's alternative to compartmentalization?

13. How, and on what basis, do we distinguish the main historical periods of Western philosophy?

A HISTORY
OF WESTERN THOUGHT
BEFORE THE RISE OF SYNTHESIS

II. B.
Introduction to the First Main Period

The ancient Greeks were part of a long line of "no"-sayers going all the way back to Cain. What they were saying "no" to was nothing other than God and his word. But, of course, one's view of reality, humankind, and knowledge is seriously affected when God is not taken at his word. Without the revealed word of God the cosmos can no longer be acknowledged as his creation, as the result of a covenanting God's creating and leading activity. Realities such as the God of Abraham, Isaac, and Jacob, cosmos as creation, a realm of heavenly creatures doing God's will, earthly creation's mediators, and the human heart, to mention just a few, are all lost sight of sooner or later when this sin of the fathers is perpetuated in their children. The end result is a darkened and reduced cosmos in which "wise men" yearn after wisdom but find only whispers and echoes of the truth.

In their analysis of reality the Greeks could not acknowledge that the orderliness of the creation is to be attributed to laws that God in his sovereignty has put to the cosmos. As a result, a variety of distortions arose, as we will see in a moment. Greek anthropological reflections brought about serious confusion as well. When it comes right down to it, the Greeks were unable to understand who man is. And no wonder! Without the word of God to instruct us, we remain hopelessly in the dark. True self-knowledge cannot be obtained by theoretical analysis and reflection. Knowing one's self is dependent on the power of God's word which discloses to us who we are, namely, creatures made in the image of God, called to serve our creator in faithful and loving obedience. And finally, with respect to epistemology, the Greeks bequeathed to the Western world the notion that true knowledge is a matter of rational, logical, and theoretical perspicuity. The rationalism and intellectualism that has characterized the Western world for centuries is the direct result of a Greek epistemological distortion.

The period of pagan or pre-synthesis thought can be conveniently divided into two parts, namely, (1) Greek philosophy (before 320 B.C.) and (2) hellenistic philosophy. Philosophy before 320 B.C. developed in Greece and its colonies and is marked by ontological and anthropological preoccupation. Hellenistic philosophy, associated with the Hellenistic Age that came about as a result of the campaigns of Alexander the Great, was widespread throughout the Mediterranean world and is characterized by a stress on questions related to epistemological matters. The year 320 B.C., roughly speaking, does indeed form a dividing line: Alexander the Great died in 323 B.C., and Aristotle, a student of Plato and the last of the classic Greek philosophers, died a year later in 322 B.C.

1. GREEK PHILOSOPHY BEFORE 320 B.C.

Introduction

This era, in which we find the earliest philosophies of the Western world, is crucial for an understanding of the history of Western thought, not only because in it we encounter influential figures such as Plato and Aristotle, but especially because the period affords us the opportunity to study a relatively simple formulation of foundational problems. In these early years the questions were by and large free from the complexities that arose as time went on. Furthermore, subsequent theorizing, including contemporary philosophy, owes its character in large part to combinations of problems raised in antiquity.

The earliest professional thinkers appearing at the dawn of Greek history focused on questions of ontology and cosmology: What is the nature of the cosmos? How did it come into being? What relationship is there between the gods and the world? Mythology often played an important role in these early cosmological philosophies (a).

As Greek civilization developed and flourished in the 6th and 5th centuries B.C., a new climate of philosophic opinion—a new time current or "spirit of the age"—arose. Interest in broad cosmological questions declined. Instead, the Greeks began to inquire about the role of the individual in the life of the *polis*, the city-state. The Sophists in particular contributed to the growth of interest in the individual citizen. This new time current we will call Classical Greek Individualism (b).

In the final century of the pre-hellenistic Greek world, in the fourth century, we see the arrival of two giants who will tower over the world of philosophy, Plato (c) and his student Aristotle (d). These men developed highly sophisticated philosophies, sufficiently distinct to deserve separate attention.

Early Greek Cosmological Philosophy

The earliest Greek philosophers found themselves, like everyone else, to be somewhere in the world (that God created, orders, and upholds). They, too, experienced the order and many of the relationships within that world. But along with their forefathers, not taking God at his word, the early Greeks did not understand that the regularity and order in the universe are rooted in the laws and ordinances of the God who calls all his creatures to covenantal faithfulness. They could not see that the reason things are what they are is to be found in God's powerful, almighty, creating, and upholding Word. Genesis 1, Psalm 33:6-9, and Hebrews 1:3 were out of the question. Nevertheless, driven ultimately by the creation or "cultural" mandate, the early Greeks attempted to account for the orderliness they experienced. The fragmented sources and extant writings of this people (see, for example, Kirk, Raven and Schofield's *The Presocratic Philosophers*) record a preoccupation with the question, "What determines the nature of the cosmos?" Or, to put it differently, "What and where is the *ordering principle* of all reality, the law for all that is?"

The earliest cosmological philosophers replied unanimously: "The ordering principle is (somewhere) in the world, within things." One will claim the origin of things to be water, another air, another fire. Contrast these this-worldly answers with the other-worldly answer Plato later gave: "The ordering principle cannot be found within the cosmos, but behind the cosmos—in another world."

Let's illustrate this concretely by examining the positions of some early Greek cosmological philosophers. One of the earliest of Greek thinkers whose work has come down to us is Hesiod. Hesiod was a farmer-philosopher who lived about 800 B.C. In one of his books, titled *Works and Days*, he gives us a fascinating

glimpse of his times. In another, philosophically more important, book called *Theogony*, about the coming-into-being of the
gods, Hesiod explains that all things have sprung forth from an
original "gaping" or "yawning" that he called in Greek "chaos."
Scholars today are still embattled about what Hesiod really
meant by the "chaos." Did he simply mean empty space, such as
the space between heaven and earth? We may never know for
sure.

Thales' answer is somewhat less difficult to understand.
Thales was regarded in antiquity as an extremely wise man. He
lived about 580 B.C. along the coast of Asia Minor, where there
were many Greek colonies. He, too, addressed the question,
"What is the fundamental principle of reality?" and answered it
by claiming that everything is basically water. We know so little
about Thales that we cannot be sure why he would choose water
as the fundamental stuff of the universe. One of Thales' pupils, a
fellow by the name of Anaximenes, also of Asia Minor, disagreed with his master and suggested that everything is basically air: "Being made finer it becomes fire, being made thicker it
becomes wind, then cloud, then (when thickened still more)
water, then earth, then stones; and the rest come into being from
these." Heraclitus (about 500 B.C.), on the other hand, declared
that the origin of all reality is fire: "The world-order did none of
gods or men make, but it always was and is and shall be: an
everlasting fire, kindling in measures and going out in measures." Pythagoras (about 530 B.C.) did his work in Greek
colonies in Italy. He is famous for the theorem about the hypotenuse of right triangles he is said to have discovered. Pythagoras
provided a more obscure answer by postulating that the essence
of things is to be found in number. The Pythagoreans were fascinated by mathematics; hence they believed that the fundamental
explanation of the nature of reality is to be looked for in the
realm of number, measure, and harmony. Still another answer
was given by the so-called Atomists, who asserted that everything in the universe is a combination of indivisible particles and
the void: "The elements are the full and the void.... Being is full
and solid, not-being is void and rare. Since the void exists no
less than body, it follows that not-being exists no less than being.
The two together are the material causes of existing things."

Note the common assumption of these presocratic philosophies: they all claim to have found the ordering principle somewhere within the cosmos: in space, or water, or air, or fire, or number, or in atoms. Observe also that a good deal of current thinking is still oriented to the world of things and relationships that surrounds us. Think, for example, of materialistic philosophy, which claims that all reality is nothing but a composite of physical and chemical matter. Think of evolutionism, which believes that everything complex evolved from what is less complex according to inherent laws and lines of biological development. This-worldly philosophy did not die with the early Greek cosmological philosophers; it persists to this very day. The assumption remains the same: something within the cosmos is the key to the cosmos. The only thing that has changed over the course of time is the answer to the question, What in the world is that "something"?

In addition to the difference between "this-worldly" and "other-worldly" thought patterns, we can discern the development of other topics of disagreement in early Greek thought. One important set involves the question about cosmogony, that is, the coming-into-being or genesis of the cosmos. Some of the Greek thinkers placed great stress on the need to explain how the world was generated. Without an account of generation, they said, reality cannot be understood. Hesiod, for example, tried to explain the coming-into-being not only of the world but also of the gods! Thales, on the other hand, appears to have placed little emphasis on genesis. Although we can't be entirely sure because of the paucity of sources, it seems that he preferred to investigate the structure of things as they are. Thales' position, therefore, was not cosmogonic but structuralistic. Structuralism in this context generally pays little attention to cosmogony, or, if it does, tends to regard genesis as merely an aspect of structure. The early Greek philosophers tended toward cosmogonism. Heraclitus, for example, laid great stress on such concepts as change, development, and becoming.

One important example of early Greek structuralism, however, merits some attention, namely, the philosophy of Parmenides. Parmenides was born about 600 B.C. and lived and worked in Elea, a city in southern Italy. His philosophic conception is very difficult to understand and continues to be the subject of much debate. In broad lines, Parmenides believed that existence, "*being*," does not come into being or ever perish. Being is truth, well-rounded, rationally balanced, without beginning or end. *That which is*, Parmenides insists, is actually static, ever-lasting, indivisible, immutable, and immovable. Nothing that truly is moves or changes. There may appear to be motion, says Parmenides, but that is only appearance. In reality, which is to say, when we think about it, there is no change or motion whatever. Change and motion are merely illusions. The structuralism is evident in this position: there is no room for change, hence no room for coming-into-being or cosmogony. Parmenides' philosophy influenced both Plato and Aristotle, as we shall see. A great defender of Parmenides' position, by the way, was Zeno of Elea, who postulated a number of famous paradoxes designed to prove that motion is an impossibility.

Thus far we have discovered two sets of questions being asked by Greek thinkers, namely, (1) Is the ordering principle of the cosmos to be found in this world or in another world? And (2) What deserves our attention, structure or genesis? We now move on to consider a third controversy that emerges from the earliest Greek speculations: Is reality reducible to one principle or to two or more? Those who say that the universe is essentially reducible to one principle are *monists*. Those who postulate two or more principles are *dualists* or pluralists.

Just as the trend of early cosmological philosophy was toward cosmogonism, so it also tended toward monism. Take Hesiod again: everything is derived from one source, "chaos." Or Thales: everything is basically just one kind of stuff, water. Heraclitus was also a monist. He was convinced that all things are one, one universal law of natural warring tension: "war is the common condition, strife is justice, and all things come to pass through the compulsion of strife." The origin of everything, according to Heraclitus, is eternally living fire. While disagreeing with Thales, he had to admit that water did have something to do with the basis of reality: fire, he says, inverts into its opposite and becomes sea, which in turn diverges in heaven and earth (in his anthropology, into soul and body). That, however, is only one side of the story or, as he put it, only one side of the *logos*. The other side is the movement in the opposite direction. Heaven and earth converge into sea, which again inverts into eternal fire. These two simultaneous movements take the same road, so to speak, but follow the opposite route. The world itself is filled with contradictory opposition—salt water kills and gives life, depending on whether you immerse men or fish. The only thing that does not change is change itself, and the real is at root one element, fire. And that is why we refer to Heraclitus as a (contradictory) monist.

Calvin Seerveld reflects on the pagan tenor of this thought pattern, contrasting it to what was going on among God's remnant at the time:

> When you realize that Heraclitus was figuring these things out in the dark of Asia Minor shortly after Daniel was given dreams from Yahweh in Babylon about the fall of civilizations foreign to His Rule, and about the same time as Zechariah was receiving visions at night straight from the Lord and Nehemiah was building up the little tumble down wall of Jerusalem, ending his diary entries at night so plaintively, "Please think well of me, O my God! for the little things I've been able to do for You," then you understand why the apostle Paul, after passing through Heraclitus's home-town 600 years later could refer to such patterns of thinking as *atheoi* [without God] (Ephesians 2:11-22) and plead with Christians not to lose their minds that way but to get their whole consciousness truly new in Jesus Christ (Ephesians 4:1-24). (1975, 277)

I will want to cite Seerveld again, because he traces the recurrence of this type throughout various time currents. As we will see, Eckhart of Strassburg and the twentieth century German thinker Ernst Cassirer were (contradictory) monists as well.

But there were dualists also. The Atomists, for example, believed that there are two constituent elements to the world, namely, "the full," consisting of the indivisible atoms, and an infinitely extended "void." The Pythagoreans, too, tended toward dualism, ordering their principle of number into the categories of the odd and the even: limit and unlimited, one and plurality, right and left, resting and moving, straight and curved, light and darkness, good and bad, square and oblong. (It should come as no surprise that Pythagoreans did not find women odd: as most Greeks, Pythagoreans considered men a cut-above.) Men were odd and women even.

Monism is still current. For example, when people describe complex things and events with the explanation that what is happening is "nothing but . . ." this or that, then some kind of reductionism is present. Evolutionists, too, frequently postulate a single origin for all of the rich diversity of life. Note also that evolutionism is cosmogonic: strong stress is placed on the question of how things came into being.

A final controversy we must consider has to do with the categories of universalism and individualism. The term "universalism" might be familiar from catechism class. There it refers to the claim that everyone will eventually be saved. The philosophic meaning of universalism is quite different, and is most easily understood as the contrast of individualism. Individualism is the position that asserts that only the individual is real and important. A true individualist will say, for example, that only the individual counts. There is no such thing as France, only millions of individual Frenchmen living in a certain part of the world. This kind of individualism is very common, especially in North America. Who has not heard of "rugged American individualism"? Even the courts pass their judgments almost exclusively on the basis of "individual rights." The rights of marriages, families, and communities are practically ignored. This kind of individualism presents a danger to Christianity, for it cannot do justice to the biblical concept of "body of Christ" or "community of believers." To individualism these are mere concepts, not realities. Note also that a strong stress on individual conversion and on "saving the individual soul" reflects a long tradition of individualism.

Universalism is the opposite of individualism. Universalism submerges the individual into a universal whole. Individual people or things are merely minor parts or offshoots of the cosmic whole. Pantheism, for example, is a form of universalism: the pantheist says that the whole world is god; individual things or people are only reflections, manifestations, or dimensions of a divine whole.

There is a third position possible, midway between universalism and individualism. We call it partial-universalism. By trying to do justice to both the universal and the individual, partial-universalism recognizes the one-sidedness of universalism and individualism. But rather than acknowledging that the universal and individual always occur together, partial universalists either maintain that both are on a par with each and avail themselves of a macro/micro thought pattern, or claim that both are to be found in every thing and can best be represented in terms of higher/lower. Macro/micro positions claim that the whole and the part, often the world and man, or the one and the many, reflect each other, are constructed according to the same proportions, and are rationally attuned to each other. In the higher/lower scheme of things, either what is universal and common to all is taken to be higher and more noble and what is individual is considered of less merit, or individuality is praised and what all things have in common is considered less worthy.

The early Greek cosmological philosophers tended strongly toward universalism. They were concerned about the whole, only secondarily about the individuality of things. Consider some of the figures already mentioned. Hesiod, in his book *Theogony*, sets out to explain how all existence came into being. The surviving fragment of Thales reads: "All things are water." Note the emphasis on the universal whole. Heraclitus, too, talks about all of reality, as does Parmenides.

We have seen that the early Greek cosmological philosophers, often referred to as the Presocratics, were primarily concerned with questions of ontology—about the nature and sources of reality. What did they contribute to epistemology and anthropology? On the whole, we find very little epistemological reflection during this first time current of Western thought. Regarding anthropology, however, we must single out an important and influential group of Greeks, the so-called Orphics.

Orphism was more a mystery cult than a philosophic movement. Its members thought of themselves as followers of the legendary Orpheus, a mythical figure from the mists of Greek prehistory. Orpheus' prowess as a musician enabled him to enchant rocks and trees with his fabulous lyre. The real origins of orphism are obscure. It seems to have developed in the 6th and 5th centuries B.C. The entire movement continues to be a subject of scholarly dispute.

There is an echo of original sin in orphism. The story, however, is quite different from the biblical account in that it involves the murder of an infant god. In any case, myths about the coming-into-being of the gods led the Orphics to conclude that humans are composed of two conflicting elements, a divine part and a mortal part. The soul is divine and destined to be immortal. The body, on the other hand, is no more than a tomb and doomed to mortality. This view led the Orphics to develop a complicated set of initiation and purification rites designed to liberate the soul from the body. They also believed the doctrine of the transmigration of the soul, that is, the transmission of the soul through a succession of bodies, including those of animals. Hence the Orphics did not eat meat: the soul of your uncle might well be in the animal you slaughter!

The orphic anthropology appears to have influenced the Pythagoreans. Again, there is much scholarly debate about this question. It is clear, however, that the Pythagoreans, too, believed in the transmigration of the soul and practiced strict rites of purification. What we see in orphism and pythagoreanism, then, is a dichotomy, a division into two, in their anthropology: humans are made up of two conflicting constituents, namely, a divine soul locked up in a mortal body. This view of human beings might have died a natural death in ancient Greece had it not been for the fact that it is essentially the anthropology adopted and developed by Plato. Plato, in turn, strongly influenced, among others, the early Church Fathers, whose attempts to harmonize this unbiblical anthropology with the Scriptures created serious tensions in the christian community, as we shall see.

Classical Greek Individualism

In the 5th century B.C. Greek civilization attained its greatest glory. The era of Periclean Athens, for example, is generally acknowledged as the "golden age" of Greece. The Greeks had beaten back the onslaught of the Persian giant; democracy was in the air; arts and letters were flourishing; the economy appeared stable.

For the Greek, life was lived in the context of the *polis*, the city-state. Particularly in leading city-states where a democratic system of government was practiced, as in Athens, the political life was of the highest importance. This situation naturally led to the growth of interest in questions as to the role the individual citizen was to play in the state. We see, then, a new age or time current emerge, a new spirit of inquiry, now no longer interested in the broad cosmological questions about the nature of the universe, but increasingly fascinated by problems of the individual life. This new time current, classical Greek individualism, is represented primarily by Socrates, the Sophists, and the so-called Minor Socratic Schools.

Socrates was born about 470 B.C. Stories about his life abound, but it is not easy to sort fact from fiction. He is reported to have worn the same clothes summer and winter. He always walked about barefoot. Presumably his gait resembled the strutting of a duck. He was also said to engage in long periods of deep thought that would make him totally oblivious of the world around him. Famous is Socrates' report of his "demon," an inner voice that told him what course of action to pursue. And then, of course, there is Xanthippe, his wife, widely rumored to be of shrewish character.

In his younger days Socrates apparently studied the cosmological speculations of the earlier philosophers but did not find them exciting, useful, or satisfying. He gave them up entirely when the oracle of Delphi declared that there was no man wiser than Socrates. Socrates eventually took this to mean that his wisdom must lie in his own realization that there was so much that he did not know. From that point on, his program was to find truth and to teach wisdom. (To recognize one's own ignorance, of course, should not be confused with the fear of the Lord. So also, one can safely conclude that the wisdom of which the oracle spoke was a wisdom different than that of Scripture.)

Socrates embarked on his career as philosopher, seeking, as Plato tells us in his dialogue the *Apology*, "to persuade every man among you that he must look to himself, and seek virtue and wisdom, before he looks to his private interests, and look to the state before he looks to the interests of the state, and that this should be the order that he observes in all his actions." Note the emphasis on the role of the individual. This program eventually ran into conflict with the Athenian authorities, particularly at the time of the end of the Peloponnesian Wars, when there was much political turmoil, confusion, and suspicion. In the year 399 B.C. Socrates was brought to trial on charges of not worshiping the state gods and of corrupting the youth. He was condemned and executed. The execution of Socrates and the events leading up to it are described, often movingly, by Plato in his very readable dialogues the *Apology*, which reports the trial of Socrates and why he was not afraid to die, the *Crito*, which explains why Socrates refused to escape from prison while awaiting execution, and the *Phaedo*, which examines the question of the immortality of the soul and reports the actual execution.

Since Socrates wrote nothing, it is not always easy to determine precisely the content of his philosophy. Most of what we know about his philosophic activity we learn from the writings of Plato. It is frequently difficult, however, to distinguish between Plato's own philosophy and the doctrines of Socrates. Suffice it to say that, like his predecessors, Socrates appears to have defended a "this-worldly" philosophy that favored individualism. He also contributed significantly to the development of epistemology. He was particularly interested in definition. The Sophists, as we will see in a moment, tended to relativism, asserting that there is no stable truth anywhere. Socrates opposed such relativism by demonstrating that certain difficult concepts, such as justice, piety, courage, and so on, acquire a certain stability and constancy when properly defined. For example, if I define the word "wind" as a "flow of air from one place to another," then I have captured the unchanging element that characterizes all sorts of wind, from breezes to hurricanes.

Although Socrates did not work out precise rules for definition, he did employ what came to be known as the "socratic method," a kind of questioning still used in law school classrooms today. To get at the true definition of some term, Socrates would engage in conversation with someone who claimed to understand the term. By careful probing and persistent questioning, Socrates would elicit from his opponent all sorts of definitions and show their inadequacy, until finally a correct version was obtained. Naturally this approach tended to be unnerving and humiliating to those with whom the discussion was carried on and who confidently, sometimes arrogantly, thought they knew it all. Crowds enjoyed hearing the philosopher destroy "expert" arguments.

Socrates also held a position that we call "practicalism," and others call "ethical intellectualism." Practicalism claims that good insight will automatically lead to good action. In Socrates' view, knowledge and virtue are identical; truly wise people will do the right and virtuous thing once they know what it is. Already in ancient times this view came under criticism. Aristotle, for example, recognized that Socratic practicalism is rather naive: there are many instances of someone knowingly doing

wrong. And indeed, Socrates, as a pagan Greek, did not acknowledge the sinful nature of human beings. Just because we
know what is right does not mean that we will practice it. Note
that practicalism is still in vogue today. It is sometimes reflected
in some theories of sex education: all we need to do is to tell our
youngsters about the birds and the bees and how to cross the
street safely, and they will know enough to stay out of trouble.
Or again, practicalism shows up in the idea that education will
solve all social ills.

Socrates was not the only representative of classical Greek
individualism. There were also the Sophists, itinerant teachers
who claimed to teach true *sophia*, true wisdom. Moving from
place to place the Sophists offered, for a fee, to train the young
and ambitious Greek in the noble arts of politics and persuasion.
They were frequently very successful, sometimes gathering a
large following and amassing wealth and fame. With few exceptions the Sophists were regarded highly by the Greeks. But
Socrates, Plato, and Aristotle opposed them, mostly because they
believed that the Sophists did not teach real truth, but only
clever ways of winning arguments. Due to the criticism of
philosophers such as Plato and Aristotle the term "sophism" has
acquired derogatory connotations, so that we now think of
sophistry as beguiling and fallacious reasoning.

Like Socrates, the Sophists were individualists, uncon-
cerned about broad cosmological questions. And although some
were monists and others dualists in both the cosmogonic or
structuralistic camps, the Sophists, like Socrates, worked mainly
in the area of epistemology. They concentrated on teaching, on
the acquisition of knowledge, on the ability to engage in dispu-
tation, and on education in general.

On the other hand, the Sophists differed from Socrates in
several ways. In the first place, they were not practicalists. Second, the Sophists, as indicated earlier, differed from Socrates in
that they tended toward relativism. Whereas Socrates believed
in stable truth, the Sophists rejected absolutes. As Protagoras, a
leading early 5th-century Sophist declared, "Man is the measure
of all things." Third, unlike Socrates, the Sophists exhibited a
tendency toward skepticism. Gorgias, for example, appears to
have maintained that nothing can be known with certainty.

An important topic of debate among the Sophists was the question of the law individuals should obey. Some claimed that the laws of nature are to be regarded as ultimate. Others, however, advocated that the laws enacted by the city-state are determinative for human life. Those who held to the former position, insisting that the laws of the city-state are in conflict with the laws of nature, defended a variety of theories, such as "might makes right" or anarchy. Callicles and Thrasymachus, for example, argued in support of the "might makes right" theory on grounds that natural law requires that the stronger rule the weaker. Antiphon, another Sophist, also believing that the laws of the state are contrary to the laws of nature, suggested that the abolition of state law, and hence anarchy, is the solution to political and social problems.

Observe that the Sophists, in dealing with the question of law, are struggling to understand God's ordinances *for* creation in terms of the laws *of* nature. Their conclusion that there is an inherent contradiction between a so-called law of nature and the laws of government is, of course, mistaken. In the first place, there is no such thing as "natural law." All of creation is subject to the laws of God and these laws are just and right, as the psalmist tells us. Furthermore, while it is true that officials, ignoring God's commands, frequently enact unjust legislation, the Lord nevertheless intends governors to rule justly and lovingly. After all, all authority, and therefore all legislation, is responsible to the Lord. Conflict between legislation and God's ordinances is not something natural and unavoidable, as some of the Sophists argued, but is the result of disobedience on the part of those whose office it is to serve the Lord in the political arena.

Somewhat less important for the history of philosophy is a third group of representatives of classical Greek individualism, the so-called Minor Socratic schools. These were not schools officially founded by Socrates, but merely loose associations of philosophers who continued the line of thought begun by Socrates. Most famous of these groups were the Cynics. Antisthenes, an early Cynic, placed strong stress on personal independence. This reflects his individualism. Diogenes of Sinope (along the north coast of Asia Minor), a 4th-century Cynic and perhaps the most notorious of them all, placed even greater stress on individual freedom and independence, deliberately flouting all social norms and conventions, even behaving indecently in public. Still today we call those who sneer at sincerity, helpfulness, and other laudable activity as being inspired by ulterior motives, "cynics." Diogenes also taught that there is no essential difference between humans and animals; a human, in fact, should live like an animal. The philosophy of Diogenes the Cynic is a sad picture of the bankruptcy of paganism.

Plato

Plato was born in 427 B.C. of a wealthy and important Athenian family. In his youth he seems to have been attracted to politics as well as to the arts. The execution of Socrates, to whom he had been devoted, apparently caused a disappointed Plato to become thoroughly disenchanted with political activity and democracy. Nevertheless, when he traveled to Sicily later on in his life, he attempted to put some of his own political theories into practice.

In the year 388 B.C. Plato founded the Academy in Athens. This institution has been called the first European university, and not unjustly, for, in addition to philosophy, studies at the Academy ranged over a wide area. Soon the Academy acquired a splendid reputation, attracting students from far and wide. The school continued to be the center of Platonism for nearly a thousand years after the death of its founder in 348 B.C.

Plato laid down his philosophy in the form of dialogues, that is, compositions portraying conversations between a protagonist and other discussion participants. Frequently Plato makes Socrates the leading character. The dialogues not only display Plato's philosophic insight, but they are literary masterpieces as well. We are very fortunate indeed to possess all the dialogues ever written by this great thinker.

A careful study of his works reveals that Plato slowly developed and revised his thinking. At first, because of his close association with Socrates, he tended toward individualism, but as time went on he switched to partial-universalism. In addition, he changed from monism to dualism and back to monism. By and large his philosophy displays a strong cosmogonic flavor. We will briefly describe the prevailing contours of Plato's ontology, epistemology, and anthropology.

The key feature that distinguished Plato's ontology from that of his predecessors is his recognition that the ordering principle for the cosmos cannot be located within the cosmos itself. Unfortunately, he consequently developed a form of "otherworldly" philosophy in which his so-called theory of Ideas or Forms plays a major role.

In order to understand clearly the nature of Plato's theory of Ideas, we do well to remind ourselves of the kinds of discussions that had taken place earlier in the history of Greek philosophy. Cosmogonic thinkers such as Heraclitus had placed strong stress on coming-into-being, on utterly permanent change, and on flux. To Heraclitus the process of becoming characterized reality. Parmenides, on the other hand, had in structuralistic fashion argued that the heart of reality is static immobility and everlasting immutability. Motion and change, he had claimed, is merely appearance and illusion. The really real is and remains the same, yesterday, today, and forever immutable, that is to say, continually unchanging.

Plato's theory of Ideas reflects the polarity between change and permanence. From Socrates he had learned, moreover, that it is important to search for stable truth. By tracing out definitions Socrates had looked, in the face of varying degrees and instances of justice and courage, for the unchanging essence of justice and courage. These considerations led Plato to postulate that our world of experience, our world of change and flux, our world of more or less justice, more or less courage, more or less goodness, is governed by another world beyond, where pure, perfect, and unchanging justice, courage, and goodness abide forever. Our daily world of experience, which is a temporal world of change, is determined by another, unchanging, eternal world beyond. We see, then, that Plato realized that the ordering principle, the law for our experienced reality, is not to be found in that reality itself, as the earlier cosmologists had thought, but must be sought in a realm beyond the limits of the cosmos.

But what is this "world beyond the world"? Plato pencils it in as the world of Ideas or Forms. The term "Idea" must not confuse us. "Idea" in this context does not mean "notion" or "concept" or anything that I just have in my head. The word "Idea," related to the Greek "*oida*" or Latin "*video*," that is, to "comprehend" or "see," is used to denote actual, concrete, existing models for what we experience. For example, as I walk from my home to the college I notice a number of maple trees. Some are smaller, some are bigger, some are neat, and some are scraggly. Yet they are all maple trees. Why? Because, according to Plato's theory, in the world of Ideas beyond the cosmos there exists one abiding unchanging perfect Idea of a maple tree, the maple tree in all its essence, the model or prototype maple tree after which all the maple trees in our world of experience are modeled. Hence, for everything that I see in this changing world of ours there exists, in a world beyond, an unchanging Idea or model that determines the nature of the thing I see.

Plato is groping after the true state of affairs. He realizes, as Christians do, that the nature of things is not determined by the things themselves. Unlike "this-worldly" thinkers who talk about inherent "natural laws," Plato recognized that we must look past things to find that which orders them. But lacking the light of the Word revelation, he could not see that it is God's mighty Word in Christ that has created, structured, and now maintains all things. The maple tree is a maple tree not because of some inherent biological law; nor, as Plato would have it, is there an eternal idea of a maple tree; rather, the tree is structured and determined by the Word of the Lord which created and upholds all things, each after its own kind through his law *for* creation. The maple trees along my path to school, too, find their ultimate meaning in Jesus Christ, the Word of God in whom all things cohere.

Observe that there is a sharp difference between Plato's Ideas and the biblical concept of God's ordinances. Plato's Ideas are mere models, dispassionately residing in a world beyond which our world merely imitates or poorly reflects. God's word and ordinances, on the other hand, exert a constant maintaining and upholding power. Not only that, God's word, unlike the Ideas, requires obedient response. The maple tree, in growing from a sapling to a large shade tree, obeys the requirements of God's ordinances for the tree. The most crucial difference between Plato's Ideas and the word of God, however, is that Plato's Ideas are divorced from God himself. In fact, according to Plato, the "god" who brought the universe into being is also subject to the Ideas. The Ideas exist in themselves and of them-

selves, independent of and transcending everyone and everything. In contrast, the Bible tells us that it is the Lord who issues
his word and commandments. All the creation shakes and
trembles at the mighty power of God's Word. Plato's Ideas,
however, evoke no fear or trembling whatever, but, as we shall
see, merely intellectual contemplation—what the Greeks called
"*theoria.*"

The biblical idea of creation is not present in Plato's philosophy. In the *Timaeus*, one of his later dialogues, Plato explains
how the world came into being. A subordinate deity, a god he
refers to as the "demiurge," an artificer or craftsman, modeled
the world after the pattern of the Ideas. (See quotation #4 on
page 51. Plato's cosmogonism stands out in this dialogue.)

As indicated earlier, Plato seems to have hesitated between
dualism, monism, and pluralism. At a certain stage in his career
he merely postulated a plurality of Ideas. But later on he became
interested in the relationship among the Ideas, finally concluding
that there is one governing Idea, the Idea of The Good, to which
all other Ideas, including the The True and The Beautiful, are
related. We see the tendency toward monism here.

A consideration of Plato's ontology naturally leads us to
examine his epistemology, for, as is often the case, epistemologies tend to follow patterns set by ontologies. Plato's epistemology takes its starting point from the distinction between the
world of experience and the world of Ideas. Since the world of
Ideas is eternal and immutable, it is the *really* real world. Our
world of experience is, in contrast, a constantly changing world,
lacking reliable reality. As a consequence, knowledge of the
world of experience is inferior to knowledge of the world of
Ideas. If we have knowledge of the Ideas, we have knowledge
that is certain and stable. It is really true knowledge. Knowledge of the changing world of our everyday lives, on the other
hand, is not really knowledge at all: it is mere belief or opinion.
In sum, the distinction between the world of Ideas and our
changing world below leads Plato to distinguish between true
knowledge and mere belief and opinion. As we will soon see,
few people are in the know, most just believe.

How do we obtain knowledge? Plato recognizes that we
are all born into our everyday world of experience. But, he says,
unless we strive to gain knowledge of the Ideas, we will remain

bound to our sense experience, beliefs and opinions, and thus never know the truth. The way to the Ideas and to truth is not the way of the senses (or body) but of the mind (or soul). (See quotation #2 on page 50.) Only after carefully developing the ability to contemplate what is real, to think logically and theoretically, to complete a long study of mathematics and philosophy, will one be able to discern the true nature of the Ideas. True knowledge, therefore, is a theoretical, scientific kind of knowledge. It follows that only those who are experts in mathematics and precisely articulated scientific thought have true knowledge. Plato describes this situation graphically in his famous allegory of the cave, in Book 7 of the *Republic*, one of his most influential dialogues. (See quotation #1 on page 50.) Humans, Plato tells us, are like a group of prisoners in a cave, chained, facing a wall, unable to turn around. Behind them is a platform on which certain men carry a variety of objects. Farther back behind the platform, toward the mouth of the cave, there is light. What do the chained prisoners see? Only shadows cast by the objects behind them. They never see the concrete objects themselves nor the light. Only when one escapes from one's bonds after a long struggle and great pain and becomes accustomed to the light, ultimately to the light of the sun outside the cave, can one discern the true situation. Once that is accomplished, the former prisoner is told to return to the depths of the cave and tell his former cohorts about the real world. But the response he gets is only laughter and ridicule for suggesting that their world is not where it's at. So it is with the philosopher, for those who love wisdom. He must loosen himself from the slavery of a world of shadows, that is, from our daily experience and the body's senses, none of which yields true knowledge, and ascend, by way of methodic contemplation, to the reality of the Ideas.

Observe that Plato's epistemology leads to elitism. Only certain professional, thoroughly trained, scientific thinkers have access to the truth. Everyone else lives in an inferior world of shadows and uncertainty. It is to these that the philosopher must "return" in the allegory. In the *Republic*, after these philosopher-kings have fulfilled their obligations of ordering and teaching, Plato assures his readers that they will stand in good stead. Or as he writes in another dialogue (*Symposium* 212a) about the philosophers, about those who fix their mind on

The Good, The True, and The Beautiful: "Don't you realize that
the gods smile on such a person who bears and nurtures true
goodness and that, to the extent that any human being does, it is
he who has the potential for immortality?"

This kind of elitism has plagued Western civilization, including Christianity, for a long time. In the Middle Ages, for example, it was only the clergy, the theologically trained, who presumably *knew* the way of salvation; the laity *just believed* it. In
our times platonic elitism has manifested itself in profession-
alism. Professional people, such as doctors, lawyers, ministers,
and professors, were often regarded as superior to those who
worked with their hands—an echo of Plato's doctrine that the
scientific application of the mind is superior to anything else
humans can do. A change in the financial status of those who
work with their hands has done much to undo the old elitism.
But still today Christians, among others, unfortunately often
have less regard for graduates of technical training schools than
for those with a liberal arts education.

Note also that Plato's epistemology is outspokenly intellectualistic. The intellect, the mind, scientific thinking, all open the
door to "salvation." The intellect alone provides access to the
truth. The senses, in contrast, cannot be trusted. The senses tell
us only about the changing world of experience, which, after all,
is only a world of appearance, a world of opinion.

We move on to consider Plato's anthropology. Plato's view
of humans was influenced by orphism and pythagoreanism. As
a result, for most of his career, he believed in a dichotomy, a division, within human beings between soul and body. The soul is
immortal and akin to the divine, while the body is little more
than a tomb or a prison. (See page 50 for quotation #3.) The
soul exists in the body like a bird in a cage. In his later years,
however, Plato began to develop theories about a closer connection between soul and body.

Although he retained a vital interest in individuals, Plato
always saw them against the background of the entire cosmos.
In fact, Plato looked at a human being as a small (micro) image
of the whole (macro) world. Human beings and the world
resemble each other: every person is a microcosm of the whole
world, while the whole world is a macrocosm of the human
being. That means, for example, that the world has a soul—the

power that keeps everything in motion—as well as a navel—the celestial north pole, around which the heavens rotate.

Throughout most of his career Plato further postulated the tripartition of the soul. The soul, he explains in the *Republic*, in the *Timaeus*, and in other dialogues, is composed of three "parts": a rational part, a spirited part, and an appetitive part. The rational part is, of course—in view of Plato's intellectualism—the highest part, the appetitive the lowest. The spirited part of the soul is responsible for human emotions, while the appetitive part accounts for our desires and drives. One knotty problem about all this is the question whether the entire tripartite soul is immortal or only its rational part. Plato seems to give conflicting answers to this question.

In addition to his work in ontology, epistemology, and anthropology, Plato developed important theories of the state, of the physical world, and of art. A discussion of these theories, however, more properly belongs to their respective disciplines.

Plato's ontology, epistemology, and anthropology have had an enormous impact on the subsequent Western world. We have already spoken of elitism. More importantly, Plato's view of our everyday world as mere appearance yielding no more than opinion tended to impede scientific, empirical observation. Artistic activity, however, was ranked even lower: to make copies of a world that is itself a shadow of what is really real diverts the mind from what should be foremost. Early Christianity was powerfully affected by Platonism, as it developed a marked other-worldliness and world-flight mentality. The idea that the soul must eventually escape from the body led to numerous forms of asceticism—practicing strict self-denial as a measure of personal and especially "spiritual" discipline. Finally, the intellectualism of Plato contributed significantly to the idea that our mind, our rational, analytic function, is the only human tool to be trusted as our sure guide in life. The rationalism and a faith(!) in science of a later age are the distant results.

Undoubtedly Plato was one of the greatest minds of the Western world. He did much to raise the level of scientific thinking and philosophy. This calls for recognition and tribute. At the same time, his greatness and frequently acclaimed nobility must not blind us to the distortions he bequeathed to the Western world.

A few representative quotations from

PLATO

1. "And now, I said, let me show in an illustration how far our nature is enlightened or unenlightened: Behold! human beings living in an underground den that has a mouth open toward the light and reaching all along the den; here they have been from their childhood, and have their legs and necks chained so that they cannot move, and can only see before them, being prevented by the chains from turning round their heads. Above and behind them a fire is blazing at a distance, and between the fire and the prisoners there is a raised way; and you will see, if you look, a low wall built along the way, like the screen that marionette players have in front of them, over which they show their puppets...."

"[Dear Glaucon,] the prison-house is the world of sight, the light of the fire is the sun, and you will not misapprehend me if you interpret the journey upwards to be the ascent of the soul into the intellectual world.... In the world of knowledge the idea of Good appears last of all, and is seen only with an effort, and, when seen, is also inferred to be the universal author of all things beautiful and right, parent of light and of the lord of light in this visible world, and the immediate source of reason and truth in the intellectual; and that this is the power upon which he who would act rationally either in public or private life must have his eye fixed."   *Republic* vii

2. "[This] fact is manifest to us: if we are to have clear knowledge of anything, we must get rid of the body, and let the soul by itself behold objects by themselves. And one day, we may suppose, that intelligence which we desire and whose lovers we claim to be will be ours: not while we yet live..., but when we have died.... While we are alive, it seems we will come nearest to knowledge if we have as little as possible to do with the body, if we limit our association with it to absolute necessities, keeping ourselves pure and free from bodily infection until such time as god himself releases us. And being thus made pure and rid of the body's follies we may expect to join the company of the purified, and have direct knowledge of all truth unobscured; for that the impure should apprehend the pure, heaven will hardly permit."   *Phaedo* 67

3. "Thus the soul, since it is immortal and has been born many times, and has seen all things both here and in the other world [of Ideas], has learned everything that is. So we need not be surprised if it can recall the knowledge of virtue or anything else which, as we see, it

once possessed. All nature is akin, and the soul has learned everything, so that when a man has recalled a single piece of knowledge —learned it, in ordinary language—there is no reason why he should not find out all the rest, if he keeps a stout heart and does not grow weary of the search; for seeking and learning are in fact nothing but recollection [*anamnesis*]." *Meno* 81

4. "All men, Socrates, who have any degree of right feeling at the beginning of every enterprise . . . call upon god. And we, too, who are going to discourse of the nature of the universe . . . must invoke the aid of gods and goddesses and pray that our words may be acceptable to them and consistent with themselves. . . .

"First then... we must make a distinction and ask, What is that which always is and has no becoming; and what is that which is always becoming and never is? That which is apprehended by intelligence and reason is always in the same state; but that which is conceived by opinion with the help of sensation and without reason, is always in a process of becoming and perishing and never really is. . . . Now that which is created must, as we affirm, of necessity be created by a cause. But the father and maker of all this universe is past finding out; and even if we found him, to tell of him to all men would be impossible. And there is still a question to be asked about him: Which of the patterns had the artificer in view when he made the world,—the pattern of the unchangeable, or of that which is created? . . . Every one will see that he must have looked to the eternal; for the world is the fairest of creations and he is the best of causes. And having been created in this way the world has been framed in the likeness of that which is apprehended by reason and mind and is unchangeable, and must therefore of necessity... be a copy of something. . . . As being is to becoming, so is truth to belief." *Timaeus* 2-8

Aristotle

Aristotle, the second of the two towering figures in ancient Greek philosophy, was born in 384 B.C. in Stagira in northern Greece. As a young man of about 16 he traveled to Athens and entered the Academy of Plato. There he became a loyal and devoted pupil and friend of the great master for more than 20 years. When Plato died in 348 B.C., Aristotle left Athens and traveled to various places in the Aegean world, including Pella in Macedonia, where he tutored the young Alexander, later called the Great. In 335 Aristotle returned to Athens and founded his own school, the Lyceum. He died in 322 B.C.

Like Plato, Aristotle developed and changed his philosophy as he matured. While a student at the Academy he undoubtedly shared the perspective of Plato. But later, as an independent thinker, Aristotle rejected the doctrine of the Ideas and returned to a one-world philosophy. Reality was here in the concrete things around us, not in some other world. To suggest that there are two worlds only doubles the problems and does not help us know anything any better.

The precise story of Aristotle's development is not clear. Unfortunately, the works of Aristotle that we now possess are not like the polished dialogues of Plato. Rather, they consist of a collection of what appears to be sets of lecture notes that were put together after Aristotle's death; frequently different, sometimes even contradictory sections from different stages of his development are found right next to each other. This situation makes Aristotle's challenging philosophic writings even more difficult to understand.

Aristotle's ontology hinges on his concept of "being." *Being*, Aristotle says, is the foundation of reality. When I look around I see all sorts of things in the world—people, trees, houses, and what have you. Though they look different, we may nevertheless say about all of them that they *are*, that they have being. Every existing thing is at root a manifestation of *being*. But since things are in fact different, it follows that the being of things is *being* expressed in different ways. Aristotle explains that there are different "categories" of being, various ways in which things can be different. The two most basic categories are *substance* and a set of *accidents*, in the sense that every thing is a substance and every thing has accidents. Take a chair. The chair exists and is therefore fundamentally a form of being. After all, if it had no being, it would not exist. The being of the chair, then, can be described in terms of the two "categories" of being, substance and accidents. We begin with the "accidents" of the chair: the variable characteristics or attributes that the chair displays. For example, the size of the chair is one of its accidents. So is its place and its color. All of these could change without changing the chair into something else. These accidents—and there are a least nine of them, Aristotle claims—do not drift loosely in the void, but are attached, as it were, to the essence of the chair. This essence, underlying all the accidents, is the substance, the *it*, of the chair. If I could think away all the accidents, I would have just the substance left. Substance, in other words, functions as the substratum of, that which lies "under," the accidents. This theory of being, often referred to as "metaphysics," bristles with complexities and difficulties. Yet it became a hallmark of the history of Western philosophy. Medieval philosophers and theologians, for example, made extensive use of it. Today Roman Catholic philosophers still hold international conferences to discuss the subtleties of "being." Actually, the theory of "substance," though much more sophisticated, is as mistaken as Thales' claim that everything is water. There is, in fact, no such thing as "being" or "substance." It is no more than a metaphysical abstraction, an attempt to give reality independence and to ground it on some sure footing. Aristotle's notion of "being" is another pagan attempt to find the ordering principle in a world without the God of Scripture. Again, without the enlightenment of the Word of God, distortions are inevitable.

Although we cannot go into detail, a brief exposition of another ontological theory of Aristotle is not out of place, namely, the doctrine of hylemorphism. According to Aristotle, hylemorphism is still another way in which we may understand the ontological structure of things. The term itself is a combination of two Greek words meaning "matter" and "form." Aristotle argues that every existing thing is not only substance and accidents, but that its substance—what makes it it—is composed of two constituents, form and matter. Let's look at the chair again. It is made of wood. The wood, Aristotle would say, is the "matter" of the chair (a particularly apt example, since the original meaning of "hyle" is "wood"). But, of course, the chair is not just simply a chunk of wood. It is wood in the form of a chair. Hence we may put it this way: the "form" of "chairness" has been imposed on the "matter," that is, the wood. Actually, the form supplies what is universal about the chair—its "chairiness," its "there-to-be-sat-upon-ness"—and the matter is what individuates the form, making this chair *this* chair. The theory of hylemorphism reflects Aristotle's dualism: all things are made up of two principles.

Aristotle combined the theory of hylemorphism with still another relationship, namely, actuality and potentiality. This distinction can be clarified by looking again at the chair. Originally the chair was just plain unformed wood. Nevertheless, the wood had the potential of being made into a chair. In fact, the finished chair is the actualization of the wood's potential. Take, as another example, the relationship between an acorn and an oak tree: an acorn is a potential oak tree, while the oak tree is an actualized acorn.

By using hylemorphism, the actuality-potentiality relationship, and other theories, Aristotle attempted to understand change. All things are in a process of change. We experience this daily, of course. Plato, you will recall, had declared the world of experience and change to be unreal, merely a reflection or transitory imitation of the eternal, immutable Ideas in the world beyond. But since Aristotle had rejected the theory of Ideas, he needed another explanation of what stayed the same and what changed in our world. Every thing, he concluded, every substance stays the same but is also changing as it moves from potentiality to actuality. Everything moves toward the fulfillment of a goal (*telos*) or purpose. The stress on the role of purpose gives Aristotle's ontology a teleological character. We should note that Aristotle's preoccupation with teleology does not make him a cosmogonic thinker. On the contrary, Aristotle's thought is essentially structuralistic. While he tries to explain change, coming-into-being and passing away, he maintains that such change is merely a part or an aspect of an eternal structure of things. The world as a whole has never come into being and will not ever go out of existence.

Because Aristotle believed that being at rest is the natural state, he had to explain what the motion and change that we experience is all about. Where is this self-contained eternal universe going? He therefore postulated the eternal existence of an Unmoved Mover, a divine substance, eternally actualizing the world. There is no "matter" in the Unmoved Mover; he is pure Form, pure Actuality, the Final Cause of all that is. Note that Aristotle is not speaking about an originator, a divine creator in some sense. Rather, the Unmoved Mover—Aristotle's god—can best be compared to a magnet: it causes motion without itself moving. Change *must* be due to something that is unchanging: there is change, therefore "god" exists. "The first mover of necessity exists," argues Aristotle, "and in so far it is necessary, it is good, and in this sense a first principle on which depend the heavens and the world of nature" (*Metaphysics* 1072b11). According to Aristotle's theology god is unchanging (immutable), perfectly simple (an indivisible substance), separate from sensible things (complete in itself), eternal (untouched by time), and entirely self-centered and dispassionate (impassive and unalterable). Hence no personal relationship with him is possible. One cannot come into meaningful contact with him. This conception of a highest being with which no union is possible we call monarchianism. It is an important strand in the historical web of Western thought.

An examination of Aristotle's epistemology reveals a tension between two theories. (See quotation #1 on page 57.) On the one hand, a strong current of empiricism runs through Aristotle's thought. Empiricism holds to the idea that our knowledge is derived for the most part from the senses. I see, hear, feel, taste, and smell the world around me, so that all sorts of impressions are transmitted through my senses into my head where my mind becomes conscious of them. In this way I gain knowledge, the empiricist claims. On the other hand, Aristotle also seems to have worked, more platonistically, with a form of intellectualism. Intellectualism disparages the senses and assigns the primary role in the development of knowledge to the intellect. At one point Aristotle seems to have postulated the existence of a "Universal Mind," some sort of "thinking spirit" that hovers above all people and activates human thought. This Universal Mind is the actualization of the human potential to think. It is as if Aristotle was trying to answer the question, "How do youngsters mature to an age of discretion? What stimulates their ability to think?" However, as on so many other topics, Aristotle is notoriously vague and ambiguous about the matter, and scholarly debate about his views about knowledge continues.

Aristotle's intellectualism is also carried over to his Unmoved Mover. The Unmoved Mover, he says, is Pure Thought thinking itself: "Thought thinks itself, so that thought and object of thought are the same." It is clear that on this point Aristotle has not rejected the intellectualism of Plato. Aristotle agrees with Plato that the intellect is more than truly human; it is a divine, godlike function in man: "god is always in that good state in which we sometimes are," pines Aristotle. Intellectual contemplation is the highest goal achievable. True happiness, in fact, is to be looked for in the exercise of the mind, in *theoria*.

We must stop to recognize at this point the very great contribution Aristotle made to the development of logic. In view of the little that was known in his day about the reasoning process, it is no less than astonishing that Aristotle was able to make such advances. He was the first to understand the law of non-contradiction, claiming it to be the firmest principle of all, a principle about which it is impossible to be in error, and one understandable to anyone who understands anything: "For the same thing to hold good and not to hold good simultaneously of the same thing in the same respect is impossible." Aristotle also clarified the relationship between terms, propositions, and arguments and worked out the many ways in which a syllogism is valid. "All animals are mortal; all men are animals; therefore, all men are mortal" (or "All B's are C's; All A's are B's; therefore All A's are C's") is a prime example of a valid syllogism. Indeed, Aristotle's contribution to deductive logic has remained significant until this very day.

It remains for us to consider briefly Aristotle's anthropology. As in his ontology, so also in his anthropology, Aristotle departs from the position of his mentor Plato. Aristotle rejected the sharp dichotomy between body and soul. He could not accept the idea that the body is merely a tomb. Instead, he postulated a much closer connection between body and soul. Using his theory of hylemorphism, he argued that soul and body constitute the form and matter of each human. We see, then, that whereas Plato had advanced an anthropology of dichotomy, Aristotle promoted an anthropology of composition. Soul and body do not form two separate incompatible entities, but a composite. Death, as with Plato, is assumed to be the separation of soul and body. For Aristotle, this implies that death is the end. The most that lives on is you (or your thoughts) in the thoughts of others.

Plants and animals have soul too, according to Aristotle. Plants contain a vegetative soul responsible for growth, animals a sensitive soul. These two souls are present in human souls as well. Human souls are distinguished, however, by their rational element. Here Aristotle's intellectualism takes over again. Men, in effect, are rational animals; an animal endowed with a rational soul. Women are that too, but always one notch down: "The female is as it were a male deformed...."

Besides his work in philosophy and logic, Aristotle also wrote about aesthetics, ethics (see quotation #2), politics, biology, astronomy, and physics. A man of enormous learning, Aristotle remained a dominant figure in the intellectual world of the West for centuries after his death. In fact, there are many Christians still today who, with St. Thomas Aquinas, simply refer to him as The Philosopher.

A few representative quotations from

ARISTOTLE

1. "All men naturally desire knowledge. An indication of this is our esteem for the senses....

"Now animals are by nature born with the power of sensation, and from this some acquire the faculty of memory, whereas others do not. Accordingly the former are more intelligent and capable of learning than those which cannot remember. Such as cannot hear sounds (as the bee, and any other similar type of creature) are intelligent, but cannot learn; those only are capable of learning that possess this sense in addition to the faculty of memory.

"Thus the other animals live by impressions and memories, and have but a small share of experience; but the human race lives also by art and reasoning. It is from memory that men acquire experience, because the numerous memories of the same thing eventually produce the effect of a single experience. Experience seems very similar to science and art, but actually it is through experience that men acquire science and art.... Art is produced when from many notions of experience a single universal judgment is formed with regard to like objects. [E]xperience is knowledge of particulars, but art of universals;... we consider that knowledge and proficiency belong to art rather than to experience, and we assume that artists [including, e.g., physicians] are wiser than men of mere experience ...; and this is because the former know the cause, whereas the latter do not....

"The difference between art and science [is found in the greater degree of wisdom]. Wisdom is concerned with the primary causes and principles. [The] wise man knows all things, so far as possible, without having knowledge of every one of them individually; ... in every branch of knowledge a man is wiser in proportion as he is more accurately informed and better able to expound the causes....

"[The] knowledge of everything must necessarily belong to him who in the highest degree possesses knowledge of the universal.... These things, namely, the most universal, are perhaps the hardest for man to grasp, because they are the furthest removed from the senses. Again, the most exact of the sciences are those that are most concerned with the first principles.... Moreover, the science that investigates causes is more instructive than one that does not.... And that science is supreme... which knows for what end each action is to be done; i.e., the Good in each particular case, and in general the highest Good in the whole of nature....

"Now there are four recognized kinds of cause. Of these we hold that one is the essence or essential nature of the thing [the formal cause]; an other is the matter of substrate [the material cause]; the third is the source of motion [the efficient cause]; and the fourth is the opposite to this, namely, the purpose or 'good'; for this is the end [the final cause] of every generative or motive process."

Metaphysics Book I

2. "By the mean of the thing I denote a point equally distant from either extreme, which is one and the same for everybody; by the mean relative to us, that amount which is neither too much nor too little, and this is not one and the same for everybody.... In the same way then an expert in any art avoids excess and deficiency, and seeks and adopts the mean—the mean, that is, not of the thing but relative to us....

"Virtue then is a settled disposition of the mind determining the choice of actions and emotions, consisting essentially in the observance of the mean relative to us, this being determined by principle, that is, as the prudent man would determine it. And it is a mean state between two vices, one of excess and one of defect.... The observance of the mean in fear and confidence is Courage....

"In respect of truth then, the middle character may be called truthful, and the observance of the mean Truthfulness; pretense in the form of exaggeration is Boastfulness, and its possessor a boaster; in the form of understatement, Self-depreciation, and its possessor the self-depreciator....

"This is why it is a hard task to be good, for it is hard to find the middle point in anything: for instance, not everybody can find the center of a circle, but only someone who knows geometry....

"Hence the first rule in aiming at the mean is to avoid that extreme which is the more opposed to the mean...."

Nicomachean Ethics 1106b-1109b

Both Plato and Aristotle wielded enormous influence. In fact, it has been said, with only some exaggeration, that all of Western philosophy is but a footnote to Plato. It certainly is true that the thinking of the entire Middle Ages was effectively determined by platonic and aristotelian thought. Christianity, whose formative years occurred during the early part of the Middle Ages, was confronted by these powerful pagan forces, and, as we will see, too often capitulated to them after only a brief battle.

II. B. 1.
Guide Questions

14. Why did the absence of biblical insight adversely affect the philosophy of the early Greeks?

15. Understand how the following terms are used and be able to indicate how these (pseudo-)controversies show up in some of the early cosmological philosophies:
   - "this-worldly" vs. "other-worldly" philosophy
   - cosmogonic vs. structuralistic
   - monism vs. dualism
   - universalism: emphasis on that which is universal; e.g., people are not important, but humanity; not rocks, but the mountain
   - partial universalistic: acknowledges both that which is universal and that which is individual, but either understands the one to be next to the other (macro/micro) or to be above the other (higher/lower)
   - individualistic: ontological priority given to that which is individual; there is no mountain, only a collection of rocks; no humankind, only many individual persons.

16. What "contribution" did the Orphics make to the anthropology of the pagan Greeks?

17. What does Socrates' ignorance have to do with his acclaimed wisdom?

18. What was Socrates' method and why did he find its intended results relevant?

19. Socrates and the Sophists are both representatives of classical Greek individualism. How did the Sophists differ from Socrates?

20. How is sophistry related to the Sophists?

21. What did Protagoras mean when he said, "Man is the measure of all things"?

22. Understand how Plato's "theory of ideas (or forms)" relates to his ontology, to his epistemology, and to his view of human beings.

23. Explain the deeper meaning of the "allegory of the cave."

24. What is the difference between Plato's "ideas" and the biblical concept of God's ordinances?

25. Explain, in an initial way, Aristotle's concept of "being," "substance," and "accidents."
26. What is Aristotle's theory of hylemorphism? That is, explain the basic contours of an ontology, an anthropology, and an epistemology that maintains that all things are composed of form and matter.
27. How does potentiality and actuality tie in with the teleological character of Aristotle's ontology?
28. Describe Aristotle's god.
29. On which important point does Aristotle differ with Plato's anthropology?

2. HELLENISTIC PHILOSOPHY

Introduction

The campaigns of Alexander the Great between 336 and 323 B.C. changed the world. Gone was the autonomy of the individual city-state. Gone was the security and distinctiveness of the Greek citizen. Suddenly the localism and provincialism of an earlier time was exchanged for a large cosmopolitan world in which Greek and barbarian, East and West, mingled and mixed in ways unknown before. Such a change affected every member of ancient society. Philosophic thought, too, could not escape the effects of a new age.

We speak of the philosophy in the ancient world after 320 B.C. as "hellenistic philosophy" to indicate that philosophy also acquired some different features. Just as the civilization of this time became hellenistic, that is, Greekish, in that Greek civilization was spread far and wide and mixed with various eastern and oriental cultures, so philosophy began to exhibit hellenistic traits.

We have already mentioned one important respect in which hellenistic philosophy differs from the thought of the earlier Greeks: the emphasis shifts from ontology to epistemology. This is somewhat understandable when we remember that in the hellenistic world the individual had lost the security of the small city-state and was plunged into a situation in which he had to cope with formerly unknown and now terrifying circumstances. As a result, hellenistic people were beset with uncertainty.

Many began to ask: "Is what I have always thought to be, really true? Is my knowledge really sound and trustworthy?" The reality of loneliness, isolation, and worry led to another distinct feature of hellenistic philosophy: a stress on practical living. Gone was the fascination with cosmological questions that could be debated in leisurely fashion in the marketplaces of the city-states. Instead, how to cope with a rapidly changing world became a burning, practical issue. Hellenistic thinkers began to address themselves to the new questions of the day, as the Sophists had done at an earlier time.

In many ways the Hellenistic Age represents a confused world. Nevertheless, some main lines have become clear. In this section we will concentrate on three major developments, namely, (a) the rise of skepticism and the theory of the a priori, (b) the hellenistic schools of philosophy, and (c) neoplatonism. Historically, these movements overlap with each other at various points. This book devotes a separate section to each.

Skepticism and the a priori

Unlike in the earlier Greek world, hellenistic philosophy came to expression in a variety of schools, rather than through individual sages such as Heraclitus and Parmenides or through towering figures such as Plato and Aristotle. A number of these schools, like the Stoics and the Epicureans, will be discussed straightaway.

The point here is that as the schools of the Hellenistic Age got under way a new time current began to make its appearance among them. A spirit of skepticism set in. This development is clearly compatible with the general hellenistic preoccupation with epistemology. Can we be sure of what we think we know, especially in a world that seems to be riddled with uncertainty and change? In itself the very presence of a process of change raised suspicions: Had not Plato declared that truth can be found only in the stable and eternal immutable world of Ideas?

In general, hellenistic skepticism developed in two stages. At first there arose a questioning of the knowledge of the ancient philosophers. Plato, for example, had confidently asserted the existence of the Ideas and the immortality of the soul. But the Hellenistic Age was not so sure. Soon the skepticism took on a more radical character: the question no longer concerned merely

philosophic knowledge, but whether we can know anything at
all.

At the beginning of the third century B.C., a good deal of
the skeptical spirit came to be expressed in a full-fledged school
of Skepticism, said to have been founded by Pyrrho of Elis.
According to Pyrrho, we can never say, "This is so." All we can
say is, "This appears to me to be so." As a result he urged that in
all matters we withhold or suspend judgment. This kind of
skepticism created difficulties, of course, as the ancients themselves already perceived. Indeed, consistent skepticism, like
consistent relativism, seems to be an impossibility. If the Skeptic
says, "All things are uncertain," then he has just stated one
undisputed certainty, namely, that all things are uncertain, just
as the relativist contradicts herself when she claims that everything is relative: for such a claim asserts an absolute amidst the
relativity.

As skepticism pervaded most of the hellenistic schools of
philosophy, a reaction set in. And no wonder. For true skepticism is incompatible with life itself. There are all sorts of cer-
tainties (besides death and taxes) that we daily experience and
that skepticism cannot argue out of existence. In the final analysis skepticism remains merely a theory.

In any case, in the Hellenistic Age the skeptical question
"How can we be sure?" came to be answered by the theory of the
a priori. This theory runs as follows: our senses provide us only
with uncertain knowledge of a changing world. Plato had been
right: we can trust neither our senses nor our experience. True
certainty, however, is nevertheless available. Where? It is to be
found in our mental apparatus. Everybody, so the theory of a
priori claims, is born with a set of innate (inborn) ideas. These
ideas and concepts are true and reliable, and part and parcel of
our make-up. What we need to make it in the world comes as
standard equipment! Every mature adult has what it takes to
find peace and happiness. The very structure of our mind, therefore, guarantees the certainty of knowledge. All men, according
to the theory, have certain trustworthy notions about the gods,
about right and wrong, and good and bad, and so on, built right
into their heads, as it were.

Now, note carefully: these innate concepts and notions are
not affected or changed by our experiences. The truth and relia-

bility of these a priori concepts cannot be touched by life or circumstances. They are independent from and had prior to our experience, before encountering and undergoing the things of our daily lives.

We must stop for a moment to consider the crucial importance of this hellenistic development. What is happening here? The theory of the a priori is nothing less than the beginning of the concept "human reason," a concept that was destined to have a long and distinguished career in the history of the West. In the theory of the a priori we find the origin of the belief that all men have in their heads a faculty called "reason" that we all share and all have in common. From here on in, then, reasonable men, i.e., those who are able and willing to reason, can sit together and discuss reasonably and agree on reasonable conclusions, no matter what their beliefs, commitments, or presuppositions. This idea, that arose in the Hellenistic Age, was adopted in the Middle Ages as the "natural light of reason." There it came to be regarded as an independent and separate "light" not in need of the light of God's Word, and, in the modern world, gave rise to powerful movements of Rationalism.

The concept "reason" as an independent a priori faculty, common to all men and functioning as an autonomous source and guide for life, is a myth, a pagan invention designed to give mankind, lost in uncertainty and sin, a solid mooring, an anchor. But human "reason" is no more trustworthy than anything else outside of the Word of the Lord. To put one's faith in "reason" is idolatry.

Note, of course, that we do not deny human rationality. All healthy people exhibit a discerning, analytic mode of human functioning that plays an important role in the understanding and insight to which they attain. But, as we will discuss toward the end of our study, our analytic ability is very much woven in with our other functions, such as beliefs and feelings and our physical existence, and has no independence or autonomy whatsoever. It is interesting to note that in our own age the disastrous implications of the concept "reason" have begun to be recognized. But we tell that story later.

Hellenistic Schools

Perhaps one of the most significant and influential of the hellenistic schools was the philosophy of the Stoics. *Stoicism* was founded by Zeno of Citium around 300 B.C. This Zeno should not to be confused with Zeno the pupil of Parmenides, famous for his paradoxes. From Zeno's beginnings Stoicism spread through the hellenistic world and later throughout the Roman world. For example, Marcus Aurelius, the Roman emperor from A.D. 161 to 180, was a Stoic. So were Cicero, Seneca, and Epictetus. As stoicism grew and spread, it changed from a philosophic system to more of a guide to conduct. A number of important Stoic themes are noteworthy.

Stoics were especially interested in the problem of human conduct and basically equated human virtue with right knowledge and intellectual understanding. Once a person achieves the right state of mind, complete well-being, whatever comes your way, is guaranteed. The goal then is to strive throughout one's life to gain this wisdom—which is, ultimately, to know Destiny's purposes.

The wisdom needed comes with the use of reason, a natural light, a spark, within the soul. This light shines brightest when we free ourselves from the physical demands of our bodies, like the emotions and pleasure-seeking desires. Circumstances of the outer life tend to create disorder in the soul. True enlightenment comes through acting in accordance with one's inner nature; for we are, by Nature, rational beings. And, wouldn't you know it, say the Stoics, what reason (= Destiny) dictates is that we conform to the Maker's design and act in accordance with Nature.

The Stoic doctrine of the *Logos* laid down many of their presuppositions. The Greek word "logos" has many different meanings, such as "word," "reason," "pattern," and so on. (The Gospel of John, for example, speaks of Christ as the Logos, that is, the Word of God.) In the Stoic sense "logos" means "reason" or "pattern." The Stoics regarded "Logos" as a divine cosmic spirit, conceiving it as a living fiery *aether*—a rarified element, believed to fill the upper regions of space. This Logos expresses itself by means of "rational seeds" or "seminal reasons" (*logoi spermatikoi*): in humans and animals as soul, in the plant kingdom as growth, and in inorganic material as cohesion. Hence, the Stoics were essentially pantheists (and therefore universalists): god, the Logos (= Zeus, Providence, Universal Reason) is diffused throughout the universe. The "Logos" is "rational" —"logos" translates into Latin as "ratio"—and the Stoics were therefore convinced that the universe is pervaded by a rational order. They likewise believed that the path of each soul is predetermined by the comprehensive plan of the Logos and that there is an infinite series of causes that logically necessitate everything that occurs. (The notion that both god and the cre- ated order are characterized by rationality became an important line in Western thought.)

To the Stoic, a life of virtue is a life lived in accordance with "Nature," with the universe as governed by the "Logos," "Reason." The law of Nature (= god) commands what is right and god (= Nature) knows what every future event will be. Vice is merely ignorance as to Nature's plan; virtue lies in coming to know the plan. Note how the Stoics do away with the power of sin. Observe also that the Stoics, like Socrates, were practicalists: once one knows about the true "logos" one will automatically behave virtuously. Once again, good insight is supposed to guarantee good action.

The Stoic ideal was the sage, a man calm, serene, and un- moved by passion or circumstances. The sage understands "Na- ture." He is not disturbed by any event because what happens was meant to be. So accept it. Nothing happens without rhyme or reason. The experience or fear of pain in connection with bodily suffering comes only because you judge that pain to be evil, which it is not. It, too, was meant to be. Freedom comes in doing what Nature wants. So, desire what you get; want, apa- thetically, what is the case; and whatever you do, don't become ecstatic(!).

Clearly, Stoicism was an attempt to give people certainty, some solid ground in a chaotic, rapidly changing hellenistic world. In Stoicism we can plainly see the religious condition of humankind, a desperate need in a sin-darkened world.

A few representative quotations of

STOICS

1. "The Stoics believe in only one cause, i.e., the Maker. [This maker] must be simple inasmuch as matter, too, is simple. Do we ask what cause is? It is surely Creative Reason, i.e., god." Seneca (*SVF* II, 346a)

2. "The Stoics are accustomed to trace all things back to an elemental
   force of a fiery nature...; their doctrine is that all force is of the nature
   of fire, and that, because of this, animate creatures perish when their
   heat fails; also in every domain of nature a thing is alive and vigorous
   if it is warm. [They say that] there is no animate being contained
   within the whole universe of nature except fire...."

   Cicero (*SVF* II, 421)

3. "Zeno said the fundamental substance of all existing things is
   fire...and the principles of fire were matter and god.... Next, the
   whole world, at certain fated periods, is dissolved by fire, and then
   formed again into a world. Now the primary fire is like a kind of
   seed, containing the reasons of all things and the causes of everything, past, present, and future. Now the union and sequence of
   these things is an inevitable and unavoidable fate, knowledge, truth,
   and law of existing things. And in this respect the events of the
   world are arranged very well, as in a well-governed city."

   Eusebius (*SVF* I, 98)

4. "Again, living virtuously is equivalent to living in accordance with
   experience of the actual course of nature, as Chrysippus says in the
   first book of his treatise *On Ends*; for our individual natures are parts
   of the nature of the whole universe. And this is why the end may be
   defined as life in accordance with nature, or, in other words, in accordance with our own human nature as well as that of the universe, a
   life in which we refrain from every action forbidden by the law
   common to all things, i.e., the right reason that pervades all things,
   and is identical with this Zeus, lord and ruler of all that is. And this
   very thing constitutes the virtue of the happy man and the smooth
   current of life, when all actions promote the harmony of the spirit
   dwelling in the individual man with the will of him who orders the
   universe."   Diogenes Laertius (*SVF* III, 4)

5. "What upsets men's minds is not events but their judgments about
   events. For instance, death is nothing dreadful (or else Socrates
   would have thought it so). No, the only dreadful thing about death
   is men's judgment that it is dreadful. And so when we are hindered,
   or disturbed, or distressed, let us never lay the blame on someone
   else, but on ourselves, that is, on our own judgments. To accuse others for one's own misfortunes is a sign of want of education; to accuse
   oneself shows that one's education has begun; to accuse neither oneself nor someone else shows that one's education is complete."

   Epictetus (*Handbook* 5)

6. "Never say of anything, 'I lost it,' but say, 'I gave it back.' Has your child died? It was given back. Has your wife died? She was given back. Has your estate been taken from you? Was this also not given back? But you say, 'He who took it from me is wicked.' What does it matter to you through whom the Giver asked it back? As long as He gives it you, take care of it, but not as your own; treat it as passers-by treat an inn."   Epictetus (*Handbook* 11)

7. "On every occasion we must have these thoughts ready:
   'Lead me, O Zeus, and lead me, Destiny,
   Whither ordained is by your decree.
   I'll follow, doubting not,
   But even if I do not wish to, because I'm bad,
   I shall follow still.' [Cleanthes]
   'Who rightly with necessity complies
   In things divine we count him skilled and wise.' [Euripides]
   'Well, Crito, if this be the gods' will,
         so be it.'" [Plato]   Epictetus (*Handbook* 53)

Epicurus, the founder of the school of the *Epicureans*, was born about 340 B.C. on Samos, an island in the Aegean Sea. His school was very strongly oriented to earlier Greek Atomism, the view that all of reality consists of indivisible particles. Like the Stoics, the Epicureans placed much stress on the question, How should we live? Observe the religious character of this question. In what way can we be fully human? Epicurus does not know the answer either. His hedonistic system of controlled pleasure, with pleasure defined as freedom from pain and fear, constitutes his method of salvation. To eliminate the fear of death is the ultimate criterion. For example, Epicurus wrote the following in his "Letter to Menoeceus":

Become accustomed to the belief that death is nothing to us. For all good and evil consists in sensation, but death is deprivation of sensation. And therefore a right understanding that death is nothing to us makes the mortality of life enjoyable, not because it adds to it an infinite span of time, but because it takes away the craving for immortality. For there is nothing terrible in life for the man who has truly comprehended that there is nothing terrible in not living. So that the man speaks but idly who says that he fears death not because it will be painful when it comes, but because it is painful in anticipation. For that which gives no trouble when it comes, is but an empty pain in anticipation. So death, the most terrifying of ills, is nothing to us, since so long as we exist, death is

not with us; but when death comes, then we do not exist. It does
not concern either the living or the dead, since for the former it is
not, and the latter are no more.

No act should be undertaken except for the pleasure in which it
results, and no act should be rejected except for the pain which it
produces. Again like the Stoics, the Epicureans were practicalists.

The a priori here is not the guidance of reason, but that provided by feelings, specifically those of pleasure and pain: "For
we recognize pleasure as the first good in us and from pleasure
we begin every act of choice and avoidance, and to pleasure we
return again, using the feeling as the standard by which we
judge every good." The hedonism of Epicurus should not be
confused with the hedonism of "eat, drink, and be merry." Epicurus's hedonism required little more than a bed, a table, and a
chair, and just good bread, clean water, and a little wine only
once and while. He was convinced that the real needs of the
body are met with simple provisions at modest expense. Anything more than that yields diminishing returns.

The Epicurean school continued into the Roman Empire.
The most important and influential expounder of Epicureanism
was Lucretius, a Roman of the first century B.C. In his poem *On
the Nature of Things* he explains the world in terms of atomism,
and attempts to show that "religion" and the fear of death are the
sources of all our woes.

The history of Plato's Academy and Aristotle's Lyceum is
long and complicated. Both of these schools passed through a
number of stages substantially altering their original character.
A particularly notable feature of hellenistic platonism is its pronounced eclectic tendency. Eclecticism, as we noted earlier,
simply means the selection and uncritical assimilation of various
doctrines from numerous sources.

One platonic development during this period is sufficiently
important to describe in some detail, as it became a significant
element in early medieval christian thought. It concerns a shift
in the location of the Ideas. In Plato's philosophy the Ideas were
self-existent entities eternally and immutably abiding in a world
beyond. Even god itself was subject to the Ideas. In hellenistic
Platonism, however, the conception began to grow that the Ideas
are not simply independent law-essences out there, but that they

exist *in the mind of god*. The Ideas, in other words, form the content of god's mind. This shift came about partly as a result of the eclectic tendency to combine Platonism with Aristotelianism. Such eclecticism produced the concept of god as an aristotelian Unmoved Mover equipped with platonic Ideas.

The aristotelian school, however, in some ways remained distinct from Platonism, particularly in regard to its tendency toward monarchianism. Recall that monarchianism postulates an unbridgeable gap between god and the cosmos. Nevertheless, some of the Aristotelians (also called "Peripatetics") could not escape the influence of Plato and adopted platonic themes.

Besides Stoicism, Epicureanism, Platonism, and Aristotelianism, other schools flourished in the Hellenistic Age. The Cynics and Neo-Pythagoreans, for example, saw a widespread revival in the second and first centuries B.C. and became an influential ingredient in the life of the Roman Empire.

Neoplatonism

Although rooted in the Platonism of the hellenistic ages, Neoplatonism constitutes a philosophic system sufficiently distinct and important to warrant separate treatment. Literally Neoplatonism means "new Platonism." It could also be described as old other-worldliness in new sheepskin.

Chronologically Neoplatonism represents the last great pagan philosophic attempt of the ancient world. Note, however, the late date of its appearance: it flourished from the third to the fifth century after Christ. Neoplatonism, therefore, was a contemporary rival to Christianity. While in the course of time many Neoplatonists were converted to Christianity, it is on the whole probably true to say, unfortunately, that Neoplatonism exercised a more penetrating influence on Christianity than the other way around. As the christian church father Augustine would later say, "There are none nearer to us than the Platonists" —by which he meant the Neoplatonism of Plotinus. At the same time we may gratefully acknowledge that Christianity persisted and grew, while Neoplatonism eventually declined and disappeared as a viable philosophic option in Western civilization.

The heyday of Neoplatonism began with the great philosopher Plotinus, who was born in Egypt about A.D. 204. After extensive studies in Alexandria—one of the great centers of learning in the hellenistic world—and participating in an expedition to Persia, Plotinus settled in Italy where he opened a school. Soon he acquired the reputation of being a kindly, spiritual, and learned man. Many came to seek his advice and counsel. Though physically frail, he enjoyed what was for that time a relatively long life. He died in A.D. 270.

Plotinus constructed a complex system composed of many strands from many philosophies. Though an original thinker to some extent, the eclectic character of much of hellenistic philosophy is evident. Predominant in his thought, however, were platonic and aristotelian themes. These show up clearly in his ontology, which is essentially a picture of a hierarchy of being stretched between a supreme god (BEING) and a lowest level of evil matter (nonbeing). At the highest level of reality, according to Plotinus, god exists in utter transcendence. This Being or god is the absolute ONE, a perfect unity about which nothing can be said and who remains forever incomprehensible. We sense here a streak of aristotelian monarchianism. Plotinus' tendency to call the absolute One the "absolute Good" reflects, on the other hand, the platonic view of the supreme Idea as "Goodness Itself." Note the paganism in Plotinus's concept of god: this god is not the creator and upholder of the universe to whom we can draw close in Jesus Christ and with whom we can engage in a covenantal relationship of love, but an immovable, ineffable, other-worldly being, in effect no more than a projection of our mathematical concept of unity.

Does the Plotinian god not relate to the world at all? Here the ambiguity and tensions, so characteristic of much pagan and secular thought, manifest themselves. On the one hand, as we saw, god is utterly transcendent. But on the other hand Plotinus claims that this god is the origin, the original source of everything that is. At this point Plotinus introduces the concept of emanation. What is emanation? Literally the word means "a flowing out of," "issuing forth from," or "proceeding from." All levels of existence, Plotinus explains, have flowed forth or proceeded from the ineffable One. It must be observed that the process of emanation has not altered the state of the One. The issuing forth has not diminished or affected god in any way. It is, at the same time, not "an act of god." Emanation happens almost in spite of this divine unity; a sort of involuntary emission. A favorite neoplatonic example used to illustrate the meaning of emanation is the picture of the rays of light and warmth proceeding from the sun. Not knowing the physical facts of solar energy emission, the Neoplatonists believed that light and heat radiated forth from the sun without diminishing or affecting the sun in any way. So it is with the coming-into-being of reality, they said.

Observe that the doctrine of emanation is basically a pagan version of the divine creation of the world. Emanation is the neoplatonic explanation for why anything exists at all. Note also that the stress on emanation gives neoplatonic philosophy a decidedly cosmogonic stamp.

The Plotinian tension between god as utterly transcendent and god as the source of all existence reflects a tension between dualistic and monistic lines of thought. The writings of Plotinus, by the way, are sufficiently difficult and obscure to allow for either interpretation. If we emphasize the otherness of god as distinct from the world, then we must call Plotinus a dualist. If, on the other hand, we interpret the emanation process as primary, we will type Plotinus a monist.

The emanation process, according to Plotinus, proceeds in stages. At the first level of emanation below the One, Plotinus locates "Mind" or "Thought," the seat of the platonic Ideas. The concept "Mind" as first emanation is actually an amalgamation of Aristotle's unmoved mover—to which Aristotle had referred as "Thought thinking itself"—and Plato's demiurge, the super craftsman who modeled the world after the pattern of the Ideas. From "Mind," Plotinus continues, emanates a double-sided soul, a higher and divine world soul that looks up to the Ideas, and a lower world soul that looks down to the world below. From this soul proceed the numerous individual souls of men. Farther down, and thus at a still greater distance from the One, we find the world of material things and nature.

Plotinus believed that the matter contained in the material world is inherently evil, not in any substantial sense, but in the sense that because of its remoteness from absolute goodness —Being itself—matter is deprived of goodness. Evil, according to Plotinus, is essentially privation—*non*being—the absence of good. As described in the works of Plotinus, this theory bristles with difficulties. Particularly vexing is the question whether this

theory implies a dualism between absolute goodness and absolute evil. But we leave this discussion to the scholars. To be
noted, however, is the fact that the idea of evil as essentially a
lack, a privation, exercises a powerful influence on the church
fathers and the later medieval church.

We may consider Plotinus's epistemology in the light of his
dichotomistic anthropology. Humans, in platonic fashion, are
composed of soul and body, in effect, a composite of being and
nonbeing. The interaction between soul and body is evidence
that the soul has become contaminated with matter. Hence it is
necessary for humans to look upwards, from whence their soul
came, and to attempt to eliminate the evil effects of the body.
The ultimate goal of mankind is to scale an ascent upwards
toward union with the One. Plotinus outlined four stations.

First, one must have complete control over one's body and
purify oneself from all matter, that is, from all evil. One must
therefore become an ascetic. The second stage is the way of philosophy, where the soul, now freed from the body and purified,
rises beyond sense perception to contemplate what moves this
world—the world-soul. Completion of the second station clears
the way to intellectually approach the universal Mind (of god)
that contains, as we saw, the eternal Ideas. In this third stage
there is a self-conscious union with Mind. And fourth, in the final stage, experienced only by a select few, there is a mystical
union in ecstasy with the One. As long as we are in the flesh,
such ecstatic union can be achieved only momentarily. In the
afterlife, however, it will be permanently enjoyed by those who
have persevered to the end.

It is clear that Neoplatonism was more than an abstract sys-
tem of thought. Instead, it offered a way of salvation from "sin."
Neoplatonism was a religion as much as it was a philosophy,
complete with purification rites, a gospel, and an eschatology.
As a result it continued to attract many pagan Greeks and
Romans.

Following the death of Plotinus, a variety of neoplatonic
leaders and schools appeared in various parts of the Roman
Empire. In Rome itself Plotinus's celebrated pupil Porphyry did
much to disseminate the doctrines of his master. Another
famous Neoplatonist was Iamblichus, a pupil of Porphyry, who
figured largely in the Syrian school of Neoplatonism. Proclus,

who led the Athenian branch of the school in the fifth century, was one of the most learned men of antiquity. He made great strides in the systematization of all ancient knowledge. His influence was felt throughout the christian Middle Ages.

Neoplatonism, in sum, was a powerful force at the time when Christianity struggled to gain the upper hand in a decaying society. Neoplatonism kept alive the flames of Platonism, thereby strengthening the hold of such pagan views as a dualistic anthropology, the inferiority of sense perception, a depreciation of created reality, and the unreality of evil. How these views affected the course of Christianity we will examine in the next chapter.

Review

In this section we have surveyed the philosophic developments of the Hellenistic Age, a period initiated by the conquests of Alexander the Great and carried over well into the Roman Empire. We saw a new spirit take rise. It is the spirit of skepticism. Nothing can be known with certainty in this uncertain age, it came to be believed. Such destructive skepticism did not continue long, however, and soon it began to be replaced by the theory of the a priori, a position that claimed that there is indeed reliable knowledge to be found. Where? Answer: in our minds. We are all born with certain kinds of trustworthy, innate knowledge, about the gods, for example, or about the difference between good and bad, pleasure and pain. Thus the idea of "reason" as an innate faculty or mechanism was born.

For the masses this era constituted a time of confusion; consequently a variety of thinkers focusing on practical knowledge instead of abstract speculation became enormously popular. The majority of these thinkers appeared in the form of schools. Most notable in the early stages of the Hellenistic Age were the schools of Stoicism and Epicureanism. Many other schools, however, such as those of Platonism, Aristotelianism, Cynicism, and Pythagoreanism flourished during this period.

Finally we examined the powerful philosophy of Neoplatonism, the final effort of pre-synthetic, pagan thought, developed by Plotinus and carried on by a variety of successors.

II. B. 2.

Guide Questions

30. Which two features distinguish the philosophy of the Hellenistic Age from the thought of the earlier Greeks?

31. What is inherently amiss when someone claims that you can know nothing for certain?

32. The theory of the a priori: Within human beings there are certain innate forms of knowledge that are not derived from experience, but instead are had prior to and determine the nature of our experience. Given the two stages of development in hellenistic skepticism, what is the importance of the theory of the a priori?

33. Briefly explain the Stoics' doctrine concerning the "Logos" and the *logoi spermatikoi*.

34. What is the Epicurean answer to the question, "How then shall we live?"

35. What does it mean to be a hedonist?

36. Which important development occurred in hellenistic Platonism?

37. Describe Plotinus's neoplatonic ontology, taking particular note of the One, and of the stages of emanation.

38. Describe Plotinus's anthropology, including his view of the individual's return to the One.

A HISTORY OF WESTERN THOUGHT DURING THE PERIOD OF SYNTHESIS

II. C.

Introduction to the Second Main Period

Confusion results when biblical themes, such as creation, sin, being created in the image of God, and being born again, are combined with pagan thought patterns. Actually, this combination, though still a persistent pattern of thinking, is always an *attempted* combination. There is no lasting unity and in the long run both the pagan way of putting things and the biblical insight are distorted. To grasp the Good News with bad categories warps the Gospel and twists the truth.

In light of the preceding discussion, it will be clear that Christianity faced no easy task when it burst into a thoroughly pagan world. The christian community was confronted by a critical situation: an apostate Greek mind had a fairly exclusive hold on the ancient world. The Gospel was proclaimed and the Church did grow. At the same time, the radical antithetical nature of the christian message often became infected and contaminated by paganism. In the succeeding centuries Christianity had to fight for its life, both against external pressure and against internal heresies. In spite of the successes scored, Christianity developed an increasingly powerful synthesis mentality, that finally culminated in the great scholastic systems of the Middle Ages.

For Christians today an understanding of what took place in this second main period is vitally important. The synthesis mentality has so powerfully affected the course of Western civilization that Reformed Christians today are still very much in the grip of a scholastic frame of mind. To a large extent our views of Scripture, theology, the Church, sin, our attitude toward society, and our understanding of the meaning of Christianity have been colored and in part determined by what took place in the first fifteen centuries of the christian Church.

Why were the early Christians unable to sustain their momentum? What caused them to adopt pagan thought patterns, so that the christian world-and-life view all too often became a variation on pagan themes? How could it be that Neoplatonism influenced Christians more than Christianity influenced Neoplatonists? Once we understand the situation a bit more fully, we will not want to blame or condemn the church fathers for their synthesis. We are not out to point a finger, to blame or condemn. Of course not. What good would that do? Nevertheless we need to evaluate critically in order that we may arrive at an understanding of the dynamic of history. Such understanding is indispensable if we are to carry out our task christianly as we face the twenty-first century.

The early Christians correctly realized that God in his Word had revealed the truth to Adam and his seed. Furthermore, they recognized their calling to obedience, and therefore also to be busy in the academic world of learning. Finally, they were aware of the fact that Greek philosophy had attained many moments of insight. After all, the Greeks were experienced observers of an ordered creation and hence in limited states of affairs could achieve great things, such as Aristotle's tremendous system of logic.

In spite of these correct realizations, a synthetic mind arose with vigor for several reasons. First of all, a few of the christian converts had been schooled in philosophy, and many had been influenced by the answers of hellenistic philosophy to the question, "How then shall we live?" As a result, they often unconsciously carried a tradition informed by pagan thought patterns. For example, stoical fatalism or a notion of an innate spark of the divine were often "baptized" with an appeal to the *logos* and light of the first chapter of the gospel according to John. Second, paganism launched a hostile attack upon the Church. In order to make their defense intelligible, the Christians needed terminology, which they borrowed from pagan philosophy and literature. Champions of the Greek tradition were hailed as protological anticipations of The Way. As a result, many Greek ideas crept into christian thought. In the third place, internal heresy demanded a clearer articulation and definition of dogma. In the attempt to accomplish this, Christians sometimes fell back upon pagan philosophy for their arguments and for their understanding of the Scriptures. Just because the Nicene Creed reaches out beyond words found in Scripture and uses the term "substance" to explain the unity of the Trinity is no grounds for theologians to begin thinking about "the attributes" of the God of Scripture as though he were an aristotelian substance.

The era during which synthesis thinking predominated can best be treated in four sections. First, mention must be made of the attempts of hellenistic Jews, prior to the christian era, to construct a synthesis between the writings of the Old Testament and Greek philosophy. Second, the period of the early church, the Patristic era, from about 50 A.D. to the beginning of the Middle Ages, saw the first attempts on the part of Christians to unify or harmonize basic themes of Scripture with pagan conceptions and thought patterns. The third period concerns the Middle Ages proper, characterized by Scholasticism. The Bible was still a source of study at this time, but the works of the church fathers and pagan thinkers usurped an increasingly important place in christian thought. Finally, there is a period that is usually not distinguished from the preceding one. Here we find a rejection of Scholasticism and a return to the emperors and church fathers.

1. JEWISH SYNTHESIS

"Synthesis philosophy" simply refers to the combination of nonscriptural conceptions with Scriptural themes. Synthetic thought and biblical Christianity did not arrive on the scene hand in hand. Just as pagan philosophy thrived for centuries after the time of Christ, so also evidences of synthesis can be found prior to the time of Christ. This synthetic philosophizing was not the work of Christians but of Orthodox Jews.

The earliest form of Jewish synthesis philosophy flourished especially in Alexandria in Egypt, where there were many Jews in dispersion. Jewish synthesis is typically a hellenistic phenomenon. The Jews away from home wanted to assimilate hellenistic culture, yet at the same time did not want to abandon their Jewish heritage and the Old Testament revelation. The desire to maintain *both* readily resulted in synthesis. Such synthesis seemed to offer two advantages. First, it enabled the Jew to make his beliefs acceptable and credible to the non-Jew by coating them with hellenistic flavors, and, second, it allowed the

Jews to accept pagan hellenistic thought patterns by "sanctify-ing" them with the divine authority of the Old Testament.

Note the pattern set here. The easiest (and perhaps most pernicious) way to synthesize a pagan thought pattern with bib-lical themes is to declare the pagan pattern to be a teaching or doctrine supported by Scripture. We commonly see this happen to day: capitalists still claim that the Bible teaches capitalism; communists used to claim that the Bible teaches communism, and so on. This method of *eisegesis-exegesis*—reading in between the lines and then taking out of Scripture what is actually not there—was especially characteristic of the medieval synthesis period. But it has never left the christian church.

The most important figure in early Jewish synthesis is Philo of Alexandria (25 B.C.-40 A.D.). Philo, although he acknowl-edged the Old Testament as the Word of God, was steeped in Platonism and Stoicism. He wrote a variety of works. Most of them are take-offs from Scripture, usually commentaries, full of allegorical interpretations. Philo's attempted synthesis was achieved by (1) selecting certain themes from the pagans and (2) using the method of *allegorical exegesis* to interpret the Old Testament. This kind of exegesis assumes that the literal sense of the Scripture is for the common, uneducated people, while the philosopher or theologian sees the deeper, allegorical meaning. Some examples: Allegorically, the three men visiting Abraham at Mamre are three Powers just below God, namely, the Logos, the Power of creation, and the Power of rulership. Or, when we read that manna came down from heaven, then the common people simply interpret that literally: God fed his people. The philosopher, however, sees more—the manna is not merely bread, but the knowledge that descends from the divine Logos. This (unscriptural!) method of exegesis was freely employed throughout the Middle Ages.

To Philo everything in Scripture is subject to allegorical interpretation. Certainly nothing that Scripture says about God can be taken literally, for, Philo says, "God is not as man" (Num. 23:19). Many of the Old Testament stories Philo rejects outright as "myth," as "nonsense," or as "incredible." The creation of the world in six days is a myth, he says, since the days are measured by the sun which did not appear until the fourth day. What Genesis 1 records is the creation of ideas in the mind of God, according to which he then set about to actually create the heavens and the earth, as recorded in Genesis 2:4 and following! Not that that chapter should be read any more literally than the first however: The creation of Eve from Adam's rib and the speaking of the serpent, he claims, is "mythical nonsense." And many other stories cannot be believed literally, according to Philo.

Throughout all his allegorizing Philo believed that Moses was the greatest of all philosophers; in fact, he was the source of all philosophy from whom the Greek philosophers borrowed. The idea that the Greeks had borrowed their wisdom from Moses came to be commonly accepted by the church fathers and persisted for a long time. It induced a number of christian thinkers to synthesize more readily.

Philo combined many platonic and hellenistic thought patterns with his Old Testament faith, such as Plato's world of Ideas —which was the world God created first (Genesis 1) as a model for the creation of our world that followed next (Genesis 2)—and the theory of the a priori—we can borrow from pagans for they too are equipped with the seed of divine reason. By adopting such pagan notions, Philo sacrificed the authority of God's word. As in all synthesis, Scripture's directing power is lost: the Scriptures do not allow themselves to be accommodated. That Christianity nevertheless sets out on the path of synthesis is the subject to which we now turn.

2. THE PERIOD OF EARLY CHRISTIAN THOUGHT: THE PATRISTIC ERA

The first writings of the christian Church were written by its leaders, the *Apostles*, and many are recorded for us in the New Testament. These gospels and epistles are directed in the first place to the small struggling communities or *ecclesia* that had been planted by Paul and others. These communities were beset both by Jewish, hellenistic, and pagan hostility, as well as influence. And yet these Scriptures are free from abstract philosophical and even theological reflection. Talk of the *essence* or *substance* (*ousia*) of God comes only later.

The next generation of leaders consisted of the so-called *Apostolic Fathers*. These were all before A.D. 150. They were the

immediate successors of the Apostles themselves. Faithfully, by
and large, they preserved and taught THE WAY as outlined by the
Apostles and their Lord. Like the Apostles, they were more concerned with pastoral care than with abstract ideas. They, too,
write directly from the heart to the concrete situation of the early
Christians. Clement of Rome, Ignatius of Antioch, and Polycarp
are names worth mentioning in this context.

Following the Apostolic Fathers was a group of leaders we
call the *apologists* (from the Greek word "to defend"). These were
Greek and Latin Christians whose primary work of defending
the faith was directed against the pagans. Their writings generally exhibit explicit strains of synthesis. The same is true of the
Greek and Latin *church fathers*, who were primarily engaged in
defending the Church against heresies within the Church. In the
pages that follow, we discuss two important apologists (a), a
number of church fathers (c), and, briefly, Gnosticism (b), a sort
of heretical halfway house between paganism and Christianity.

This first period of christian thought, the patristic era, is
characterized by a certain amount of spontaneity, that is, the
Church's leaders responded spontaneously and readily to both
the Gospel and pagan philosophy. Generally speaking, these
early Christians were not aware of the synthesis they were con-
structing. As a matter of fact, the intentions were often good and
they meant well.

The Apologists

A famous early apologist was Justin Martyr. He was very
much enamored by Greek philosophy. Justin incorporated the
theory of the a priori into his christian thought. It is instructive
to observe how this was done, for it gives us another clear example of the *eisegesis-exegesis* method that we found Philo applying
earlier—reading something into and then taking out of Scripture
what is actually not there. The Bible text in question is John 1:9.
In the Greek original the text is ambiguous and can be read in
two ways. The ambiguity is reflected in the translations of the
King James and the American Standard versions. The King
James translates: "That was the true light, which lighteth every
man that cometh into the world." The American Standard Version corrected this translation and renders: "There was the true
light, even the light which lighteth every man, coming into the

world." What is the difference? The King James (and Rheims translation) ties the "coming into the world" to "every man," whereas the American Standard (and the New International, New Revised Standard, New American, and Amplified versions) connects the "coming into the world" with the Light. Justin Martyr was quick to seize upon the first interpretation—clearly, he said, the Bible teaches that every human that comes into the world, including Greek philosophers, is enlightened by the Logos—understood here as the "natural light of reason," which of course Stoics and the pagan theory of the a priori had said all along! Justin's interpretation reads the theory of the a priori into the text (= *eisegesis*) and then exegetes accordingly. It ignores the true import of the text, which says that Jesus Christ is the Logos, he is the light that came into the world to lighten every human, but the world knew him not (vs. 5 and 11). Not a light in every human, but a world that rejected the light (note John 3:16-21; 12:35-50).

One of the most influential of the apologists was Quintus Septimius Florens Tertullianus (160-225). A lawyer of pagan origin, Tertullian was converted to Christianity about A.D. 195. Of his many works still available to us, many display a paradox: he appears to reject and to accept paganism at one and the same time. That is, on the one hand, he retains a strong sense of the antithesis, in other words, of the radical, thorough-going opposition between the Kingdom of God and the influence of the devil. "What has Jerusalem to do with Athens, or the Academy with the Church?" he asks, claiming Plato to be the father of all error and philosophy, the mother of heresy. For him, Christianity is best served by ignoring philosophy altogether. But in the process of trying to develop his own christian perspective on things, we find that he reverts to the categories and thought patterns of the Stoics!

In Tertullian we still see the spontaneous apologist, yet there is also a developing theoretical theology in his works. In his attack on paganism he is concrete and personal; in his attack on heresy he becomes very abstract and loses the confessional focus of the apologists. He has been rightfully called the "father of theological terminology." He Latinized numerous Greek words and coined many of his own.

Tertullian originated, furthermore, a number of theological doctrines, such as the doctrine of *traducianism*. This doctrine asserts that at conception the soul is passed on along with the body by the parents. He postulated this theory in order to remain consistent with the doctrine of original sin. Traducianism is contrasted with *creationism*, that is in this context, the idea that God creates the soul and implants it into the body at a very early stage. Both these positions bristle with difficulties, and no wonder: the problem is a pseudo-problem! It presupposes a Greek dichotomistic view of a substantial soul in a substantial body. Nowhere do the Scriptures teach us a doctrine of soul and body as two substances. The Bible's words "heart," "mind," and "soul" must never be taken in a Greek sense. (This question is not as medieval as it may first appear. In 1996 Pope John Paul II declared, on the one hand, that evolution is "more than just a theory" and is fully compatible with the Christian faith. At the same time, in a letter to the Pontifical Academy of Sciences, he also reaffirmed the church's creationism teachings that, while the human body may have evolved gradually, the soul "is immediately created by God" in each person.)

Tertullian's desire to be antithetical must be commended. However, his way of thinking helped set the stage for a world-flight mentality, a kind of gnosticism. Just as fevers kill the body, so heresies kill the soul. Heresies are fostered by philosophy, which is the wisdom of the world. Therefore, Christians should withdraw from the world. Cultural life, business, politics, and the arts are all dirty, tainted, the very playground of the devil. The world out there is evil and must be avoided. The ultimate consequences within the Church of this unbiblical position were asceticism and monasticism. As Richard Niebuhr has pointed out in his book *Christ and Culture* this "Christ against culture" mentality is unfortunately still with us today.

Gnosticism

In the early stages of the history of the Church, a very great danger to the Gospel appeared in the form of Gnosticism. Gnosticism knows many variations, a dozen or more rival sects. It is usually obsessed with evil, which they claim inheres in matter, and it always stresses *gnosis*, that is, intellectual knowledge, as much more important than uneducated faith or beliefs. Gnostics not influenced by Christianity constructed similar theories or doctrines about reality as bases for a way of "salvation" from this world. Babylonian astrology, Persian religion, Greek mystery cults, the book of Genesis, Plato's dialogues, and Stoicism were all considered to be helpful sources.

The conceptions of "christian" gnostics incorporated a number of biblical themes into what they already knew from oriental and hellenistic sources. For example, they would confuse the Old Testament with myth or claim that the Hebrew *JHWH* was a wicked demiurge (creator), that the serpent was sent to warn Eve against this Jehovah's deceptions, and that the true God was revealed only in the New Testament. Jesus was the Redeemer because he came down from heaven with the saving *gnosis* (knowledge) needed to strengthen the elect for their ascent to the Father. Others, convinced that God could not have anything to do with mortal flesh or suffering, claimed that the Redeemer entered Jesus at his baptism and withdrew at his crucifixion. That the Savior was possessed of a material body they found to be inconceivable. Gnosticism was vigorously combated by the Church, especially by the church fathers Irenaeus and Hippolytus.

The Church Fathers

Irenaeus (c.140-202) and Hippolytus (c.180-240) were not strictly speaking apologists because they combatted heresy rather than paganism. Both of these men strove to fight gnosticism and both sensed that the source of the trouble with heresies lay in the speculations of Greek philosophy. Irenaeus's major work, *Against Heresies*, testifies to a much keener sense of the antithesis than we find, for example, in Justin Martyr. We also encounter various biblical themes: he strongly stresses the unity of the christian community. He was the one who introduced the term "holy catholic [i.e., universal] church." The creation, fall, redemption motif comes through in his denial of pre-existent matter, in his denial that matter is evil, and in his emphasis on the radical nature of the Fall. In spite of these sound biblical themes, the doctrine of the a priori remains very much in evidence, as he repeatedly refers to the implantation of a divine *logos* into the human mind.

Another important group of early christian leaders whose synthesis thought exerted a tremendous influence on later medieval philosophy is the so-called Catechetical School of Alexandria. The most outstanding figures of the school were Clement of Alexandria (c.150-213) and Origen (c.185-254). Origen's thoughts clearly betray the influence of Philo, of Plato, and of the Neoplatonists. There was nothing subtle about Origen's synthesis. Although this influential church father died a martyr because of his christian faith, the Church in the sixth century condemned his theories as heresy.

Many of the church fathers laid a stress on spiritual reality and on the ascent of the soul to God. At the same time they were not averse to studying the literary culture of the ancient world. St. Basil (d.379), for example, in his "Address to Young Men," argues that just as the soul is more precious than the body so too education should ultimately prepare for that other life which is more precious than the present one. But, because Scripture's mysteries are too deep for the minds of young men, they should turn to preliminary readings in the pagan authors in order to exercise and prepare their minds. After all, didn't Moses learn the wisdom of the Egyptians too? Students, of course, had to be careful to stick to passages describing behavior suitable for Christians and not allow poetic language to lead them down the garden path. Christians know what the goal of life is and with the help of the intellect, like a ship's captain, should make straight for that safe harbor. The christian classicist Wendy Helleman explains St. Basil's anthropology:

> The soul is not to be enslaved to the body but through philosophy to free itself from the body, as it were from a prison. Quoting Plato, Basil says that the soul should attend to the body only as much as it will serve it in its pursuit of wisdom, for Paul (Rom. 13:14) also tells us not to attend to the desires of the body. We are instead to concentrate on the purification of the soul (*psuche*) or mind (*nous*) so it will be able to behold the truth and come to proper self-knowledge.

The influence of platonic thought patterns on Basil's understanding of biblical themes is evident in the difference between this life and the next that he describes in terms of body and soul, or dream and reality. The soul is to be taught and purified by means of analogies, shadows, or temporal reflections, as it prepares to look at the source of light, namely, eternal truth itself. The goal of education is to purify the soul's eye, the *nous* (nüs), which is to guide the soul on the journey to its other-worldly destination. Basil was on that score not an exception among the Greek church fathers. Like for Origen and Gregory of Nyssa, Plato was not just one of the pagan authors to be read in the schools; in the search for truth, Plato was regarded an ally.

Among Reformed Christians Augustine (354-430) is the church father *par excellence*. John Calvin, who quotes Augustine incessantly, regarded him as a saint. Such an attitude is not misplaced: Augustine was without a doubt great in the Kingdom of God. He battled with great diligence and power against all kinds of heresies. The church was built up by his work.

Augustine was born in Thagaste, North Africa, and experienced rather unsettled years of adolescence and youth. A book by Cicero awakened his interest in philosophy, with the result that he adhered successively to several pagan philosophic schools before becoming a Christian in 385. He became Bishop of Hippo in North Africa, where he spent the rest of his life defending the Church from heresy and producing voluminous writings. His *Confessions* and the *City of God* rank as the most famous of these. From a philosophic perspective, we may say that of all the church fathers he was the most aware of the integral character of Christianity. As he developed and matured, he increasingly saw the danger of synthesis, and thus his struggle to be antithetical grew. He not only tried to articulate the difference and relationship between believers and unbelievers, but also began to recognize questionable elements in his own thought. In his later years he even retracted some of his earlier claims. As such he was a blessing for both the Church and christian thinking for centuries to come. Nevertheless, though we respect and admire him, we may not close our eyes to the platonistic synthesis that permeated much of his thinking.

Augustine follows hellenistic Platonism by placing the Ideas, Plato's intelligible world of Forms, in the mind of God. Augustine believes that the eternal Ideas in the mind of God form the pattern and design for all creation. This view is frequently called "exemplarism": God's mind contains the model (the exemplar) in light of which everything (the *exemplata*) is patterned. This Augustinian theory, which is platonic rather than biblical, did much to initiate notions of "God's plan" and "divine decrees" within christian theology.

Augustine was also strongly influenced by Neoplatonism. For example, he sees the creation in hierarchical fashion, levels of being ranging from the inferior—mere matter—to the superior, from the temporal to the eternal. For example, for the neoplatonist Plotinus the distinction between time and eternity was fundamentally a distinction in the great chain of being. In the hierarchy of reality, time is distinct from but dependent upon eternity just as an image is distinct from but dependent upon its archetype. For Plotinus eternity fills the changeless and self-identical life of the universal Mind (of god). Time as its image permeates the changing and successive life of the world and what moves it. For Augustine, too, the difference between enduringly changeless eternal being and forever-changing temporal existence is a distinction in degrees of being. God, for Augustine, is eternal because God is immutable. Divine being is for Augustine (as it was for Parmenides, for example) per definition unchangingly self-identical. Creation, on the other hand, is temporal because it is mutable. Its existence is an endless succession of moments because it came into existence out of nothing and constantly tends toward nothing. Therefore, its existence is secure only insofar as it depends upon the unchangeable being of its Creator. So also, like the Neoplatonists, Augustine believes evil to be a negation, that is, the absence of good. See quotation #2 on page 90.

Augustine's conception of God illustrates this synthesis with Neoplatonism quite clearly. One could say that in his writings two Gods appear. On the one hand, there is the covenanting God of Scripture, the Lord and Creator who loves Augustine and who is loved by Augustine. It is the God with whom Augustine engages in conversation, the God with whom Jacob struggled at the Jabbok. On the other hand, there is the neoplatonic ONE: a god who is a self-identical, uncompounded essence, "being" in the absolute sense. Augustine reads such a mathematically unified god into the Bible, for example, into Exodus 3:14: "I am who I am. You will say to the children of Israel: He who is has sent me to you." According to Augustine, God displays basically two attributes: eternality and immutability. Thus, he conceives of God as an eternal unchanging substance. In the subsequent Middle Ages one can easily recognize Augustinian theology when one meets descriptions of God as the "eternal and immutable being." As Augustine grew older, however, his more pagan conception of God began to disappear. Augustine's epistemology is thoroughly platonic. He depreciates sense experience for it produces only changing and worthless knowledge. Reason is the highest and most reliable human function. Abiding truths can be attained only by the intellect. Augustine's epistemology is strongly oriented to the a priori theory as well: he is fond of quoting John 1:9, after the fashion of Justin Martyr. Augustine expands the notion of the natural light of reason into the so-called "doctrine of illumination." How is it that all human beings recognize mathematical truths? It is because of the illuminating light of God's wisdom shed directly on the human mind. Here too we detect the intellectualistic influence of Plato(nism).

A number of things should be said about Augustine's anthropology. The Neoplatonists believed that the human soul was contaminated by the body. Augustine, too, initially thought the body not only as inferior, but as evil. After his years as a student, he had a very low view of human sexuality in particular, associating sexual desire with original sin. But many passages of Scripture referring to the holiness of the body later led him to modify his views. Nevertheless, at all stages he regarded the soul as rational and closer to God than the body. At the same time Augustine disagreed with the claim that souls of human beings are self-sufficient in their ability to access eternity. Augustine insists that since human beings are mortal and miserable, they need an immortal mediator who has participated in their mortality and hence can lift them to his own immortality.

Augustine also wrestled with the problem of traducianism versus creationism. He could not really make up his mind. He tended toward traducianism, since it best explained original sin. His battle against the Pelagians, who denied original sin and asserted that people essentially on their own can attain to righteousness, led Augustine to write extensively about the nature of the human will. The will, he says, was created free, that is, free to turn toward or away from God. But after the Fall the will became a slave to passion and required grace to be set free again. Grace, then, sets the will free so that it is really free to love that which it was made to love from the beginning. Augustine's consideration of the question of sin and grace led him to develop an elaborate theory of predestination. God's electing grace, eternally fixed in the divine Mind, is part of God's eternal plan of predestination.

Augustine's anthropology reflects a kind of "macrocosm-microcosm" theory, especially in his view of the image of God. God—the macrocosm—is reflected in man—the microcosm. Human beings are created in the image of God and in that image parallel the Trinity: our memory parallels the Father, our reason and understanding reflect the Son as the Logos, and our will to love is the firstfruit of the Spirit. Augustine also mistakenly draws a sharp distinction between "image" and "likeness" (cf. Genesis 1:26). The "image," according to Augustine, represents the intellectual qualities of remembering, understanding, and loving God, while the "likeness" refers to "moral" qualities such as justice, temperance, and goodness.

His massive (1091-page) book *The City of God* is a lengthy *apology* or defense in which Augustine lays the foundation for a christian philosophy of history. His original audience consisted of learned pagan Roman exiles in Carthage who had fled Rome when it was sacked in 410. They were proud of their Roman heritage and were suggesting that the fall of Rome was at least in part due to Christianity. In the first part of this book Augustine reviews the history of Rome to show that the worship of the Roman gods neither built moral character nor guaranteed national security. He then sets christian teachings of eternal life, faith, and grace over against their pagan ideas of happiness and ways to attain it. Augustine argues that their false religion stands in opposition to the true religion, namely, to the ordering of this life under divine direction and with divine assistance so as to eventually enjoy peace with God in eternal life; true religion is a life of faith, hope, and prayer.

Augustine sketches this radical, thorough-going opposition, or *antithesis*, using the image of two cities, the "city of God" and the "city of the earth." The picture he paints is of two communities, two societies, that encompass all rational creatures, human and angelic. They are religious communities, that is, they are known and characterized by their loves. The one, the earthly city, loves itself above all and sets its sights on the enjoyment of some earthy good.   The other, the heavenly city, loves God above all and subordinates every desire to the ultimate enjoyment of God. As Theodore de Bruyn explains,

> These two communities move together through time from the fall to the last judgment, but because of the difference of their loves they regard their progress in time from quite different points of view. The earthly city has made this life its home. It has settled down to enjoy the goods of this life and believes that by its own efforts it can attain happiness in this life. The heavenly city, on the other hand, regards this life as an exile and longs for the next life as its home. It expects happiness not from the goods of this life but rather from God in the next life and appeals for God's help so that it may finally enjoy God forever. Time is thus the scene of a great drama in which human beings play out their part, joined in an invisible fellowship from the moment when Cain and Abel founded the two cities on earth, guided by God's providence through prosperity and adversity, and eventually gathered together with all their fellow citizens to the place of eternal life or the torment of eternal condemnation.... But, on the other hand, this also means that Augustine espouses an otherworldly view of salvation which limits the role of the Christian in the empire to that of a homesick exile. (58, 65)

The pilgrimage of the heavenly city in this theory is ultimately an other-worldly movement through the changeable existence of time to the stable being of eternity.

For Augustine this view of history did not mean that christian emperors are guaranteed prosperity in the world and that Christians, far from enjoying a millennium of peace, can be assured of troubles and persecutions to the end of time. Augustine wants to hold human beings responsible for the restlessness they suffer in time. Deficiencies in their present temporal existence are the result of their turning away from God in the fall. The two cities likewise do not admit of easy distinction in the course of human history and cannot be identified with particular historical institutions, for example, with the Church and the state. There are unbelievers in the Church and believers in the state. Augustine did claim, however, that the state can only become christian when it subjects itself to the guidance and authority of the instituted church, a suggestion that represents the beginning of the medieval view of the Holy Roman Empire.

Augustine recognized that human thought is not autonomous, but that its direction is determined by faith, either christian or apostate. However, instead of working out this thesis in the direction of a reformation of philosophy, he came to believe that philosophy needs to be subjected to theology in order to become christian. The relationship between philosophy and theology became a real bone of contention in the Middle Ages. According to Augustine and other medieval theologians, because faith leads to understanding, and theology is a study of the faith, theology is obviously the "queen of the sciences." The other disciplines are all "handmaidens" of theology. This idea is sometimes still expressed in Reformed circles. The notion is derived from Aristotle, who called metaphysical theology the "queen of the sciences," which other sciences, as its slaves, may not contradict (cf. Aristotle, *Metaphysics*, B, 996b10-15). See quotation #1 below.

The influence of Augustine on the subsequent Middle Ages was nothing less than enormous. He initiated what came to be known as the Augustinian tradition. This tradition carried a good deal of Platonism along with it. And yet it must not be concluded from the above that Augustine was practically a pagan. Far from it. He not only repudiated Roman polytheism, he challenged some assumptions of the Platonism of the day with such christian teachings as creation, fall, incarnation, resurrection, grace, and faith. Undoubtedly he was the greatest of all the church fathers, and because of his labors the Church grew and prospered and was safeguarded against all kinds of heresies. Further, as we indicated, Augustine, more than anyone else of his time, understood the radical nature of the Scriptures and stressed the depth of our fall into sin and our desperate need for grace. He was a devout Christian who walked with the Lord. We need not hesitate to revere him for his ability and his achievements. At the same time we must not be blind to the effects of paganism, even on so great a man as Augustine.

A few representative quotations from

AUGUSTINE

1. *crede ut intelligas:* "Believe in order that you may understand."

2. "What is time? Who can easily and briefly explain this? Who can comprehend this even in thought, so as to express it in a word? Yet

what do we discuss more familiarly and knowingly in conversation than time? Surely we understand it when we talk about it, and also understand it when we hear others talk about it.

"What, then, is time? If no one asks me, I know; if I want to explain it to someone who does ask me, I do not know. Yet I state confidently that I know this: if nothing were passing away, there would be no past time, and if nothing were coming, there would be no future time, and if nothing existed, there would be no present time. How, then, can these two kinds of time, the past and the future, be, when the past no longer is and the future as yet does not be? But if the present were always present, and would not pass into the past, it would no longer be time, but eternity. Therefore, if the present, so as to be time, must be so constituted that it passes into the past, how can we say that it is, since the cause of its being is the fact that it will cease to be? Does it not follow that we can truly say that it is time, only because it tends toward non-being?"

Confessions Book XI, 14

3. There are two kinds of men in this world, "one of those who live according to man, the other such as live according to God; these we also call figuratively two cities, that is, two societies of men, one of which is predestined to reign eternally with God, the other to undergo eternal torment with the devil."

De civitate Dei (The City of God) XV 1.1

4. "Both feel the same vicissitudes of fortune, good or bad; but they do so not with the same faith, nor with the same hope, nor the same love—until they shall be separated in the last judgment."

De civitate Dei XVIII 54.2

A Comment on Kinds of Synthesis
(past and present)

When we go to the history of Western thought and ask the question as to how the combination of pagan thought patterns with Scriptural themes has been attempted, it is possible to distinguish at least three basic "methods." Because synthesis philosophy remains a reality among Christians still today, use of the present tense is not inappropriate to this brief detour.

(1) By far the most pervasive way in which biblical themes are mixed with nonbiblical conceptions is the method of *eisegesis-exegesis*. We have already mentioned this method explicitly in

connection with Philo and Justin Martyr. What does this method involve? The words "eisegesis" and "exegesis" are derived from Greek compounds meaning "to bring into" and "to lead out of." In effect it involves unconsciously reading into Scripture what is not there, yes, even what is in conflict with the Scriptures. Then, when these foreign elements have been read into the text, they are taken out again, exegeted. Pagan philosophic ideas are unwittingly carried into the Scripture, in such a way that it seems that the Bible sanctions them! Often it happened that the Christians in their debate with the pagans would say: "We believe it, not because you say so, but because we know it from the Bible." In such cases they were trying not only to reckon with what Scripture reveals, but to extract—in a chapter and verse, biblicistic fashion—a complete philosophy from the Scriptures. But what in fact was happening was that they were simply making explicit what was implicit to their understanding already before they went to Scripture. It is not difficult to imagine the endless grief this type of synthesis causes the Church: Christians read different conceptions into Scripture and consequently run into conflict with each other.

(2) A second kind of synthesis is that of the *paradox*. This method is very hard to comprehend because it implies a contradiction in one's thinking: a point of view is accepted that is at the same time realized to be contrary to Scripture. In other words, paradox synthesis believes Scripture—because it is the word of God—*and* current philosophy—philosophy after all is philosophy, all the while recognizing that "here and there" they are in conflict with each other. Hence the paradox: both the Scriptures and the pagan mind are true. Something similar is going on when a christian pedagogical institute says on the one hand to do everything to the glory of God and, on the other hand, advocates a behavioristic vision of culture that, along with B. F. Skinner, is optimistically convinced that we have as yet to see what man can make of man. Clearly this is an untenable position. Yet it constitutes an improvement on the method of eisegesis-exegesis, for it realizes that pagan thought cannot simply, without critique, be incorporated into what we know on the basis of Scripture.

(3) A third kind of synthesis or accommodation to pagan thought was quietly developing during the years we have dis-

cussed, although it did not surface before the sixth century. We call it *nature/grace* synthesis, for reasons to be explained below. This type of synthesis not only prepared the way for medieval Scholasticism but also produced conditions for a process of secularization that ultimately resulted in the triumph of humanism. Even today the christian community is plagued by the effects of a nature/grace mentality. Any sacred/secular dualism heard of today has its roots here.

In 529 bishops of the church meeting at the Council of Orange articulated canons condemning a group called the semi-Pelagians. This group which had earlier helped condemn the Pelagians (see p. 87) did not agree with all that Augustine had said. Especially his views on the doctrine of predestination evoked dissatisfaction. This increasingly vocal element in the Church began to reassert that the Fall did not totally corrupt humans. John Cassian, a vigorous opponent of Augustine's views, wrote: "It cannot, therefore, be doubted that there are by nature seeds of goodness implanted in every soul by the kindness of the Creator" (*Collationes*, Bk.XIII, ch.12). In condemning the semi-Pelagians, however, especially where the Council's canons deal with the state of humankind before and after the Fall, terms were used that distinguished and seemed to accept a difference between "natural grace" and "supernatural grace." And once the distinction between nature and supernature was implicitly made, the door to a nature/grace framework was open. How?

For a century already there had been extensive discussion about human nature, both before and after the Fall. In this way the stage was set for the idea that the Fall caused humans to lose something "super-natural." It was merely a matter of time before it was "determined" which attributes could be assigned to "supernature," and which ones to "nature." Hence we see that, in effect, the anthropology implied by the Council of Orange presents human beings as follows: before the Fall "natural" man possessed a special measure of "supernature." When he fell, the "supernature" was lost, while his "nature" remained essentially intact. This common "nature"—weakened by the Fall, but nonetheless present in everyone—still functioned normally under the guidance of the "natural light of reason." For as Aristotle(!!) had

said long ago: "reason" is the determining characteristic of "natural man."
This view of humankind became the basis for Scholasticism. According to the Scholastics, there are two areas in life, namely, the area of "nature," which includes among other things the state, society, philosophy, "reason," law, and the sciences; then there is the area of "supernature," which includes grace, the Church, theology, faith, and "religion." The theme of nature and grace regards (pagan) philosophy as "natural," as an expression of the "natural" man and therefore acceptable. Likewise, astronomy is astronomy and zoology zoology. Consequently, there is no perceived need for a christian philosophy on the one hand and, on the other hand, usually a receptive attitude to what is called "natural theology."
Natural theology attempts to know and describe God by means of "reason," by means of rational arguments, without using "the means of grace," like faith or Scripture. The medieval Scholastics became very adept in the use of "natural theology." Witness their extensive "proofs of the existence of God" and their attempts at a logical explanation and description of, for example, the Trinity.   John Calvin combated natural theology (cf. *Institutes*, I,5,9), and rightly so. He affirmed that we cannot reason and philosophize about God, nor ever fathom his essence: we can only worship him.   Nevertheless, in Reformed theology there are still clear traces of such "natural theology," as there are also definite hangovers from a nature/grace secular/sacred mentality in the lives of Reformed Christians.
Synthesis philosophy, whatever its method, is always an *attempted* combination, like trying to connect iron and clay. And the result is always an artificial entwining, a forced mixture of two mutually exclusive principles. It can never result in a fully unified conception. A true synthesis, in the sense of attained unity, between what Bible-believers know from Scripture and the conceptions of pagan thought is actually impossible. To use the words of Alvin Plantinga, the result at best is an unintegrated pastiche.

In Conclusion

The battles and heresies in the early church were caused by synthesis. For example, some of the early Christians favored a

monistic position, others a dualistic one. As we have seen earlier, this dilemma is not christian at all. Christians can be neither
monists nor dualists, universalists or individualists, subjectivists
or objectivists. Yet church fathers fought with each other about
these thought patterns.

Another example is the battle about the Trinity. Some
Christians, for instance, who were oriented to aristotelian
monarchianism, saw God the Father as the "forever beyond,"
untouchable, not even by Jesus Christ, who was considered by
them to be a mere man endowed with the supra-personal
thinking spirit. Other Christians, oriented to platonizing monarchianism, saw the unity of Father, Son, and Spirit in the aristotelian god, and the distinction of persons in the thinking processes of the Universal Mind. Tremendous battles ensued.
Furthermore, certain Christians variously identified Jesus Christ
with the Stoic *Logos,* or with the neoplatonic mind of the One.
Endless were the varieties on these and other themes.

We have now become acquainted with the situation in the
early church. We have seen that paganism and apostasy came to
infect the christian message. Humanly speaking, the christian
church seemed a lost cause. The same holds true today. Look at
the irrelevance and impotence of Christianity in our modern
humanistic world! It might be there, but what difference does it
make?! Many Christians take a synthesis mentality for granted!
Too much of our thinking is thoroughly secularistic! It would
appear that those who struggle for the welfare of the christian
church have bet on the wrong horse.

Synthesis causes the christian church nothing but grief. We
do well to reflect on this situation in the early church, and on the
fact that Christians, all Bible-believers, could diverge on so many
issues simply because they synthesized. The reforming and
renewing power of the Word of God was seldom applied to
philosophic thinking during these early years. An inner reformation of Western thought did not take place, nor, to put it differently, did a christian mind develop. Instead, that renewing
power was undercut and watered down by the wholesale acceptance of nonchristian constructions. Synthesis always breaks
the power of the Church.

Those who seriously wish to promote the unity of the
Church and carry out an ecumenical task should not sacrifice the

truth for the sake of love. Instead of saying, "Let's be friends and forget about doctrinal matters and creeds," we should together combat the influence of unbiblical and nonchristian ideas that have infiltrated our minds: "Do not conform any longer to the pattern of this world, but be transformed by the renewing of your mind. Then you will be able to test and approve what God's will is" (Romans 12:2). At the same time, we must remember that today, as in ancient times, Jesus Christ rules his church. He has already attained the victory for us, in spite of our weakness, sin, and synthesis. And it is in response to his victorious call that we are to arise and carry out our task in his Kingdom.

II. C. 1 and 2.
Guide Questions

39. What were the reasons for the early development of synthesis?

40. What is synthesis philosophy?

41. What is *allegorical exegesis*? Explain how Philo of Alexandria used it in his synthetic understanding of Scripture.

42. What is *eisegesis-exegesis*?

43. What is the difference between apostles, apostolic fathers, apologists, and church fathers?

44. How does Justin Martyr's reading of John 1:9 illustrate the method of *eisegesis-exegesis*?

45. What does Tertullian mean when he asks, "What does Jerusalem have to do with Athens?"

46. Why is the "traducian/creationism" controversy which Tertullian focused on a pseudo-problem?

47. What is gnosticism?

48. What does it mean when we say Augustine "struggled to be antithetical"?

49. Talking about Augustine: What do you think "theologizing about God in terms of the neoplatonic One" implies?

50. How does "illumination" fit into Augustine's theory of knowledge?

51. In what sense does Augustine's discussion of the *Civitas Dei* and the *Civitas Terrena* lay a foundation for a christian philosophy of history?

52. Why did Augustine claim that theology is the queen of all the sciences?

53. How does the anthropology implied by the Council of Orange open the door to nature/grace synthesis?

54. What is "natural theology" and why did Calvin combat it?

55. Compare and contrast the three types of synthesis.

3. SCHOLASTICISM IN THE MIDDLE AGES

Introduction

The philosophy of the Middle Ages (ca. 500-1300) is characterized by Scholasticism. What does this mean? Scholasticism incorporates the thought of the church fathers into standard books and teaching materials. In other words, the writings of the early Church take on a didactic, but also sacrosanct character. As teaching materials, the works of the church fathers and the pagan philosophers come to stand *alongside* the Scriptures. This situation requires some reflection: what happens when the Word of God is treated on a textbook level?

We need to observe the historical context. The Roman world had disintegrated. The barbarians had overthrown society and culture. The monasteries, however, had managed to save books. These books—both pagan and christian—became the source of authority. They were collected and compiled, and studied with excruciating care. Wherever texts differed in opinion, attempts were made to harmonize them. Medieval scholars wrote lengthy commentaries. It is easy to see why the Age of Scholasticism is sometimes called the Age of Schoolmen.

The church was headquartered at Rome, of course, but was developing a world-wide establishment that officiated as the veritable custodian of Western civilization. The institutional church would almost totally dominate human life for a millennium. Seerveld describes how indebted the people were.

> Worship services on Christmas and Easter in a twelfth or thirteenth century cathedral—overwhelming height inside, massive statuary in stone, gold-brocaded vestments in processions, with incense, stained glass colored light, mellifluously haunting plainsong crescendoing at the high point of the raised host and celebration of the mass, thronged by the whole countryside—epitomized incantationally the power and glory forever and ever of the church. Only its priestly rites guaranteed you as a man a heavenly eternity; so you were utterly beholden to it. And it was this "Mother" church which had given her blessing, officially and unofficially, to the habit of supplementing Platonic philosophy with the insights of supernatural revelation. (Seerveld, 1975, 277)

With the Church's stamp of approval, joining the thought patterns of pagan minds with the truths of Scripture became the unquestioned method of educated leaders: reinforce the

Church's theological deposits by combining them with the older (and, to their minds, hence authoritative) results of "natural reason" in order to arrive at a cumulative, definitive synthesis of truly dependable knowledge on all matters. That driving spirit formed the scholastic mind that controlled the Western world unchallenged until William of Ockham and the Black Death Plague of 1348-50.

We can distinguish three periods: the rise, height, and decline of Scholasticism. We shall treat these periods in three subsections.

The Rise of Scholasticism

The patristic period discussed above was characterized by the synthesis of Christianity with all kinds of pagan philosophies. A general trend emerged, however, that affected the Middle Ages. This trend consisted of a predominantly platonic (and neoplatonic) influence. Augustine, for example, had been very strongly affected by Platonism. Meanwhile, the church fathers had articulated, often in great detail, their theological positions. In the struggle with heresy, the Church had adopted canons and creeds, many of which bore a decidedly platonic stamp. As we begin the study of Scholasticism, it is important to remember that christian theology at this point tended to be colored by Platonism. As we shall see when Aristotelianism is revived, a conflict ensues not only with christian dogma, but also with the platonic element in that dogma. That this state of affairs seriously complicates the situation is lamentable.

A few important figures in the early scholastic period demand our attention.

Boethius (480-525)

Boethius has been called the "last Roman and first Scholastic." He got in trouble with the emperor and, after a lengthy jail term, was executed in 525. While in jail, he wrote the famous *Consolation of Philosophy*. His reflections there rested in the conviction that the greater one's level of spirituality is (read: the greater one's mental aptitude is), the greater is one's consolation and freedom (from nature, pain, and evil).

In his writings Boethius passed on platonic theories of god, happiness, the constitution of the world, and a Stoic concept of nature, natural law, fate and providence. Aristotelian tendencies are also evident. It should be noted that at the time of Boethius, most of the writings of Aristotle were not available. Plato's works were widely circulated, but his as well as Aristotle's were in Greek. Boethius's plan was to translate into Latin the entire works of both Plato and Aristotle, convinced as he was that they were in basic agreement. Of Aristotle's books only the *Organon*, his writings on logic, was translated and only part of Plato's *Timaeus* was put to Latin. (And, of course, what people cannot read, they soon ignore.)

Boethius wrote an interesting little tract on the Trinity. In this work he explains the nature of the Trinity in strictly aristotelian terms. It is a fine example of scholastic synthesis and natural theology: God is described in terms of "Pure Form." The God of the Scriptures is altogether lost in such a description.

For quite some time Boethius was regarded as the "teacher of the Middle Ages." His translations of the classical texts from Greek to Latin and his writings on logic, arithmetic, and music were used for centuries as handbooks of instruction in the so-called "liberal arts."

Anselm of Canterbury (1033-1109)

Anselm has been called the "Father of Scholasticism." He was appointed Archbishop of Canterbury (England) and he strove to preserve a healthy church life.

Anselm was an Augustinian thinker. Even his style of writing betrays the influence of Augustine. He too tended to think in a platonizing fashion. For example, he believed the theory of Ideas. The Ideas, however, are not located in an other, unchanging, eternal world, but, as they were already for Augustine, in the eternal "mind" of God.

Anselm is best known for his so-called ontological argument. This argument supposedly proves the existence of God. Anselm, like Augustine, believed that faith leads toward understanding. See the quotation below. Anselm took this to mean that it was the task of the believer to probe intellectually the mysteries of faith. This expectation accounts for the desire of many medieval theologians to seek ways of "proving" that God exists. Of such proofs, the ontological argument of Anselm is one of the most discussed. As a matter of fact, philosophers today are still debating the validity of the argument.

The actual argument is very brief: "God is a being than which nothing greater can be conceived. Therefore, God exists." You see, if God did not exist, we could conceive of a greater being, namely, one who does exist. A being who exists is always greater than one who does not exist, not only in one's mind, but in reality the more so.

Already in Anselm's time the argument met with much debate. We shall have a little more to say about these proofs of God when we deal with Thomas Aquinas.

One representative quotation from

ANSELM

"I acknowledge, Lord, and I give thanks that You have created Your image in me, so that I may remember You, think of You, love You. But this image is so effaced and worn away by vice, so darkened by the smoke of sin, that it cannot do what it was made to do unless You renew it and reform it. I do not try, Lord, to attain Your lofty heights, because my understanding is in no way equal to it. But I do desire to understand Your truth a little, that truth that my heart believes and loves. For I do not seek to understand so that I may believe, but I believe so that I may understand. For I believe this also, that 'unless I believe, I shall not understand.'

"Well then.... God is that-than-which-nothing-greater-can-be-thought. Whoever really understands this understands clearly that this same being so exists that not even in thought can it not exist. Thus whoever understands that God exists in such a way cannot think of Him as not existing.

"I give thanks, good Lord, I give thanks to You, since what I believed before through Your free gift I now so understand through Your illumination, that if I did not want to believe that You existed, I should nevertheless be unable not to understand it...." *Proslogion*

In this first period of Scholasticism we see various pagan conceptions synthesized with Christianity. Note that the history of Western thought presents a picture of currents and types. Remember that we are concentrating on only a very few individuals who represent such movements. This survey presents only a bird's eye view, so to speak, of the history of thought.

Another point is that throughout the early part of the scholastic era there occurs a solidification of the nature/grace theme. As more and more aristotelian influences begin to exert themselves, the more solid this theme becomes. The notion that philosophy (including natural theology) belongs to the lower level of nature, while "revealed theology" belongs to the higher level of supernature takes an increasing hold on the scholastic mind.

The Height of Scholasticism

The period of the height of Scholasticism (1100-1300) was heralded by the invasion of Jewish and Islamic philosophy from Northern Africa into Europe via Spain. Up to this time Platonism had been the most influential factor in medieval thought. The bulk of Aristotle's work was not known to the Latin West. The Arabs, however, had obtained these lost works, translated them, and absorbed them into their Mohammedan thinking. Meanwhile, the Moslems had been on a conquering spree and had also acquired Spain. From there it was an easy jump for a well-developed islamic philosophy to the rest of Europe.

Observe that the philosophic contacts were not made by the crusaders. The crusades were the work of knights, soldiers, and merchants who were not schooled in theology and philosophy. Rather, the invasion of islamic thought was due to the west-european youth, who went to Spain to learn the newest in intellectual trends.

Two points need to be noted. First, it must be remembered that most of the Aristotelianism that entered the West at this time came in the form of an islamic-Greek philosophic mixture. Hence, together with Aristotle came an islamic interpretation of Aristotle. Incidentally, Plato had also been translated into Arabic. His influence on islamic philosophy is therefore evident as well.

Second, when christian thinkers learned that the Arabs, too, used Greek philosophy, they were strengthened in their belief that this Greek philosophy was a universal, perfectly natural way of thinking. They concluded that all real philosophy is Greek philosophy. As a result, the nature/grace framework became still more firmly entrenched in medieval thought.

The clash between Aristotelianism and Platonism came to a head in the era of the scholastic masters. The majority of theologians wished to remain orthodox in their theology and were forced either to reject certain pagan themes or to adopt extreme positions such as the "double truth" theory of the so-called Latin Averroists. The "double truth" theory made a sharp distinction between faith and reason, allowing the believer to hold to doctrines the philosopher had to deny. It reflects a paradox synthesis position.

Scholastics were often oriented to partial-universalism. Furthermore, their conceptions were dualistic. Their dualism consisted, for example, of a view of God as transcendent pure Form and a nontranscendent material world. Sometimes the notions form and matter were held up as two eternal constituents determining all of reality. This dualism in scholastic thinking goes hand in hand with a tendency to regard genesis as merely an aspect of structure. It may be asked, did the scholastics not believe in creation, and were they therefore not concerned with origins? Yes, they did believe the creation act of God as revealed in Scripture but restricted the creation theme to an idea of structure. The act of creation, they believed, says something about the structure of reality and nothing more. That God should start and then stop doing anything would also suggest a change in him who knows no change. The world as it appears now could not and will never look like anything else.

The fact that scholastic thinking was filled with pagan problematics created an enormously tense situation. The heresy trials of the Middle Ages were only one result. The tension between the power of the Word-revelation and pagan philosophy's attempt to restrict that power reverberated throughout the entire philosophical and theological enterprise. The effects of this state of affairs were felt everywhere, also in the distorted views of the relationship between pope and emperor, church and state. Once again, synthesis brings nothing but grief.

We shall discuss some of the most important figures of this period.

Islamic and Jewish Philosophy

No history of Western thought can neglect to mention the great Arab thinkers who synthesized Greek systems with Islam and passed the results on to the Latin West. Especially two important figures stand in the foreground, Avicenna (11th century) and Averroës (12th century). These men exerted a powerful influence on scholasticism. Both Avicenna and Averroës were monarchianists. They differ, however, in that Avicenna's monarchianism is platonizing, whereas Averroës' is not. This difference is manifested by the fact that Avicenna accepted the neoplatonic theme of emanation, while Averroës rejected it. The platonizing character of Avicenna's thought made him much more acceptable to the Latin West than Averroës—remember the platonic influence on early medieval theology! In the long run, however, Averroës was to have the greatest influence.

Jewish philosophers, like Islamic thinkers, worked hard to reconcile their arguments with their faith. For the Jews this meant that their philosophy had to fit with what the Old Testament and its study guide, the Talmud, said. Moses Maimonides was a contemporary of Averroës and one of the greatest medieval Jewish thinkers. His book *Guide for the Perplexed* was written to help people harmonize reason with their faith. When things were not so apparent, he urged his readers to interpret what they believed allegorically: for then it would surely fit with what the great teacher Aristotle had written so very long ago! Conservative Jewish scholars soon branded Maimonides a heretic, but that did not stop him from influencing Christian scholars, the chief of whom was Thomas Aquinas.

Bonaventure (1221-1274)

In a sense Bonaventure was a strange fish in the scholastic pond. He was a scholastic all right! Nevertheless, he strikes our attention because he attempted—more or less unconsciously—to combat the nature/grace synthesis. Although in effect he could not break free from this mentality, his stress on faith did tend to offset the work of his contemporary Thomas Aquinas. Faith, Bonaventure maintained, determines the content of our knowledge. He denied the autonomy of philosophic thought and also seriously questioned the use of Aristotle's philosophy. In fact, he thought that no pagan philosophy could adequately describe even the realm of nature. He adopted an essentially Augustinian position. As in the case of Augustine, however, Bonaventure failed to see that philosophy as philosophy needs an inner reformation. Instead, he, too, theologized philosophy, i.e., subordinated philosophy to the authority of theology and gave it a theological content.

We can understand Bonaventure's opposition to the aristotelian monarchian influence when we realize that his philosophic position was one of semi-mysticism. Semi-mysticism
simply means that (the highest part of) the human soul must rise
to attain mystical union with the *Logos*, with Jesus Christ in the
case of Bonaventure.

In another respect Bonaventure's philosophy differed from
Thomas's, namely, in their understanding of the structure of
human beings. Bonaventure believed that we are not merely a
unified combination of form and matter, but that both one's soul
and one's body were composed of form and matter—a kind of
double dualism, in other words. In some mysterious fashion the
soul-substance (composed of form and matter) and the body-
substance (composed of form and matter) are held together.
Albert the Great and Thomas Aquinas denied any kind of double composition and asserted that a human being is a unity consisting of form and matter. It is difficult to see how such a unity
of two constitutive elements can come about, and in the Middle
Ages the matter was a topic of fierce debates. It is clear, of
course, that the problematics are purely pagan in character.

Albert the Great (1206-1280)

The life of Albert the Great spans nearly the entire 13th
century. Already in his lifetime he was recognized as an
extremely learned man. His writings are important not only for
the history of theology and philosophy, but also for the sciences,
especially botany and zoology.

Albert adopted and openly defended the newly rediscov-
ered aristotelian writings. Because of the great respect the
medievals would have for "Albertus Magnus," as he was called,
his attitude toward Aristotle made it easier for this Greek
philosopher to find inroads into medieval thought. After all,
Aristotle can't be half bad if Albert likes him! Thomas Aquinas
will refer to Aristotle simply as "The Philosopher."

Albert the Great was one of the first medievals to draw a
sharp line of demarcation between theology and philosophy.
His distinction reflects the extent to which the nature/grace
framework had taken hold of the Middle Ages. To Albert theology works with material derived from special revelation, while

philosophy depends on the so-called "unaided reason" alone, that is, on reason without the assistance of faith.

Thomas Aquinas (1225-1274)
Thomas Aquinas, the illustrious pupil of Albert the Great, can rightfully be called the Dean of Scholasticism. Unquestionably, this monk was the most significant and influential of all the medieval theologians. He taught in France and Italy. His complete works in Latin fill twenty-five volumes.

The theme of nature and grace comes to its most articulate expression in the philosophy of Thomas Aquinas. The Fall, for Thomas, is not radical: it does not affect the image of God in human beings, but effects only a removal of the likeness of God in them, that is, of certain supernatural gifts. Basically, human nature is weakened by the Fall and, since that time, directed by a common "natural law" and the "natural light of reason." Christianity, the Bible, faith, the Church are all specially added items (a *donum superadditum*). The natural man is not the radically fallen man that Paul speaks about, but a man endowed with "reason." This natural gift is one and the same in and for all men, and therefore the basis of all common, "neutral," autonomous areas of life. As a consequence, the radical antithesis is often absent in Thomas's thinking.

Implicit in this nature/grace scheme is the possibility of secularism. If it is true that there is a whole realm of "nature," and if this "nature" possesses a certain amount of autonomy, then what prevents this area of "nature" to go it alone? What need does this area have for theology and the Church? There is no reason at all why whole areas of life cannot be secular, free from church control, and free from the authority of the Word of God. This process of secularization began to surge after William of Ockham.

Thomas certainly wished to keep the two realms of nature and grace together. As he said in his *Summa Theologica* (I,8,2): "Grace does not abolish nature, but perfects it." Grace builds on and presupposes nature. The natural is basically excellent and good as far as it goes, but it does not go far enough. It cannot come to the point of complete realization of what it strives for. It is "imperfect" in the Latin sense of being incomplete, unfinished. It must be completed or perfected by grace. He writes elsewhere, "The gifts of grace are added to those of nature in such a way that they do not destroy the latter, but rather perfect them. Therefore also the light of faith which is gratuitously infused into our minds does not destroy the natural light of cognition." According to Thomas the christian life is the fulfillment of the natural order, the completion of "the natural desire for knowledge" manifested in the classical philosophic heritage.

The power of the Church was able to keep these two realms, the natural and the supra-natural, together by force for a little while, until finally the opposition became too strong, and the process of secularization set in. It should be noted that this process of secularization was initially a good thing: the institutional Church had usurped too much power and had created an ecclesiastical society. Secularization began to correct this distorted situation, but went astray when it withdrew whole areas of life not merely from the control of the instituted Church, but from the authority of the Word of God.

The nature/grace theme comes to expression especially in the relation between faith and reason. Note that the equation nature/grace = reason/faith is not correct: reason is used in both areas, both in philosophy and in theology. Not the use of faith and reason, but their source and starting point is what distinguishes them. By means of reason we know "naturally." Reason, the Church claimed, begins with "natural principles" such as the law of noncontradiction. Faith, on the other hand, gives assent to that which is known "supernaturally," to that which is known by revelation. To put it differently, reason affirms that which can be demonstrated without Scripture; faith affirms that which is given in Scripture. The difference between these two realms is still evident today in the degrees universities grant. Back then those who went to a university majored either in theology or philosophy (which included *all* the other nontheological disciplines). Today you earn either a Th.D. or a Ph.D.

Note the insidious character of this distinction. The authority of the Bible, the Word of God, is limited to an area of faith, of theology, and of the Church. "Reason" is the authoritative principle in the "natural sphere." It is precisely this scholastic distinction that has led to the impotence of present-day Christianity. The area of politics, labor, science and technology, industry and business are all areas of "nature," "neutral" areas where the antithesis supposedly does not show itself. Christianity presumably is a matter of faith, values, and morality, of living a decent life and attending church services! Here you have the nature/grace scheme all over again! If Christianity is to survive in our land we had better get rid of this mentality in a hurry and begin to see that Jesus Christ is King of kings. That Kingship includes cultural activities, not merely morality or church activities. It is of critical urgency that the christian community with one voice confront the humanistic world with the full-orbed power of the Word of God.

The Thomistic distinction between faith and reason has bequeathed to us, among other things, a perverted notion of truth. This involves a rather complex situation, although the essence of it is quite simple. Thomas had said that faith gives assent to the givens, the "data" of revelation. Theology is the systematic arrangement of such "data." This approach reduces the Scriptures to a mere collection of "data," of propositions that can be theoretically manipulated. Hence the notion of the Bible as "propositional truth." But the Word of God is not a set of logical propositions, but a power that grips our hearts and turns us around. The Word of God, also revealed in the flesh, Jesus Christ, reveals God's will for humankind and demands that we obediently bow before him. Similarly, truth is primarily not that which can be propositionally, logically asserted or denied, but lasting, steadfast stability and consistency, faithfully maintained moment by moment by God through Jesus Christ. *Truth* is ultimately the reliability and faithfulness of our Father, not the logical coherence of all of God's thoughts together nor the correspondence of human thoughts with his. Because of scholastic influences we have lost sight of this biblical meaning of truth. At the same time, it must be granted that the question of truth in the sense of "getting it right in the way of cognitive claims" is and remains a legitimate philosophic problem for christian philosophers to think about.

As is to be expected, Thomas Aquinas delves deeply into the realms of "natural theology." His proofs of God's existence demonstrate his desire to approach God through the natural light of reason. Thomas rejects Anselm's ontological argument and, instead, postulates five so-called "cosmological" proofs. Briefly, the proofs go as follows:

1. There is movement. All such movement is caused. Hence there is a first mover, which is God.
2. Events are caused by other events. Since no infinite causal chain is possible, there must be a first cause, which is God.
3. The world is a contingent world: it could easily not have been and might not exist tomorrow. An infinite series of contingent events is not possible, for that would leave unexplained why anything exists at all. Hence there must be one who began it all, and that is God.
4. Around us we see degrees of goodness, beauty, and so forth. Such degrees presuppose an ultimate standard, which is God.
5. There is design in the universe. Either there is an intelligent source that regulates the various orderly processes, or it is all due to chance. To appeal to chance is very unsatisfactory, hence there is an intelligent source, which is God.

These proofs have been subjected to much analysis and discussion. For our purposes, suffice it to say that we must reject the accessibility of God by means of logical argument. God is not the object of logical analysis. God is our Father to whom we can come through Jesus Christ. The Thomistic proofs do not prove the existence of the Father of our Lord, but rather an aristotelian god, an unmoved mover. With the traditional attributes of simplicity, impassibility, immutability, and eternality, his conception of God too often sounds more Greek than biblical. Such an unmoved mover is a logical construct, a conclusion based on the premise that immutability and immobility are divine.

A different topic is sin in medieval theology and philosophy. The concept of sin in the Middle Ages was very much derived from Neoplatonism. Remember that Plotinus had constructed a hierarchy of being with the ONE at the top, and matter (non-being) at the bottom. This stuff, matter, we said, was the principle of imperfection and evil. This same notion was carried into medieval theology and resulted in the idea that evil is the absence of good, a lack, a privation, a *privatio boni*. Thomas, too, adopted this position. Needless to say, this negative view of sin as a privation is a pagan idea and completely unbiblical. Sin is very much an apostate, parasitic power that must be reckoned with. It is a privation only in the sense that it constitutes alienation from God. But this is not what the scholastics had in mind.

We have only briefly touched upon some points of Thomas's thought. Thomas Aquinas represents the pinnacle of Scholasticism. Today we are very much afraid of neo-orthodoxy and liberal theology, and rightly so. However, at the same time we tend to overlook the fact that, by far, our biggest problem is not a rising liberal theology, but scholasticism. As long as we continue to think within a scholastic context, the christian community will continue to become increasingly impotent and irrelevant.

Duns Scotus (1266-1308)
Duns Scotus (born in Scotland) was the last of the great scholastics. Already in his thought we can detect a critical tendency that foreshadowed the decline of scholasticism.

Scotus, too, is firmly committed to the principle of nature and grace. But he allowed less of a role to philosophy in our knowledge of God than Aquinas had. Faith was given greater prominence. Furthermore, he differs from Thomas in that he asserts the primacy of the will, whereas Aquinas had proclaimed the primacy of "reason." We say, therefore, that Thomas maintains an intellectualistic position, while Duns' standpoint can be characterized as voluntaristic.

Scotus, like all the scholastics, engaged in lively debate with his contemporaries. Sometimes these debates are difficult to follow because of the endless distinctions that complicate and obscure the argument. As a result, the scholastics never seemed to be getting anywhere. This situation contributed greatly to the growing disenchantment with scholasticism.

The scene in the Middle Ages was much more complex than the brief outline in this survey would indicate. Many other currents of thought (and combinations of currents) made their effect felt. The height of scholasticism constitutes a crucial period in the history of philosophy. The preceding centuries form a prelude. From now on it's downhill for scholasticism. At the same time we must remember that the same types of problems continue to impose themselves upon the western mind.

Although the decline of scholasticism was about to set in, and the Reformation followed, it should not be forgotten that the effects of this period of nature and grace continue throughout the ages. One example will suffice: after the Reformation and the concomitant breakdown of medieval society, a scholastically-oriented theology was re-introduced in the universities. As a result, Reformed theology too, in spite of the work of John Calvin, is far from free from scholastic influence. Today we still have a tendency to theologize about God as though he were an object for theoretical analysis. We still are inclined to look upon Scripture as a collection of true-false propositions. We still tend to believe in supposedly neutral areas of public concern. We need to work this scholastic mentality out of the christian fabric of life. If we don't, then inevitably humanistic secularists will grow stronger and stronger, and more and more intolerant, until—God forbid—the christian voice will be no longer heard in our land.

The Decline of Scholasticism

In the fourteenth and fifteenth centuries we detect a rather sharp decline of scholasticism. Several factors contributing to this decline included a disenchantment with the endless scholastic distinctions as well as a growing spirit of doubt and skepticism (and subsequent rise of subjectivism). Moreover, the tension in the Church and theology, caused by continuing synthesis, was reaching a bursting point. But we must not neglect to notice that at this point in history a real decrease in interest in worship services and "religious" practices was also taking place. This decline in zeal went hand in hand with the disintegration of the power position of the Church. These were troubled, yet exciting times: national states were on the rise, and the world was being explored. Science began to develop, and with the breakdown of the authority of the Church, the process of secularization set in. All these factors signaled the end of medieval scholasticism.

Unquestionably the most influential figure—one who hastened the fall of scholasticism—was William of Ockham, an individualist. However, other trends and currents were present as well. Conflict continued between platonic and aristotelian versions of partial-universalism. Universalism was represented by Meister Eckhart. Meanwhile, the theme of the a priori prepared the way for the subjectivistic character of the modern age.

Meister Eckhart (1260-1327)

One response to (partial-universalistic) scholasticism was a movement of universalistic *mysticism*. The German monk Eckhart, a high ranking Dominican (but nonetheless popular) preacher, represented this position. Interestingly, he was one of the first philosophers to write popular works, as well as preach, in the vernacular language (the more difficult and scholarly treatises he wrote in Latin, of course).

As a mystic Eckhart insisted that the human soul should seek not just communion, but union with God, and that at the moment of union with God the soul must be "apathic" (tranquil and absolutely calm). Because God was for him the Origin of everything that is, he believed that the *being* of the entire creation is the same kind of *being* as that of God, with every creature participating in the being of God. At the same time, creatures differ from God in their essence, as far as their determining characteristics are concerned; men are not like God, of course. (The difference between *being* and *essence* is a typically scholastic distinction.) Eckhart's universalism is evident: individuals and things are but derivations, offshoots of the one, universal *being*. For example, when God made man in his likeness, God sparked the human soul to be his equal everlasting active counterpart—a spiritual powerpoint that emanates from the eternal Spirit. The emanation process from the universal to the individual is matched by another process: that from the individual to the universal. Through the active soul alone, creatures are prepared for becoming and acting Godly. In fact, it seems that the more (or less) one mirrors God in the flint-like power of one's soul, the more (or less) this God comes to be. As far as Eckhart is concerned, what you want to do as a christian soul, as God's image, is return to God and in a sense go beyond God back into the hidden inner abyss of Divinity from which all that is has come. Something along the lines of: Deny yourself and empty yourself of everything creational, for God's sake, so that your knowledge becomes purest ignorance, a dark unconsciousness into which God will come and surely fill that vacuum. You will blend with God into the Godhead when you forsake this present life of opposites; for by becoming dead to the whole world in your soul, you become singlemindedly alive in Being, in the eternal

Being where you were before your creation. This is the mystical character of Eckhart's thought.

There is an obvious similarity between Eckhart's view and that of Heraclitus. Remember that Heraclitus, too, postulated two simultaneous processes: from fire to water, and from water to fire: two opposites return into each other. This view of Heraclitus and Meister Eckhart we call *coincidentia oppositorum* (the coinciding of opposites). Such thinking is contradictory, since the two processes "contradict" each other; and in the case of Eckhart, who joins his love for God to contradictory monist misconception, it is also clearly synthetic—a pagan thought pattern filled with biblical themes. Seerveld sketches well the tension within Eckhart's world.

> Because Eckhart sees the estrangement of man from God not as a call to men for a change in direction to obedience through Jesus Christ but as a necessary return in ontic structure of man directly to God, a biblically envisioned reality is ruled out. There can be no sense of creaturely man's being covenanted to the merciful, just and faithful Yahweh fully revealed in Jesus Christ and attested to by the Holy Scriptures: God is fundamentally a hidden God who discloses his whereabouts like a man in the dark who happens to clear his throat. Sin is not something historically subsequent to creation that can be rectified and healed: for Eckhart, evil is a furtive feature of creatureliness somehow, so that it becomes either/or between Godhood and creation for man. And man is not an adopted serving son of God, through faith, thanks to the Grace of the Lord: instead, thanks to his soul's *vünkelîn* (empowering spark), man is wrenched into the superhuman task of unending mediatorial work, making him a Christ actually, and therefore burdening him like a Sisyphus in an everlasting chain of Becoming perfect. Eckhart's genial sermons of encouragement have a permanent, disconcerting edge underneath, and his "Book of Divine Comfort" is spiked with wormwood. (Seerveld, 1975, 282)

Eckhart's was not a quietistic mysticism. On the one hand, he was convinced that those who try to gain their life shall lose it and those who lose it disinterestedly shall find it forever and ever directly flowing in the heart of God. On the other hand, life for Eckhart is a constant struggle of back and forth, an ongoing process by nature, so that every gain and loss is radically relativized because our life is simply only and finally Becoming.

William of Ockham (1280-1349)

William of Ockham prepared the funeral of scholasticism. He was a keen thinker and a radical critic, and he sounded strangely out of place in a scholastic context. No wonder the Church considered him a heretic!

We have already seen that the Church maintained by force an artificial fusion of nature and grace. Only through its edicts and condemnations of "heresies" could it keep these two areas together. Such a fusion was, to say the least, rather precarious. After all, both areas were pretty well autonomous, although in Thomas's view, the realm of nature was a first step toward the realm of grace, somewhat like a "natural" porch through which one enters the halls of grace. Ockham was determined to show that in reality there was no such fusion, such a connection between nature and grace. In effect, he was out to deny synthesis.

Ockham was an excellent logician. This enabled him to demolish the fallacies of a number of scholastic notions. Besides his logic, he used another tool to destroy scholasticism, namely, "Ockham's Razor." This "razor" is the principle of economy of thought: "A plurality is not to be postulated without necessity." By applying this principle Ockham deftly got rid of a multitude of scholastic (fine) distinctions.

Ockham's philosophic position is characterized by a thorough-going individualism. He denied the existence of universals in any way. There is no such thing, he said, as universal form or matter. There is no "*being* as such," only individual man and woman. Each individual thing is a self-contained entity, an absolute, unrelated by any universal characteristics to any other individual thing. Furthermore, universals—the house, humanity—are only concepts of the mind, formed by abstracting similar characteristics from several concrete individual things— houses, people. Hence Ockham's nominalism (= universals are a concept, a name, from Latin *nomen* = name) is a natural consequence of his individualism.

Ockham was an empiricist. Only about our experience can we say meaningful things. The rest, for example, our knowledge of God, is simply faith. The result of this strict empiricism was that Ockham rejected the scholastic proofs of God's existence. Take the argument from causality, for example. Thomas had

114 PATTERNS OF THE WESTERN MIND

argued that events are caused, that there must be a first cause, and that that first cause is God. Ockham not only questioned the basis for asserting that there is such a thing as causality (all we experience is a sequence of events), but moreover objected that there is no compelling reason why God must be regarded as first cause. Could a heavenly body, for example, not be a first cause? For example, all that "reason" knows about God or the soul, Ockham concluded, is purely subjective knowledge without any basis for certainty.

Ockham was a voluntarist, that is, he asserted the primacy of the will, rather than the intellect, as Thomas—echoing the Greeks—had done. Ockham believed that God is omnipotent and absolutely free. He is really an unpredictable and capricious God, free, for example, to change the moral law at will. God can change the world order as he pleases. From this position follows the notion that everything is contingent: things exist (now) not because they are rational or good—as the scholastics had assumed—but because that's the way God wanted it (then). This view of God's will cancels out any idea of God's faithfulness. The Scripture did not norm Ockham's theory, and no wonder: for to him the Bible was little more than an ecclesiastical handbook.

Under the hammer blows of Ockham's logic, scholasticism began to disintegrate. Before we applaud, we do well to realize what Ockham really is doing. He is driving a wedge between the areas of nature and grace. This, in effect, sets the ball of secularism rolling. The area of grace, including the Bible and faith, have nothing whatsoever to do with the area of nature, with the state, society, and science. The Word of God is confined to an area of grace. This area has in subsequent history become smaller and smaller, and more and more irrelevant. Very effectively, as the process of secularization unfolds, the Word-revelation is placed on the sidelines, seemingly out of commission. Meanwhile, the world of "nature" is quickly claimed by the rapidly growing forces of humanism. This situation will be the topic of discussion in the next sections.

By now the disastrous effects of nature/grace synthesis should be quite apparent. The decline of scholasticism meant the beginning of secularistic, humanistic forces. Apostate people, remember, suppress the truth in unrighteousness, and when the scholastics articulated a theology and a philosophy that inherently contained the possibility of limiting the power of God's Word, there was no hesitation at all: eagerly the new humanistic spirit seized upon the opportunity and claimed practically all areas of life, leaving just a little bit for the christian community. The result was that the authority of the Word of God was eliminated from public concerns. Today, many political processes, for example, are inherently humanistic and unchristian because Jesus Christ and a biblical sense of normativity play less than a marginal role in politics. The scientific enterprise is thoroughly secularistic, because Jesus Christ is not recognized as King of science and technology in our modern world. Public schools and universities, certainly in Europe and North America, are bulwarks of humanism because God's Word is outlawed and ridiculed. Let's be fully aware that merely a moral reform is not going to correct this unholy situation. It will not do merely to tell people to behave properly while the forces of unbelief continue to tighten their grip on practically all of life. What is needed is an *inner reformation* of politics, labor, industry, and the scientific enterprise. This calls for communal christian action (individualism has too long sapped the strength from the christian community). What a tremendous task awaits us!

4. SYNTHESIS AT THE CLOSE OF THE MIDDLE AGES

Essentially this period represents a time of transition. We have already noted some of the factors that contributed to the decline of scholasticism. Representatives of this era are sick and tired of scholasticism. More important, however, is the desire to return to the patristic period. We can distinguish two movements, neither one of which produced philosophers of note.

The Prereformation stressed the scriptural element in the church fathers. This emphasis indicates that there was no intention to synthesize. Since Augustine was the most scriptural of all the early church fathers, he was by far preferred.

The father of the Prereformation was Bradwardine (1290-1349). He was very much oriented to the thought of Augustine, and consequently he endeavored to subject his philosophy to biblical norms. Nevertheless, he could not altogether escape the effects of scholasticism (for example, he adopted the ontological argument of Anselm).

Bradwardine had a great influence on John Wycliffe (d.1384) and John Huss (d.1415). Unlike Bradwardine, these two well-known figures came under the influence of a monarchian type of thinking. This is one of the reasons why the Prereformation failed: another example of how synthesis breaks the power of the Church.

The Christian Humanists, too, were synthesis thinkers. Like the Prereformation, christian humanism longed to return to the patristic period. But the stress was different. They appreciated not so much the scriptural element in Augustine as the fact that Augustine was both a Christian and a Roman. In other words, the Christian Humanists were seeking a return of a christianized Roman world. Petrarch (d.1374) and his friends actually tried to bring about such a world. They wanted to be Romans, rather than Italians. These Christian Humanists believed that by restoring classical culture, they could improve their own world.

The desire to return to the patristic world was very unhealthy. A restoration of the past, what we call "repristination," is not only impossible, but in conflict with the very principle of reformation. Reformation is never a return to a christian period in history, but always means repentance and a return to obedience. This wish for the past constitutes another reason why these movements failed.

We have now come to the conclusion of the second main period, the period of synthesis. It should be clear that the Middle Ages were far from "dark." On the contrary, a rich diversity of types and currents were present in practically every century. In the next main period we consider the negative response to these centuries of synthesis. That response heralds the arrival of the Modern Era.

II. C. 3 and 4.
Guide Questions

56. What is scholasticism?

57. Why did Boethius find philosophy consoling?

58. Anselm of Canterbury, "the Father of Scholasticism," is known for his "ontological argument for the existence of God." What was behind his attempted proofs.

59. How did medieval Jewish and Islamic philosophy affect the Latin West?

60. Why was Bonaventure a strange fish in the scholastic pond?

61. What is not so great about Albert the Great's way of distinguishing between philosophy and theology?

62. How does the theme of nature/grace come to expression in Thomas Aquinas' anthropology?

63. How is the possibility of secularism implicit in the nature/grace scheme?

64. How does the Thomistic distinction between faith and reason reflect the nature/grace scheme?

65. Explain two of the Thomistic proofs for the existence of God. What is problematic about all of them?

66. Why will the christian community continue to become increasingly impotent and irrelevant as long as it thinks within a scholastic context?

67. What factors contributed to the decline of scholasticism?

68. Given the mystical character of Eckhart's thought, what does he think every Christian should want to spend their life doing?

69. Describe the important role Ockham played in the history of the West.

71. How do the following apply to Ockham?
    - Ockham's Razor   - individualism   - voluntarism
    - nominalism   - empiricism

72. Summarize the similarity and the difference between the Prereformation movement and the christian humanists.

73. Why is it that synthesis brings nothing but grief?

A History of Western Thought
that Shuns Synthesis

II. D.
Introduction to the Third Main Period

To many contemporary historians of the Western world, the beginning of the modern age resembles a dawn: the first rays of humanism and secularism break through the "darkness" of the Middle Ages. The Age of Reason begins. The Church and its superstitions are done for. A bright new future beckons.

That this picture is very one-sided, to say the least, is immediately evident when one glances at the last 500 years to see what humankind come of age has accomplished. Not only did the anticipated paradise of reason fail to materialize, reason itself has been replaced by a number of irrationalistic spirits, as we will see. Though far from producing the utopia that the Renaissance foresaw, the modern era has given rise to a wide variety of fascinating attempts to define and redefine foundations and pinnacles.

It goes without saying that the rise of modern thought did not constitute a clear break with the past. Of course not. As a matter of fact, the new era depended very much on the preceding one, as does any age. Sometimes a new period in history retains very strong ties with an earlier one by means of tradition, or else, it may react very violently against the preceding period. Something of the second alternative characterizes the rise of modern thought.

The response of modern philosophy to the Middle Ages is primarily anti-synthetic in nature. We have already encountered an *anti-synthesis* feeling in the very last part of the previous main period. Now, however, it constitutes a much more definitive characteristic: modern philosophy is outspokenly against synthesis! As such, nonchristian pagan modern philosophy can never be placed on the same level as pre-synthesis pagan philosophy. Just as ancient pagan philosophy was affected by christian accommodation, so the character of modern pagan philosophy was determined to a large extent by its negative response to christian synthesis thinking.

One can respond negatively to synthetic thought patterns for two reasons: it may be that the rejection of synthesis is prompted by an aversion to Scripture, or at least contempt for the suggestion that what one believes on the basis of Scripture has anything to do with science or philosophy. The resulting conception will then bear a stamp that varies from strongly paganistic to indifferent. On the other hand, the answer may be motivated by a holy reverence for Scripture. When we become aware of the terrible effects of the attempted combination of pagan thought patterns and biblical themes, such as conflicts over pseudo-problems and divisions among Christians, then we gladly take a stand against those who have contaminated, warped, and watered down the Word of God.

A common enemy does not necessarily unite standpoints that differ in principle. The underground movement during World War Two united diverse people in opposing Hitler's Germany, but this negative unity did not bring unanimity after the war was won. Both Christians and rationalists are opposed to synthesis thinking. Does that remove the antithesis? Is "christian rationalism" in order now?

It may be instructive to draw a parallel from this state of affairs. Often it is said that our political parties are really "christian" because they are opposed to crime and immorality, are in favor of law and order, and do wish to bring about a better world. This argument has no force whatsoever when we remember that even the most thorough-going anti-christian humanism is just as much opposed to crime and immorality and also desires a better world. No one I know of is opposed, for example, to freedom (for those who deserve it). The question, then, is not which issues we are for or against, but whether Jesus Christ is acknowledged and obeyed.

We can distinguish three major currents in the modern period: the prelude to the modern period (ca.1500-1600), rationalism (ca.1600-1900), and anti-rationalism (ca. 1900-present).

1. Prelude to the Modern Period (1500-1600)

Introduction

In many ways the sixteenth century determined the shape of things to come, for in it took place the struggle for cultural control of the West. Scholasticism lay in ruins and an authoritative Christendom promising security where moth and rust do not corrupt had lost its unquestioned control of men's hearts and minds. A new vision had to be supplied. Which was it to be? Both a rising humanism and the Reformation contested for the leadership. In other words, the lines of the antithesis were very sharply drawn in the sixteenth century.

All the movements of the Prelude period displayed a strong anti-synthetic character. This characteristic by no means united them. To the contrary, we find the two types of response that we mentioned a moment ago. On the one hand there is the anti-synthesis movement that resists reckoning with Scripture, at least at certain times and places, and on the other hand there is the Reformation. Consequently we can discuss the Prelude to the modern age in two subsections, namely, (a) early unscriptural anti-synthesis thought, and (b) the Reformation.

Early Unscriptural Anti-synthesis Thought

Since practically all of modern anti-synthetic thinking is not in line with Scripture, we can designate this period as "early." We can distinguish two movements, namely, anti-synthetic humanism (in distinction from the Christian Humanism already discussed) and the Renaissance.

Anti-synthesis humanism is a nonchristian type of humanism that compares with the already discussed christian variant in that both of them share a longing for the past. Now, however, the object of this desire is no longer merely the times of the church fathers, but pagan antiquity itself. Classical culture becomes a model to be imitated, an ideal to be attained. Anti-synthesis humanism had no use for the Church and scholastic theology, and, in returning to antiquity, wanted to by-pass all of it.

This type of humanism focused entirely upon "nature": the area of "grace" had no significance at all when it came to science and philosophy. This attitude contributed greatly to the increasingly secularistic character of western civilization. Heaven was brought down to earth and man became "God on earth."

A typical representative of nonchristian anti-synthesis humanism was Boccaccio (d.1375), a friend and pupil of Petrarch. The anti-christian strain of Boccaccio is quite evident in his famous work *Decameron*. Sparked by the rediscovery of many ancient works of literature, this type of humanism did much to preserve and elevate a classical tradition. The medieval focus on an afterworldly spiritual destiny was being dislodged. Human consciousness and culture apart from the church were becoming revitalized.

The word "renaissance" means "rebirth." This is essentially a christian concept that became a secularized slogan. Therefore even the term "renaissance" hints at the apostate character of the movement. "We must be born again," they said, "but not of water and the blood, but in our own autonomous strength." The Renaissance must not be confused with Humanism. Both did elevate humankind to the center of reality. But the Renaissance had its optimistic eye only on the present and the future, and had little more than criticism for the past. The promoters of the Renaissance envisioned a bright future through the process of self-renewal. Recent scientific discoveries sparked the desire to combine such self-renewal with scientific progress.

Sometimes it is asserted that the Renaissance bore an individualistic stamp. It is true that such individualism was present, and also universalism, but the dominant position was one of partial-universalism. This position is especially evident in the great astronomers of the period, such as Copernicus (d.1543), Bruno (1548-1600), and Kepler (d.1630). For example, in Bruno, an Italian philosopher who was burnt at the stake by the Church during the Inquisition, the partial-universalism is displayed by his view of reality in terms of God as universal world-soul and a world composed of divine individual particles called "monads." The fact that Bruno speaks about God ought not lead one to conclude that his thinking was scriptural. He remained a typical Renaissance figure who believed that God must not be looked for in a special revelation, but in the orderliness of the universe—a point of view that certainly has retained an enthusiastic following.

The Englishman Francis Bacon (1561-1626) was a real Renaissance figure. He is famous for the impetus he gave to the development of the inductive method in science. *Induction* is a method of reasoning in which one relies on similar, observed cases, so as to infer that the same event or property will recur in as yet unobserved cases.

Bacon's anti-synthetic position is very clear, although the trappings are still very christian. He writes, for example, in his *The Advancement of Learning* (Bk.1.1.3):

> Let no man upon a weak conceit of sobriety or an ill-applied moderation think or maintain, that men can search too far, or be too well studied in the book of God's word, or in the book of God's works, divinity or philosophy; but rather let men endeavor an endless progress or proficience in both; only let men beware...that they do not unwisely mingle or confound these learnings together.

Let theology study its book. We scientists will put away our idols and study the other. Scientific progress, according to Bacon, can come about only when we free ourselves from "idols," namely, the "idols of the tribe" (a human nature prone to quick opinions), the "idols of the cave" (presuppositions and personal prejudices), the "idols of the marketplace" (inaccurate use of words), and "idols of the theater" (the stubborn desire to cling to outmoded philosophic systems).

Bacon believed that humanity's future lay in technological power, the road to which is knowledge: "knowledge itself is power." In *The New Atlantis* he describes an ideal society that looks to science as providing the key to happiness. Technical control of the created order constitutes the highest good. Again, however, the trappings sound so biblical: "The empire of man over things depends wholly on the arts and sciences.... Let the human race recover that right over Nature which belongs to it by divine bequest" (*Novum Organum*, Aphorism 129). One look around us, however, is enough to see the devastation the human race has wrought with this "God-given right to technically control creation." With this emphasis on scientific cultural power, Bacon stands far removed from the scholastic world of metaphysical distinctions.

Nonchristian humanism and the Renaissance easily formed a united front. After all, both movements were looking for new life, one through the rebirth of antiquity, the other via the rebirth of humans themselves. They were also both anti-synthetic, opposing the mixture of "grace"—faith, Scripture, beliefs, and the Church—and "nature"—our ability to study and control the world around us. Furthermore, it did not take much time for humanism to discover that a return to the ancient world was pretty well an impossibility. Consequently, it was absorbed in the general renaissance movement which was to culminate into the great rationalistic systems of the seventeenth and eighteenth centuries.

Whatever force scholasticism still carried was rapidly destroyed by the spirit of this new age. That is not to say that scholasticism died completely. Scholastic philosophers continued to produce, even in the period of the prelude to modern times (e.g., Suarez, 1548-1617, a fairly original thinker in the tradition of Duns Scotus). Nevertheless, this was the time when cultural control began to pass over to the humanistic, secularistic mind. Western civilization eagerly reached for the area of "nature," which promised a bright new future for mankind. This was the time when a new vision of humanity arose: man, the lord and master of the universe, shaper of his own destiny.

The Reformation

The Reformation was not a philosophic movement. Rather, it was a religiously-driven re-orientation to renewed obedience. In this sense the Reformation stood in close alliance with Augustine. Note, however, that this alliance was not colored by the unhealthy wish for the past such as the Prereformation movement had exhibited. Luther and the other reformers realized that the way of the Prereformation—with its terrible revolts in England and the wars of the Hussites—was not a good example. Hence the reformational stress on one's (and the Church's) relation to God (especially strong in Luther and Calvin) rather than to other people.

Some things about the Reformation remained embedded in the spirituality of the later Middle Ages. But many developments were refreshing and invigorating. People once again caught and disseminated the biblical vision of God's majesty in a law-ordered creation, of his righteousness and faithfulness, and of his love in Jesus Christ. Luther saw that the whole person is corrupt and in need of God's forgiveness. The problem is not just particular sins that could be covered one by one through Church-directed actions. Our souls, our very being, needs the healing that only Christ can give, and only through faith in him can we be made right with God. Although Luther was still much affected by William of Ockham, for example, he nevertheless powerfully placed the *sola fide* (by faith alone) before the western world. Calvin shared this emphasis and, in addition, posited the scriptural principle of the sovereignty of God who remains faithful to his Word and Law.

Unfortunately, the Reformation's effect was severely curtailed by the Roman Catholic counter-reformation, as well as by a liberal Protestantism that very soon succumbed to a renewed synthesis mentality.

Unfortunate as well is the fact that the Reformation did not produce a christian, reformational philosophy. This failure constituted a tremendous handicap and contributed to the success of anti-christian rationalistic spirits. The pagan world continued to articulate theoretical visions, which—for lack of a christian philosophy of its own—strongly influenced the christian community. Not until the twentieth century did such a philosophy take shape.

We as Christians today must learn to take up the banner of the Reformation. That commitment does not mean a return to the historical sixteenth-century Reformation—that would be making the same mistake as the Prereformation and Christian Humanism made! Instead, let the spirit of the Reformation—renewed obedience to Jesus Christ the King—take hold of us, so that we will be able to evaluate our own times in a truly biblical light. Let us, in addition, test the spirits within the christian community as well, to see whether they be of Christ or of a stagnant scholastic traditionalism. *Ecclesia reformata reformanda est!* The reformed church—not merely the instituted church, but the christian community in its wider sense—must be continually reforming.

II. D. 1.
Guide Questions

74. How can it be that in the modern era Christians and non-Christians are both interested in an anti-synthetic attitude?

75. What is the difference between early Humanism (e.g., Boccaccio) and the Renaissance (e.g., Bruno and Kepler)?

76. In what way was Francis Bacon a typical representative of the Renaissance?

77. Why did Bacon think that learning would advance if people would talk about the *two* books of God?

78. Why did Bacon make such a stink about idols?

79. What is the difference between the "Prereformation" and the "Reformation"?

80. The Reformation, unfortunately, did not produce a christian, reformational philosophy. Where does that leave us when it comes to taking up the banner of the Reformation today in, for example, the field of philosophy or physics or literature or ...?

2. RATIONALISM (1600-1900)

Introduction

Rationalism held sway over the Western world for three centuries, in approximate figures, from 1600 to 1900. How did this situation come about?

For one thing, the Reformation had not produced a scriptural philosophy and therefore could neither combat unscriptural thought on philosophic grounds nor defend itself against dominant paganistic influences. As a result, a synthesis mentality crept in again. Meanwhile the secularizing spirits succeeded in containing the power of the Reformation so that it could not continue to be effective in the ongoing need for reformation. And in Roman Catholic circles an out-dated scholastic tradition could not recapture the leading role that it played in the Middle Ages.

Humanism as a historical movement did not fare much better. The restoration of antiquity in a modern age proved to be an impossible dream. We should note, incidentally, that the term "humanism" is an ambiguous word. So far we have used it to signify a historical philosophic movement, such as christian and anti-christian humanism. When we speak about a humanistic spirit today, we refer to the spirit that places humankind on the throne—where God rightfully belongs. Such usage gives the term a religious, not merely a philosophic content. Secular

humanism is *religious* in character. It is a religion, not a philosophy in the proper sense of the word.

The rationalism of the 17th century grew out of renaissance
movements. The buoyant optimism of the Renaissance had been
toned down somewhat; nevertheless, the belief in humankind's
own possibilities had not decreased in the least. The individual
ego was about to be embraced as the self-determining center of
the world. Autonomy—independence, from the Greek "*autos*"
self "*nomos*" law—was in. Subjection—from the Latin "*subjectus*"
to place under—was out, except for a subjugation of "nature,"
which was soon to become man's footstool.

The term "rationalism" means the exaggeration and overes-
timation of *ratio.* What does *ratio* mean? It means "reason." But
reason is actually a human concoction. Ignoring God and his
Word, creaturely human understanding gets outfitted with universally binding and absolutely certifying a prioris that are supposed to guarantee truth and reliable meaning to everyone following it. *Ratio*nality then takes on the status of God's Word, as
it also recalls the stoic assertion that a fundamental order and
structure lies within all reality and is evidenced in the workings
of the human mind. As such, the term "reason" is a pagan concept! God did not give "reason" to human beings, but the ability
to distinguish, to discover, and to understand. The concept
"reason" with its attending a prioris is the product of an apostate
illusion.

It is clear that the full significance of rationalism cannot be
appreciated without an understanding of the hellenistic period.
In many ways the Period of Rationalism is parallel to the Hellenistic Age. Not only is the notion of a priori "reason" a determining element, but there is also a remarkable similarity in stress on
epistemology. Furthermore, the subjective character of rationalism was prepared by skepticism, just as in the hellenistic period.

The complexity of the relationship between ancient thought
and modern rationalistic philosophy is unfortunately too great
for anything like an adequate treatment in this brief survey. Suffice it to say that monarchian and platonic patterns, especially
their hellenistic interpretations, determined the varieties of rationalistic movements.

Again, the exact difference between the hellenistic a priori
and the modern "*ratio*" falls outside the present scope of this

study.   In general, the hellenistic position had "a priorized"
Plato's Ideas.   The modern *ratio* included a wider range of experience and is therefore more pronouncedly subjectivistic in character.   The subjectivism of the rationalists should be evident: the
a priori equipment of our "reason" determines the character of
our experience.   As we saw when we studied the Hellenistic
Age, the human mind is said to be the key to the world.   This
state of affairs produces a thoroughly distorted vision of created
reality.

Our account of rationalism will differ from most current
textbooks and secondary sources.   The reason for this is that secularistic historians do not apply consistent criteria for distinguishing types and currents.   For example, various trends in
rationalism are often distinguished on the basis of geography!
The result is some unsystematic distinction as the "British empiricists" and the "German idealists."

To begin, we shall distinguish two successive stages of
rationalism.   The first stage, early rationalism from approximately 1600 to 1830, is characterized by a stress on the content of
the a priori reason.   The second, late rationalism from 1830 to
about 1900, shifts the stress to the activity of the a priori reason.
This is a technical distinction, of course, yet extremely useful, for
it helps us to understand the complex nature of rationalism.   We
shall treat these stages in two subsections.

Early Rationalism

Early rationalism covers the period from ca. 1600 to 1830
(Hegel died in 1831).   Within this time we can distinguish three
successive rationalistic developments.   At first the "*ratio*" was
believed to be of a scientific nature.   The rise of the mathematical
and physical sciences and the spirit of the Renaissance contributed greatly to that notion.   The role of scientific, theoretical
knowledge, especially in terms of mathematics, came to be very
much overestimated in this early period.   We call this phase of
rationalism "scientialism."

After a while some of the early rationalists began to see that
there was such a thing as practical knowledge, in other words,
valuable knowledge not of a theoretic nature.   A large area of
knowledge does not presuppose theoretical analysis.   These rationalists placed such practical knowledge on the same level as

scientific knowledge, yes, even attributed more importance to it. Thus we see the development of what came to be called "practical reason." Hence we have a renewed, rationalistic form of what we met way back with Socrates: practicalism. In ancient times, before the theory of the a priori arose, practicalism simply meant that good insight guarantees good action. Now it acquires a rationalistic tone: the "insight" is now the practical a priori, the practical "reason." This state of affairs is characteristic of The Enlightenment.

Slowly a tension began to develop between scientialism and practicalism. Scientialism continued to stress the primacy of theoretical, scientific knowledge. The practicalists—though not denying the crucial role of scientific knowledge—felt that the nonscientific element in our knowledge is the most important. When the conflict became intense, a third reconciliatory movement arose, namely, idealism, which attempted to bring the opponents together, as we shall see.

A word about the usual distinction between continental rationalism and British empiricism: These two are not mutually exclusive, for an empiricist can very well be a rationalist, as we shall discover. The traditional grouping of Locke, Berkeley, and Hume as "British empiricists" falls therefore by the wayside, especially when we note that Locke and Berkeley were scientialists, while Hume was a practicalist.

These rationalistic developments are addressed in three subsections. We will merely touch upon some of the most important representatives of each movement.

Scientialism

This current of rationalism was built on a shared consensus concerning reason, nature, and human autonomy. With the intellectual ability to grasp the foundational order of the universe and to formulate objectively the very laws of nature, reason was to pave the way toward changing and controlling the world. By casting this project as an effort to understand God's mind by discovering how the realm of nature operates, this way of doing science did retain a religious hue. On the other hand, the universal availability of these "natural laws" transformed nature into the common court of appeal: let us bring all of life into conformity with the laws of nature as discovered by human reason. As a result, a sense'of self-certainty grew as reverence for an external authority as the arbiter of truth waned. Compliance is no longer grounded with an appeal to Scripture or doctrine but by embracing the universal laws of nature. Some of the more important representatives are Galileo, Hobbes, Descartes, Spinoza, Leibnitz, Newton, Locke, and Berkeley.

   Galileo Galilei (1564-1642) is well known for his defense of Copernicus and the subsequent conflict with the Church. His use of the telescope and mathematical demonstration to argue for a heliocentric theory did not keep the Church from censuring his views as contrary to Scripture. This situation once more demonstrates the trouble that synthesis brings about. Galileo's dismissal of the geocentric theory (of Aristotle) proved to be an attack on the Church simply because the Church had "baptized" Aristotle and adopted much of what he had said. (In 1992, Pope John Paul II declared that the church had erred in condemning Galileo in 1633 for asserting that the Earth revolves around the sun.)

   Galileo wrote the following concerning the authority of the Church and its interpretation of Scripture:

> I think that in discussing natural problems we should not begin from the authority of scriptural passages, but from sensory experiences and necessary demonstrations; for Holy Scripture and nature proceed alike from the divine Word, the former as the dictate of the Holy Spirit and the latter as the faithful executrix of God's commands. Furthermore, Scripture, adapting itself to the understanding of the common man, is wont to say many things that appear to differ from absolute truth as far as the bare meaning of the words is concerned. Nature, on the contrary, is inexorable and immutable; she never transcends the limits of the laws imposed on her, and she is indifferent whether her secret reasons and ways of operating are understood by men. It would seem, therefore, that nothing physical that sense experience sets before our eyes, or that necessary demonstrations prove to us, should be called into question, not to say condemned, because of biblical passages that have an apparently different meaning. Scriptural statements are not bound by rules as strict as natural events, and God is not less excellently revealed in these events than in the sacred propositions of the Bible. (182-183)

These are obviously the words of a Christian. But note what qualifies as "the absolute truth." What is it that Galileo finds to be steadfast and trustworthy? He so wanted to rhyme thought with scholastic church dogma, to pay unconditional allegiance to "reason" in matters of this world, but still honor God for the next. This kind of synthesis could console the historical conscience of many, but it only insured secularism's progressive hold on hearts.

Christianity has had to suffer grievously because of synthesis, as it gave rise to a continuing conflict between science and the Church. Even today this "problem" is ravaging the christian community, especially in connection with biological and geological discoveries. Here again, a scholastic mentality continues to grip us, thereby rendering the debate rather fruitless.

Part of Galileo's significance lies in his contributions to the construction of a philosophy, actually a mathematical science, that was designed to explain the orderly processes in the universe. His goal was to interpret the world from a strictly quantitative point of view.

> Philosophy is written in this great book—I mean the universe—which stands continually open to our gaze, but it cannot be understood unless one first studies the language and the characters in which it is written. It is written in the language of mathematics, and its characters are triangles, circles, and other geometrical figures, without which it is humanly impossible to understand a single word of it. (237-238)

Galileo's method, canonized by Isaac Newton (1642-1727), can be described as the *inductive, empirical, quantitative, mechanistic* observation of reality, with an eye to reducing what one finds to a single mathematical formula that can be regarded as universally valid. Galileo also stressed the distinction between appearance and reality, where appearance is supposed to be made up of "secondary" qualities (such as color, taste, emotions, and sounds) while real reality consists of "primary" qualities (such as size, position, motion, and density). To trust appearance is to embrace ignorance and miss the mark. The only real reality is that which can be scientifically explained in mathematical terms. It may appear that the sun rises in the east, but anyone in the know knows that science knows better. For years to come, however, God would still be called upon to bridge the gaps that science could not fill or explain or explain away. But as this science advanced, there was less and less a need for miraculous stop-gaps.

The claims of Galileo and Newton led modern thinkers to reject an organic view of the world and to replace it with a mechanistic world picture. Reality soon became an awesome, but yet relatively simple, static, objective universe—a very order-ly set of basic elements or elementary particles and forces. Experimentation that yields quantifiable results gave scientists the sense they were producing exact and unambiguous knowl-edge that was next to divine and, humanly speaking, almost as powerful.

Thomas *Hobbes'* (1588-1679) view of the universe drove him to the extreme conclusion that everything, including people's emotions and beliefs, is mechanically determined. Likewise, the addition and subtraction of sense data is all that is needed to explain human thinking. Truth ends up being mere convention, for as social conditions or political parties change so does the truth. Hence, his view is one of determinism.

Besides his determinism, Hobbes is known for his political theory of "might is right." He maintained that the need for gov-ernment can be deduced from certain facts about human nature: Each person is naturally inclined to do whatever will best ad-vance his own interests. Life without government—i.e., life in a "state of nature"—would be lonely, poor, nasty, brutish, and short. Only government, with its power to punish, can alter the behavior that is in each person's interest. If I know that my attacking you will result in a punishment that will outweigh anything I can gain, then I will not attack you for gain. And the same holds for you. Hence, concludes Hobbes, reason dictates the need for a king or a government that is stronger than any citizen or group of citizens. Likewise, because it was in the best interest of citizens to transfer their power to a ruling person or government, they are not entitled to resist or depose him. The ruler has been given the might, and with that comes the right to wield it.

Modern philosophy comes into its own with René *Descartes* (1596-1650). He is considered the rationalist *par excellence*. His tendency was to be skeptical about any claims to knowledge based solely on the testimony of the senses, former opinions, prejudices, tradition, or any other authority than reason. He elevated mathematics as the model of "clear and distinct" reasoning and geometry's chains of reasons as the objective means to methodological certainty. Reason is universally valid, not limited by historical happenstance, and shared by all (rational) human beings.

Descartes was a partial-universalist who thought of God as infinite substance and of human beings as finite substances. Although we are finite, according to Descartes, we are in will and understanding not imperfect. Our finite knowledge is related to God's knowledge as a part to the infinite whole. The problem is that we too easily or quickly affirm or deny what we do not understand clearly and distinctly. But Descartes found what he thought was a remedy.

In his efforts to find a sure and indubitable foundation for his thinking, he chose the route of methodical doubt as a kind of intellectual purification of self. In other words, Descartes consciously and explicitly wanted to put all philosophic tradition behind him and to start anew, from scratch. Bound and determined to find certainty somewhere, he set about to doubt away hypothetically everything he could. Whatever could possibly be doubted was not indubitable. Proceeding in this manner he discovered that he could doubt everything, except: I cannot doubt that I am doubting (which is, of course, me thinking). Hence his famous "*cogito, ergo sum*": I think, therefore I am. This belief was so "clear and distinct" that it could never be questioned. According to Descartes, this absolutely certain knowledge of one's self-existence as thinking substance is innate and a priori, had by everyone prior to all sense experience. But a strange thing happens at this point: in order to waylay the fear (of *solipsism*) that he is just stuck inside the intuited immediacies of his own head and that what he *says* is true for all is *not* true for anyone else (if indeed there are other people out there), Descartes soon falls back on an old version of the ontological argument to prove God's existence. After proving that God exists he could then demonstrate that God being good would not let Descartes be deceived in embracing as certain anything that is so clear and distinct in his mind. The result is a divinely sanctioned trust in human reason!

The significance of Descartes and his Cartesian method is hard to overestimate. His method of taking things apart and putting them back together, of "breaking down" and "building up," which takes geometrical proofs as its standard, is so ingrained in the Western world that most people reading his *Rules for the Direction of the Mind* find it surprising that Descartes had to work so long and hard at formulating what seems so obvious.

> *Rule II* "Only those objects should engage our attention, to the sure and indubitable knowledge of which our mental powers seem to be adequate." "Science in its entirety is true and evident cognition.... [T]rust only what is completely known and incapable of being doubted.... [I]n our search for the direct road toward truth we should busy ourselves with no object about which we cannot attain a certitude equal to that of the demonstrations of Arithmetic and Geometry."

> *Rule III* "In the subjects we propose to investigate, our inquiries should be directed, not to what others have thought, nor to what we ourselves conjecture, but to what we can clearly and perspicuously behold and with certainty deduce; for knowledge is not won in any other way."

> *Rule V* "Method consists entirely in the order and disposition of the objects toward which our mental vision must be directed if we would find out any truth. We shall comply with it exactly if we reduce involved and obscure propositions step by step [analysis] to those that are simpler [resolution], and then starting with the intuitive apprehension of all those that are absolutely simple, attempt to ascend [synthesis] to the knowledge [composition] of all others by precisely similar steps [demonstration]."

> *Rule VII* "If we wish our science to be complete, those matters which promote the end we have in view must one and all be scrutinized by a movement of thought which is continuous and nowhere interrupted; they must also be included in an enumeration which is both adequate and methodical."

> *Rule XIII* "Once a 'question' is perfectly understood, we must free it of every conception superfluous to its meaning, state it in its simplest terms, and, having recourse to an enumeration, split it up into the various sections beyond which analysis cannot go in minuteness." (*Rules for the Direction of the Mind*, 3-49.)

> "Those long chains of reasoning, simple and easy as they are, of which geometricians make use in order to arrive at the most difficult demonstrations, had caused me to imagine that all those things which fall under the cognizance of man might very likely be mutually related in the same fashion; and that, provided only that we abstain from receiving anything as true which is not so,

and always retain the order which is necessary in order to deduce the one conclusion from the other, there can be nothing so remote that we cannot reach to it, nor so recondite that we cannot discover it." (*Discourse on Method*, 93)

For Descartes, all certainty rests upon the a priori *ratio*, upon human reason. The self is the thinking subject; and the self necessarily perceives every other kind of thing as an object. This posture, of course, soon sets the knowing subject apart from and above, or over against, the world, which is the object of the self's knowledge. The subjectivistic rationalism is crystal clear. Because of Descartes' influence, scientialistic rationalism gained a very strong presence in Western philosophy.

Baruch *Spinoza* (1632-1677), a Jewish thinker and native of Amsterdam, was initially very strongly oriented to Descartes. He differs, however, in that he was a universalist: Spinoza recognized only one substance. There was a strong touch of neoplatonic mysticism in his thought, which explains his desire to intellectually attain to mystical union with God (= Nature). Consequently, his mysticism is of a rationalistic nature. His philosophy is—due to his universalism—pantheistic in character: the one substance is God, of which everything in the world is a manifestation.

Like Spinoza, *Leibnitz* (1646-1716) underwent stages of philosophic development. He was an able man who dreamed of uniting all the scientific minds of his time. As a step in that direction he founded the Berlin Academy of Sciences. He also strove to unify the Church. Philosophically, Leibnitz was a partial-universalist. This position is clear from his theory of monads, which resembles that of Bruno, already mentioned. What are monads? Monads are indivisible, formless kernels of power, capable of producing action. God is the great central monad. Besides him there are the numberless monads that together constitute the universe. Leibnitz was an optimist who believed that our world is the "best of all possible worlds." His optimism did much to continue the strength and vigor of rationalism.

John *Locke* (1632-1704) and bishop Berkeley (1685-1753) are traditionally classified (together with David Hume) as "British empiricists." Locke indeed was an empiricist, but certainly a rationalist as well. In spite of what the secular historians of philosophy say, rationalism and empiricism are not at all mutually exclusive. In the case of John Locke, for example, empiricism is of a distinctly rationalistic character. In his view, the knowing process begins with sense impressions; nevertheless, the a priori laws of association confer meaning on such impressions. In other words, the impressions are ordered by an a priori structure of thought, the results of which can therefore be trusted.

Locke's stress on individual introspection ultimately provided him with a rational argument for religious toleration (of everyone except atheists, the insane, and members of the Roman Catholic Church). He also contributed to the rise of the theory of "natural rights to life, liberty, and property," a theory that was destined to become a powerful force in the American and French revolutions. Today it is difficult for people used to the freedoms of democracy to imagine how radical Locke's claim was that "[reason] teaches all mankind who will but consult it, that being all equal and independent, no one ought to harm another in his life, health, or possessions."

The pressing issue at the time was religious persecution. Following the whims of the king, England was flip-flopping back and forth between being Anglican and Roman Catholic. In addition, there were a great variety of sects: Lutherans, Puritans (Calvinists), Baptists, Anabaptists, and the like. Locke set out to prove that given the nature of human understanding, reason dictated religious toleration.

The case he made went something like this. All men are born equal, that is, we all come into the world with a blank slate (a *tabula rasa* with no innate ideas) and the natural light of reason—"Light enough to lead them to the Knowledge of their Maker, and the sight of their own Duties." Like marks in soft clay, sense data make impressions on the mind. For example, almost everyone, at some time in his or her life, has sensed "red" "here" "now"—these impressions become single simple ideas. These and many other single simple ideas are grouped and combined, in a rational fashion, in the mind of each person to form more complex ideas. It is these more complex ideas, such as "duty" "value" "peace," to which the will quite understandably turns when making choices and pursuing consequences. One's sense of "justice" and "righteousness" and "worship" are all complex ideas and have never been experienced as such. Anyone then, argues Locke, anyone whose actions are the result of the rational use of the will in choosing what that individual knows to be right and good, given the (rationally constructed) complex ideas with which that person has to work, is doing the best we can expect anyone to do. Such people may not be persecuted for their practices, for they are doing what (their) reason dictates. And coercion or persecution will never convince them that their actions are wrong. Hence, reason requires religious toleration!

And what about those exceptions? Once we realize that the sole criterion for toleration is reason and rationality, the exceptions are not too hard to figure out. Atheists are not to be tolerated because reason quite obviously proves that God exists. The insane, which for Locke include religious fanatics and "enthusiasts," are likewise contraband because they too fail the test of rationality. And the Roman Catholics, while generally nice people, cannot really be trusted because at any point in time the Pope can override what their own reason dictates and simply tell them what to do.

Locke was an empiricist, but a rationalist as well. That he spent the latter years of his life writing paraphrases of Paul's epistles should come as no surprise. His appeal, here again, is to reason. Reason is God's gift to humankind, to help us determine what constitutes revelation: "I believe what I can understand."

Practicalism

It did not take very long for a reaction against scientialism to set in. Certain rationalists realized that there is more to life than merely mathematical-scientific theory. There is such a thing as practical knowledge, knowledge that is not necessarily the consequence of theoretical analysis. Such knowledge is, for example, knowledge of one's language, of business practices, of how to act properly in a given situation. These practicalists realized that distortions will inevitably result when theory controls practical life. As such they developed a broader but nevertheless rationalistic view. The result was that practicalistic rationalism spread far and wide and gained greater control than scientialism had done.

Three of the greatest Enlightenment figures were such practicalists: Hume, Voltaire, and Rousseau.

David *Hume* (1711-1776), like John Locke, was an empiricistic rationalist, but of a practicalistic, rather than a scientialistic nature. The question he tried to answer was, "How do we gain our knowledge about matters of fact?" Well, he said, knowledge about matters of fact depends on knowledge of causal relations. So the question becomes, "How do we gain knowledge of causal relations?" But, says Hume, it is impossible to know that one thing causes another, without having prior knowledge of matters of fact. Needless to say, Hume was soon chasing his tail on this one.

Hume eventually claimed that we know little more than a stream of impressions. He questioned, for example, the very notion of causality as well as the reality of a self-same *I* as experiencing substance. All we experience, Hume maintained, is a series of impressions. When such a series seems orderly, that is, when impressions follow each other time and again, we postulate the laws of causality, even though we have never actually experienced causality itself. So also, what you call "you" is nothing more than the bundle of impressions that you remember. To Hume, however, such postulates were imaginary fictions. He argues that the conclusions we reach based on experience are not the product of proper reasoning, but merely a product of habit.

Hume's radical critique did much to damage faith in "scientific reason." Truths became nothing more than psychological associations. Universally valid statements are out of the question for every science except geometry, algebra, and arithmetic. For the rest, probability is the best that one can hope for.

Voltaire (1694-1778) and Rousseau (1712-1778) were two great figures of the Enlightenment. Both of them were very sharply anti-scientialistic as well as anti-christian. Especially Voltaire has become famous for his bitter attacks on Christianity. A deist in theory, Voltaire actually took science to be "God" and left "religion" for the masses. Needless to say, his influence was a contribution to the further secularization of daily life.

Voltaire and Rousseau differed in their views of culture. Voltaire believed that human cultural development constitutes progress, whereas Rousseau held that culture corrupts. He declared that human beings are basically good, that once upon a time in the "state of nature" there were no evils and social ills. Hence Rousseau's call: Back to nature! His anti-scientialistic position is evident from his depreciation of science. Science cannot cure the world, he said, only freedom and equality, both practical situations. Men should not be subjected to each other, only to the "general will." Rousseau's ideas—especially his book *The Social Contract*—worked as a powerful catalyst in bringing about the French revolution.

Idealism

Idealism attempted to reconcile scientialism and practicalism. The father of idealism was the German *Immanuel Kant* (1724-1804). He is probably one of the most influential philosophers of modern times.

Kant's method of philosophizing—expounded in his *Critique of Pure Reason*—is called "transcendental." This means that he wanted to investigate the conditions that determine the possibility and certainty of scientific, theoretic knowledge. In other words, he set out to demonstrate what could and what could not be known for sure by the human mind.

He believed that the impressions we receive from "things out there" are shaped and determined by an a priori structure of our mind. That is to say, he tried to show that our knowledge contains components contributed by ourselves prior to all experience. It is first of all our a priori forms of time and space that determine the shape of our sense impressions. Then our a priori forms of thought, categories such as unity, difference, negation, and causality, further delineate the perceived spatio-temporal impressions, forming them into appearances of objects according to concepts in the understanding. According to Kant we can know only the thing of sensory experience (the *phenomena*), never the thing itself (the *noumenon*— Kant's "*Ding an sich*"). In effect he was rejecting the long-standing assumption that our knowledge depends on objects and was replacing it with the claim that objects depend on our knowledge. This turnabout was referred to by Kant as "the second Copernican revolution." It is reason—the *cogito* behind the categories—that orders the chaos of received impressions. Human beings make sense of reality and bring order to the world!

An example of this last point may be helpful. Kant takes the "after each other" (temporal character) and the "next to each other" (spatial character) of sense impressions to be the result of us ordering our sense impressions. In other words, we are bombarded with a flood of sense impressions and what we do with them is order them in terms of "before and after" and "next to and across from." The sciences that deal with this "after each other" and "next to each other," namely, arithmetic and geometry, actually focus only on what the mind contributes to perception. And that, says Kant, is why the results of mathematics have a universally valid character to them!

Is "reason" then the ultimate condition for Kant? Is the thinking "I" under no more ultimate condition than its own self? Kant said no; there are things like God, the soul, and the world, that ought to determine the use of the understanding in experience. These ultimate conditions or principles themselves, however, which Kant calls "ideas," exceed the possibility of experience and are beyond our ken. People can search for the soul and the world, but they will never find them. God, the soul, immortality, freedom as such (*an sich*) can not be known. Hence, the best that we can do is act *as if* we had already reached those ultimate principles, and allow these "regulative ideas" to guide us in our further investigations.

In his second major work, *The Critique of Practical Reason*, Kant explores the conditions for moral action. He finds that morality is essentially a matter of obligation and freedom. He postulates his famous "categorical imperative": He believes that persons are capable of formulating laws of conduct for themselves and that the fundamental law is that one should do an act only if one would will that anyone in similar circumstances would do the same thing. He is convinced that whenever we think about doing a particular act, we can always tell right from wrong by thinking about that act from that more general standpoint.

Kant's position represents an attempted reconciliation between scientialism and practicalism. He puts it this way: I have confined the area of science (= scientific reason) in order to make room for religion (= practical reason). Actually, the "religion" that Kant talks about is nothing else than the moralism of the Enlightenment. The moral law, being a direct result of human reason, holds a priori. Moral goodness is determined by nothing other than reason. Hence, humans, being rational, know a priori what is good, without any outside help. Right and wrong rest in one's autonomy. As a result Kant claims that all human beings have ultimate and intrinsic worth. Given their autonomy, we must treat persons with respect and never as mere means to some goal.

How did he combine the pure (scientific) *ratio* and the practical *ratio*? The answer: in the "*Urteilskraft,*" that is, in our ability to judge, an ability that Kant expounds in his third major work, *The Critique of Judgment.* In this book he tries to bring theoretical and practical reason together on a deeper level, namely, in the imagination. A complex and, as generally recognized, unsuccessful theory is involved that cannot be dealt with here.

We saw that in the Middle Ages philosophy was based on and determined by the nature/grace *ground motive,* that is, a starting-point-commitment to nature/grace. This theme of nature and grace produced intolerable tensions. The modern period can be said to have adopted a different ground motive, namely, that of nature and freedom. The problem for modern philosophy is to reconcile the two: on the one hand, there is "nature"—conceived as a set of scientifically discerned mechanical laws and processes—and, on the other hand, there is human autonomy, human freedom. The question is, "How can we maintain our autonomous freedom in a mechanically determined world? The works of Kant illustrate the idealistic solution. In the *Critique of Pure Reason* Kant deals with "nature," that is, with the problem of knowledge relative to the natural sciences. In the *Critique of Practical Reason* he discusses "freedom," his morality, "faith," relation to God, and so on. Then he attempts to reconcile the two in the *Critique of Judgment.*

Most secular historians of Western thought stress Kant's *Critique of Pure Reason,* and only to a lesser extent the *Critique of Practical Reason,* while the *Critique of Judgment* is very much neglected. This situation demonstrates a contemporary preoccupation with the natural sciences and reflects the prejudice of many, still, that our future somehow lies in the scientific enterprise.

Other prominent idealists of early rationalism were Fichte, Schelling, and Hegel. *Hegel* (1770-1831) was a very erudite scholar whose philosophy is generally regarded as the pinnacle of idealism. Hegel believed that there is only one ultimate reality of which everything is but a manifestation. This reality is the identity of being and thought: the Absolute Mind or Spirit (in

German: *Geist*), which he also refers to as "God." His system is not easy to understand, not the least because much of his writing is quite obscure.

A sample: In his *Science of Logic* Hegel sets out to study this ultimate rational reality. We read there:

> [L]ogic is to be understood as the system of pure reason, as the realm of pure thought. This realm is truth as it is without veil and in its own absolute nature. It can therefore be said that its content is the exposition of God as he is in his eternal essence before the creation of nature and a finite mind. (50)

Man—finite mind—being one with the very foundation of things, must come to know himself through his own development as linked into this larger reality of *Geist*, which in history is also in the process of differentiation. Absolute Mind unfolds dialectically in an effort to come to know itself as Mind—in the same way, says Hegel, that our consciousness strives toward self-consciousness by going back and forth (= dialectic) between what we claim to be and what we actually are. Every person and community is but a moment in the cosmic process of Being's becoming, of historical differentiation; the earlier ones are poorer expressions of what the later ones will embody more adequately. History, says Hegel, is ultimately an expression of the cosmic order and is directed toward the realization of Mind as Mind (read: of Reason as Reason). History will reach its culmination in a dynamic and living community (read: Germany) that is in conformity with reason.

Among other things, Hegel's views did much to foster a spirit of German nationalism. Nevertheless, his philosophy met with severe criticism of a nature that eventually called irrationalistic spirits into being.

Late Rationalism (1815-1900)

The idealism of the early rationalistic era failed to satisfy. However, the centrality of history, so emphasized by Hegel, would remain. A reaction set in with the rise of positivism. This shift from idealism to positivism signified the transition from early to late rationalism. Note that all these movements, including the reaction to idealism, remain rationalistic. Reason remains the totality of human worship. There is a change in emphasis, however. Whereas early rationalism had specialized in developing the theory of "Reason" in terms of a priori content, the stress now began to fall on the activity of "reason." The result was a stress on method. This emphasis on method went hand in hand with an expansion and diversification among the special sciences. During the age of early rationalism "science" was synonymous with "mathematics and physics." But in the nineteenth century we see the scientific enterprise beginning to tackle other areas as well. Biology, psychology, history, linguistics, economics, and sociology, as distinct sciences, were all "born" in the nineteenth century.

The period of late rationalism consists of three movements. They resemble the three stages of early rationalism. There is (1) the scientialism of the positivists, then (2) the practicalism of the neopositivists, and finally (3) neo-idealism, a movement that tries to combine the two.

Positivism

The scientialistic nature of positivism is clearly displayed by the position of the Frenchman August *Comte* (1798-1857), the "father of positivism," for whom the *positively given* is the sure basis of all knowledge. His primary concern was to restructure society on the basis of a re-structured science. The sciences must determine just how society is to be re-ordered. Comte recognized only six sciences: mathematics, astronomy, physics, chemistry, biology, and, on the top, sociology.

According to Comte, history has progressed in three stages: first there was the mythological or theological stage, when men explained natural phenomena in terms of supernatural causes. Societies then were run by feudal militarists. Comte included Christianity in this stage. The second phase was the metaphysical stage, in which the phenomena were attributed to abstract principles, like form and substance. During this stage, societies were jural and based on so-called "natural rights." Now, declared Comte, a new stage has begun, the stage of positive science—reason come of age. If everything proceeds as planned, an ordered society will emerge led by specialists, economists and industrialists, and supervised by (positive fact) sociologists. Philosophy's task in this new age is the promotion of a unified method in all of the sciences. Which method is this?

Method, as we noted early on, is a way of proceeding. Positive science, for Comte, is science that proceeds by taking "the positively given"—what appears to and is perceptible by the senses—as the basis for all knowledge. Positive science does not ask for motives or reasons or intentions. It is not interested in the why of events and human actions. Positivists focus on the *that* and the observable *how*. They systematically observe the following steps. By extracting the logically independent, constant factors—the recurring "hard facts"—in examined phenomena and looking for constant sequential relations—causal connections—between these facts, they arrive at scientific facts or laws. These laws, in turn, become the humanly posited means to the stated end: to altruistically predict and control—to re-structure—what happens, also in society. (B.F. Skinner's twentieth century behaviorism and methodology are prime examples of positivism in action both theoretically and practically.)

The English positivist John Stuart *Mill* (1806-1873) had much in common with Comte. Mill labored to give positivism an epistemological/logical foundation. He also saw the science of psychology as the basis for philosophy. Philosophy has to investigate the "givens," the elementary "data" of consciousness, namely, impressions and their "associations" according to the example of the natural sciences.

Mill was a staunch defender of *utilitarianism*. Utilitarianism is the view that the ultimate principle of morality is "Strive to produce as much overall happiness as possible." He argues that whatever is desired is desirable; that in the last analysis people desire happiness and nothing else; that happiness is therefore the only truly desirable thing; and that, as a result, happiness should be maximized. It comes as no surprise to read of Mill's appreciation for the Epicurean theory of life.

Though no longer prevalent in Europe, a positivistic approach continues to pervade most North American schools, colleges, and professional institutions. For example, the predominate view among social scientists in North America, in terms of numbers, is an adherence to some form of positivistic methodology. The powerful presence of positivism requires a few comments of negative critique. The concept "fact" is in fact much more complex and much more structured than positivism is willing to admit.

First of all, the suggested move from hard facts or data to scientific facts or laws is, on the one hand, misconstrued. There are no neutral facts void of a law that holds, both for the knower and the known. Nor are scientific laws a specific kind of fact. On the other hand, the "law-full-ness" in reality holds in a much more powerful, dynamic, and varied way than is ascertained in the uniformity and stiffness of "sequence" and "similarity" (or "association"). For positivists, laws are ultimately fixed mathematical formulas, and norms are nothing more than fluctuating quantifiable means (averages)—as though the majority of people, events, marriages, or whatever can or may set the standard!

Second, facts are many and diverse. Different facts have a different meaning. As facts they may have some traits in common, but an emotional fact can not be reduced to a physical fact. A lingual fact can not be reduced to a historical fact. A fact of justice can not be reduced to a religious fact. The diversity is even more varied if we think, for example, how having command of a language and having political clout, although both are kinds of "control," cannot be forced into the same basket. Similarly, there are important differences between habitual ways of thinking, buying habits, social habits, and traditional rituals.

Positivism developed into various forms and produced some important consequences, only four of which we mention here.

The first consequence involves the development of *evolutionism*. Not all positivists could subscribe to this theory because it requires a number of conditions. For example, evolutionism is never found among structuralist thinkers because the evolutionist thinks genetically. Further, evolutionism presupposes a monistic position. After all, the evolutionist is trying to explain the multitude of phenomena in terms of derivation from one source. A dualist cannot be an evolutionist.

Charles Darwin (1809-1882) was an evolutionistic positivist, whose theories were philosophically systematized by Herbert Spencer (1820-1903). Spencer's anti-christian attitude did much to make the term "evolution" a dirty word for Christians. We as Christians should keep in mind that there is a distinction between evolution and evolutionism. Evolution refers to the fact that changes in plant and animal life occur, for example, when botanists produce all kinds of beautiful roses or when the aquarist develops fantail guppies. However, when such changes are considered to contain the ultimate explanation of all life on earth, then evolution*ism* is the result; something that is true in part is elevated as the truth for the whole.

A second consequence of positivism is that it opened the door to a *marxist* critique of society and the status quo. Communism, socialism, and anarchism, movements present already in limited form among some Greek sophists, began to blossom.

When Karl Marx (1818-1883) came on the scene, European society was in the throws of economic and political upheaval—this in contrast to Hegel's totalitarian system that claimed to see everything in its rationally ordered place. Marx's question was, "What value does philosophy have in the reality of society?" His answer: to intensify a critical self-consciousness of who we are and what we are about, rather than fleeing from self-consciousness in rational or religious interpretations of society. "Philosophers have only interpreted the world in various ways: the point is to change it!" he wrote emphatically.

Marx rejected the notion that humans are what they are. Marx views man as a being that produces; a being that, in producing, historically produces himself. People make a society. This self-production is said to be characterized by dynamic desires and forces (that Marx ultimately interpreted to be economic in nature). There is discontinuity as well as continuity in this development. Revolution must be accepted as a necessity when in the course of history's development new forces (of production) cannot be incorporated in the existing societal relationships (of production). Here lies philosophy's task, according to Marx: to talk about and contradict "the establishment" and, in so doing, to open possibilities for change.

Marx appeals to historical reality and to what he calls the "self-alienation of man." People are alienated from other people: they are foreigners to each other, ships passing in the night, with no sense of being one, together. But people are also alienated from themselves: "Am I my own self or am I what others have made me or want me to be?" Self-alienation, says Marx, describes both the capitalists (the have's) and the working class, the "proletariat" (the have-not's). But it is especially the proletariat that most obviously and completely represent this negativity of historical reality, in their suffering. In the radicality of that suffering, in that boundary situation, lies the critical point where the possibility for radical self-recognition and self-recovery become real. The proletariat live this suffering and discover in it the bottom line of their existence. The proletariat person discovers himself as a being with real needs, a being that stands in need of other things and people outside himself. He discovers it in himself. And his struggle to meet those needs is a struggle toward self-realization. Marx believed that his philosophy could not have arisen earlier. Only now, in the midst of this universal negative situation, could this servile and dehumanized class arise.

We have to note a fundamental ambiguity and tension in Marx's thought at this point. On the one hand, Marx's philosophy appeals to the negative existence of the proletariat that the "natural" course of "history" has brought into being, while, on the other hand, the task of uncovering the meaning of this negative existence and of making people conscious of their suffering (and hence to experience it more intensely) is left to philosophy as such. That is to say: (his) philosophy comes in from elsewhere, as revelation—revealing the mystery *of* history to the proletariat—in order to become the ringleader of a practical emancipation *from* the process of history.

"Historical," for Marx, immediately means "dialectical." History is a development in oppositions via polarities: between forces (of production) and relations (of production), ultimately, between the person and everything and everyone else; between my needs and my possibilities, on the one hand, and that which and those who are needed in order to realize those needs and possibilities. At bottom, this dialectic lies within human existence as such. That is why self-alienation is not simply a historical accident. Self-alienation is an irreplaceable element for continuing historical development! And yet Marx remains ambivalent on this score. He sees something wrong, something antinormative in self-alienation. That is why Marx set his eye on a situation of total human communism, a "realm of freedom," in which this self-alienation is overcome. (That culmination, however, would imply that history would have to end. Although sometimes Marx seems to suggest that this would be the beginning of "true" history, making what has gone before "pre-history"!)

A no less ideologically driven twentieth century attempt to embrace only the "positively given" is Logical Positivism. Its goal was to establish a no nonsense, empirical, scientific attitude by making physics the model for all human knowing. These positivists were convinced that unifying the sciences around a single, solid method would produce a unified system of meaningful and valid knowledge. Their first step required that they clarify the language of science, and to that end they devised a standard for clarity, a criterion by which to test which sentences did and which did not express a genuine proposition about a matter of fact. Their famous verification principle laid down that the meaning of a statement is the method of its verification. Stated negatively, any statement that cannot be empirically verified (be it about God or ether or ethics) has no meaning. Language consists of words and is meaningful to the extent that these words represent facts. And so they set about logically to analyze propositions (= knowledge) and what they speak about (= facts), for true knowledge is propositional. Assertions about things and facts that cannot be observed, either directly or indirectly, were then declared to be no assertions at all. The ultimate agenda of logically reducing all (true) language to observational statements, however, proved to be its undoing. Not only could no one verify the verification principle, but they also had trouble deciding whose observation statement, whose (subjective?) experience about a physical event, would count as valid.

A close relative to logical positivism that today shows more signs of life is what goes by the name of General Systems Theory or simply Systems Analysis. This philosophy has its ear closer to the ground and presents itself as able both to diagnose and resolve the dangers and problems of our global village. Progress is no longer an alternative, however; the best we can work for is survival. Interestingly, it usually pinpoints an overly one-sided, hyper-specialistic, scientific approach to things as the culprit and a single "holistic" science, overarching all the separate sciences, as an antidote.

Egbert Schuurman, a christian philosopher of technology, explains some of the dynamics involved here:

> [In] systems theory the *whole* remains central *as a system. That whole is more than the sum of the parts.* Closer consideration shows the whole to be the sum of the parts plus the interaction between

those parts. The interaction is controlled by additional information, communication, feedback, equifinality, self-stabilization, and self-organization. This approach also attends to the system and its environment in terms of the [quantifiable] input and output of material, energy, and information. We see from this that although the method is new when compared to previous methods, the result leads to an enhanced continuation of modern technology in information technology, computer technology, and the technology of integrated systems. (48)

We will see later how important it is to have a sense of the whole, but in this case it is crucial to remember that the whole that systems analysis looks at is a constructed system of quantifiable input, output, feedback, and the like. The map it draws can at times be helpful. But one ought not to forget that such a system is constructed, a simulated whole that, like most maps, inevitably leaves many very important things out of the picture.

Neo-positivism

Neo-positivism stood critically over against the scientialism of the positivists already at the end of the nineteenth century. There is more to life than merely the positive facts of the six sciences of August Comte, they said. There is practical knowledge and practical experience as well. Doing is as important as knowing.

In this sense Karl Marx became a neo-positivist. In his later years Marx lost interest in his desire to produce a "scientific socialism." He began to concentrate on the actual, practical class struggle and to direct his philosophic thoughts pragmatically toward agitation and strategy in that struggle. This shift from positivism to neo-positivism perhaps contributed significantly to the success of communism well into the twentieth century.

The real father of neo-positivism was Wilhelm *Dilthey* (1833-1911). Of importance was his distinction between the natural and the psychological sciences. Dilthey declared that psychological (mental, spiritual) phenomena can not be explained in terms of (natural) scientific laws, but can only be intuitively grasped and understood as types of behavior. Humans are called as thinking, willing, and feeling beings to live creatively in the historical stream of life.

Dilthey was an advocate of historicism and helped to articulate a "historical consciousness" that was growing in the nineteenth century. As an interest in history grew, so did insight into historical determination. Where you are in time makes a difference. History is not juśt the lump sum of more and less interesting things that have happened to humankind in the past and that have been handed down to instruct us in the present. According to Dilthey, history is a pageant of possibilities and the human person is a mind-body unity living in interaction with the physical and social environment. All experience and therefore all thought arise out of this interaction of self and world. And from this interaction the self constructs a historically and socially conditioned view of the world (*Weltanschauung*).

One can come to know man from history, but *Man* does not represent a constant type. "The type 'man' melts in the process of history," wrote Dilthey—meaning: in history we encounter ourselves in *one* of the forms that humankind can assume. There are and have been others; still others will follow. Conclusion: There is no one right way! We must recognize that our experiences of the world are finite and must avoid claiming complete and exclusive truth for any worldview we construct. There is no social order dictated by the nature of things. Things could always have been different. It's all relative!

For the historicist, the relativity of time and place and the finitude of each is really not a problem. The historicist is gripped by a kind of superiority complex that results from being able to understand all historical periods and all foreign cultures from within. The attempt at unlimited understanding of this diversity, including the limitations and curiosities of each culture, enables one to take a position outside and above history, suggesting that at least some are or can become disinterested observers of the human drama. Only such as these, however, can recover the past as it actually was and discover the meaning of history as a whole.

In a similar vein, the Swiss linguist Ferdinand de Saussure (1857-1913) claimed that language is a changing social phenomenon that does not refer to things in the world or to the ideas that we have for them in our minds. Language is what it is within the conversation that is going on within a community of discourse. In other words, he disagreed with his predecessors who viewed language as a natural phenomenon that develops according to fixed laws, that the structure of our sentences reflects the logic of our thought processes, and that words serve simply as labels for independently given "facts." Saussure suggested that we must conceive of language as a network of interrelated sounds and meanings determined by nothing else than social convention. There are no logical reasons explaining why words mean what they do; that's simply how any particular language functions. One's language, and ultimately one's world and its values, rests in the social conventions and relations operative at a given time. The movement that followed Saussure was called "structuralism." His followers proceeded with the commitment that an objective, universal cultural system "structures" our mental processes and that this structure is evident in both human language and social institutions.

Franz Brentano (1838-1917) was another well-known neo-positivist. Like Dilthey, Brentano's emphasis is on psychology and mental phenomena. He called these phenomena "intentional acts," meaning that acts are always referential and related to some object. This intentionality, according to Brentano, is the determining element of all psychological behavior.

Neo-idealism

As in early rationalism, so now a movement arises intent on reconciling the conflicting schools of positivism. Kant had been the man to "accomplish" this reconciliation in early rationalism; hence he became the example for the neo-idealists (often referred to as "neo-Kantians"). Transcendental philosophy again became the order of the day.

Wilhelm Windelband (1848-1915) attempted to bring about peace and harmony between theoretical and practical "reason" by insisting that the sciences must be divided into two groups, neither one of which should rule the other. There are, he claimed, the "nomothetic" sciences, which investigate the orderly processes of nature, and there are the "ideographic" sciences, which explore the cultural-historical framework and involve value judgments. Heinrich Rickert (1863-1936) was closely associated with Windelband. He, too, recognized two groups of sciences, namely, the natural sciences and the "humanities." Supposedly the first deals only with "facts," the second with "values." This was Rickert's attempt to bridge the gulf between scientialism and practicalism.

This distinction between "facts" and "values" is still very current. Few today realize, however, where it comes from. According to these neokantians, facts are things that can be objectively and certainly known, while values are creations of the mind that have no validity apart from the human need to give meaning to the world. That the atomic number of barium is 56 is a fact and to think otherwise is to be mistaken. But it is only a "value" to believe that crime should be punished, that adultery is wrong, or that Jesus is the Christ. People can think differently about these matters, but they can't be wrong. Facts are true as such; values are true only to the extent they are widely held and valued. This neokantian distinction has become so pervasive, also in the social sciences, even Christians are hesitant to speak of divine ordinances and the moral order as they used to a century ago, but going with the flow refer to their "christian values." In doing so, of course, they implicitly concede the point that their convictions on these matters do not have objective validity or factual status. Given the way most people talk about "values," and what that talk usually implies, it is almost impossible for Christians, especially in an academic setting, to believe that "You shall not murder" is as much a fact as "Water freezes at 32 degrees Fahrenheit." This humanistic thought pattern continues to be subliminally propagated in our day.

A more radical resolution for the gulf between scientialism and practicalism was proposed along neoidealist lines by Ernst Cassirer (1874-1945) who confidently rooted physical as well as historical facts within the circle of Humanity: The natural sciences are human activity, are they not? Physical factual truth is not so much a matter of mental duplication of simple sense data impressions: the senses themselves are a mental apriori form of the human spirit and any sense knowledge always depends upon the act of (subjective) judgment. In other words, the mathematical-physical sciences are to be understood in terms of a unifying, general human, cultural activity.

However, even though he lauds science's constancy as the highest possible accomplishment of human culture, Cassirer also pushed the claim that there is more to the universe than can be dreamt of in mathematical categories. The realm of meaning and human life is much more important and original than any brute world of "facts" or "being." Historical facts and the living reality of language are not natural phenomena and need to be treated differently. And so, in addition to a critique of reason, this neokantian called for a critique of culture: his objective was a phenomenology of human culture, a rigorous exposition of the polydimensional ways we perceive, constitute, and indeed, construct reality.

In providing this exposition Cassirer was a committed *subjectivist*, which for him meant that "objective" and "intrinsically necessary" correctly describe whatever is culturally configured. Man, whose mission is Utopia, is in the saddle and lord over reality, after all. In fact, "things" and "the physical world" are all just theoretical constructs, sort of like grandfather Kant's regulative ideas (God, soul, and world). Language, myth, religion, art, science, history: these all are part of the process of progressive self-liberation. They make up the various sectors of "the circle of humanity," building stones from which the world of "reality" and the human spirit are constructed for us.

As Seerveld points out, proclaiming the possibility of freedom through fortitude is not peculiar to the twentieth century:

> Such faith in Humanity is an old-time religion, and Cassirer's volumes are an exceptionally grand confession of it. Anyone whose vision is shaped by the biblical Word of God, however, sees immediately that the Cultural King in Cassirer's procession has no clothes on. The stirring and intricate, probing and insightful Culturalism of Ernst Cassirer is a no-god made by a man's hand, and those who feel secure with such a brilliant man-made "god," says Psalm 115, will become like it (Psalm 115:4-8): busybusy, principled, little old-style idealists aware of tradition, open to innovation, toughened by Positivism, curbed from Romantic excess, but incurably sold on building, through ups and downs, advances and reverses, a richer and more noble Babylon in the hearts and lives of mankind. This particular idol worship allows no sabbath rest.... There is no opening for the Holy Spirit's healing, Christ's reconciling, the Lord God's establishing the beginning of *His* gentle Rule upon the earth (cf. Isaiah 65:17-25): only an unceasing, combative (cultural) imperialism proper to this Geneticistic Contradictory Monistic universe of thought. (Seerveld, 1975, 293-4)

Cassirer did not champion culture to the exclusion of nature. Nor did he pretend to evolve culture out of nature. But the contradictory, polar union, in which culture becomes the saving revelation of nature, which in turn becomes the source of life for culture, will not do. It is a world-bound position that damns humanity to a restless search for closure and final meaning that will always be frustrated.

Edmund Husserl (1859-1938) underwent quite a philosophic development, part of which was devoted to neo-idealism. He was very much influenced by Brentano's theory of intentionality. Husserl developed the method of phenomenology, which was to exert much influence on later philosophic movements. Husserl meant phenomenology to be the science of consciousness, in which all other sciences, as specific modes of consciousness, would be grounded. Phenomenology intends to look at the phenomena in a completely "objective," "unprejudiced" fashion, to disclose and describe the actual state of affairs. "Back to the things as they really are!" was the rallying cry. By means of so-called "bracketing," or the reduction of incidental subjective experience, the simple phenomena can presumably be described in such a manner that universally valid scientific knowledge results.

Phenomenology is not always easy to understand, partly because Husserl, who was the first to postulate the method, changed his philosophic position so often.

Review

Rationalism pretty much monopolized the philosophic scene for 300-plus years and its influence continues. At the beginning of the twentieth century it seemed that the rationalists were going to have the last word, that the only real philosophy is rationalistic philosophy. However, things soon began to change. As we will soon see, some irrationalistic voices were heard already in the nineteenth century. And more were on the way. The Modern Age of Reason, more than just showing some wrinkles in time, was beginning to self-destruct, ever so slowly. But before we trace that path, a brief review of the Enlightenment's vision, of its sense of truth, and of "modernism" in general would be appropriate.

A major theme of the Enlightenment was human *autonomy*, with *method* serving as the knowing subject's major means: "Dare to use your reason (*sapere aude*)!" was its motto. Take "x," whatever it be, and subject it to the scrutiny of human reason, assessing it on the basis of that criterion, and great things will happen. The general assumption was that reasoned objectivity would open the door to absolutely certain, universal, supra-cultural, timeless truth: a kind of even-handed, value-free, free-dom-securing, progress-paving, dispassionate knowledge that would ultimately be for the sake and advantage of all. To use Newton's prognosis, we'll be able "to think God's thoughts after him." But with the claim in hand to be able to view the world as unconditioned observers, from a transhistorical vantage point, outside the flux of history, it did not take long for the godtalk to fall into disuse. With science and education enabling us to free ourselves from our vulnerability to nature and to save ourselves from servitude to others, many grew in the confidence that B.F. Skinner still preached in 1971: "We have yet to see what man can make of man."

Truth, for rationalists, is theoretical and objective, a trust-worthy re-presentation of the way the world actually is. Truth is the claim to knowledge that can be validated by procedures devised by the appropriate community of scholarly experts. For such can verify the correspondence between our assertions and the objective world about which they are made. That world is real and displays an order inherent to itself and independent of human activity.   The human mind, however, is capable of grasping reality as a whole, of mirroring this external reality with increasing accuracy and, through language, of adequately declaring what that world is like. It is actually these proposi-tions that are either true or false and determined to be so by comparing them with the world "out there." The more true propositions we can compile, the more knowledgeable we are.

Modernism's goal was to unlock the secrets of the universe, to master nature for human benefit, and in so doing allow the self-defining subject to create a better world in freedom. In the twentieth century that has often meant bringing increasingly monolithic management to society and culture in order to improve human existence through technology, while at the same time advocating a highly individualistic relativism of "to each his own"—an obvious tension.

Old pagan problematics continued to determine the various types of rationalism, itself not a brand-new development, but an adaptation in modern setting. For example, there is the subjec-tivism of all the rationalists. Then there were monistic and dualistic thinkers, universalists, partial-universalists, and individualists. In other words, the problematics that we had occasion to study in a relatively simple early Greek context are still present in the age of rationalism. This state of affairs demonstrates its pagan character. Nowhere in the rationalistic camp is the light of the Word of God allowed to penetrate philosophic thought. Here and there is, on occasion, some moralistic hue discernible. And there have been a number of Christians who have tried a rational apologetic that appeals to logically warranted proofs for the existence of God or for the historicity of Jesus' resurrection. In other words, some have tried to enter the fray and play according to rationalism's ground rules. But if we ask, "Where in the 300-plus years of rationalism's presence do we detect a truly christian philosophic voice?" The answer is: next to nowhere!

As a christian community we must work to articulate a viable alternative to applying current philosophical methods to matters that concern Christians. A christian philosophy must powerfully confront the apostate spirits in the academic world. Such a christian philosophy has begun to be formulated, for which we are grateful. Nevertheless, we stand only at the beginning. We are way behind. A gigantic task awaits us. Let us boldly put our hands to the plow, our fingers to the keyboard, and our minds to work.

II. D. 2.
Guide Questions

81. What is the difference between christian humanism and nonchristian humanism?

82. What does the term "rationalism" mean?

83. In what ways is rationalism parallel to hellenistic philosophy?

84. How do scientialism and practicalism differ?

85. How did Galileo's defense of Copernicus demonstrate the trouble that synthesis brings about?

86. What does Galileo mean when he says that the universe is written in the language of mathematics?

87. Why did Thomas Hobbes never attack his neighbor or refuse the king's demands?

88. To which question is *cogito ergo sum* an answer?

89. In what sense could Descartes' method be described as one of destruction and reconstruction?

90. What does John Locke have to do with the American Revolution?

91. When Hume claims that you are nothing more than a bundle of sense impressions, what does he mean?

92. What did Kant claim was so revolutionary about his view of knowledge and its objects?

93. How did Kant explain the consistent dependability of mathematics as a science?

94. What function do "regulative ideas" play in Kant's philosophy?

95. Explain the phrase, "right and wrong rest in human autonomy."

96. What was Hegel's view of history?

97. How did the positivist August Comte view the unfolding of history?

98. What are the basic components of a positivistic methodology?

99. Given a positivistic way of thinking, how are the standards for society, its norms, determined?

100. Why will a dualist never defend evolutionism?

101. How does "self-alienation" function as a mainspring in Marx's philosophy?

102. Highlight a basic similarity between logical positivism and systems analysis.

103. How does the thought of Dilthey, Windelband, and Rickert reflect a "fact/value" dualism?

104. Why could "structuralists" not be considered positivists?

105. How does Cassirer pull most everything into the circle of humanity?

3. IRRATIONALISM

Introduction

First of all let it be said that "irrationalism" does not mean a "philosophy void of reason and deprived of sound judgment." Some of the keenest minds and most penetrating analysis of foundational issues have been employed in the service of irrationalism. Irrationalism in this context is a philosophic climate that arose as a negative response to rationalism. As such the term denotes anti-rationalism. Indeed, to the extent that we can equate rationalism with modernism, this time current can rightly be described as postmodernism.

Irrationalism has been the most profound philosophic spirit in the twentieth century. The reasons for this situation are very complex. Unquestionably, the drastic and unforeseen changes in the development of the Western world produced a certain amount of disillusionment with rationalism. In various sciences the realization grew that life is more than a matter of logically independent factors, causally related. Perhaps life is not as rational and orderly as the Age of Reason had believed. Historical development, for example, does not appear to follow strict laws of causality, and human dialogue is so much more than the output, input, and feedback of information. There are the elements of commitment, mystery, the unpredictable, the irrational.

Irrationalism gained solid support through the devastating effects of two world wars. These bloodbaths proved that humankind does not necessarily seek to live in harmony with reason. The result was that a threatened humanity began to explore the avenues of anti-rationalistic philosophies. What is more, irrationalists began to blame the rationalists for the evils that had befallen the world.

Many Christians joined in with the "criticize rationalism" chorus and joined hands with the irrationalists. There have been a good number of "christian existentialists." We find here a situation similar to that in the Prelude to the Modern Age. Then we noted that an anti-synthesis movement can be motivated by two principles, one christian, the other nonchristian. Now again, too many Christians adopted the dilemma rationalism/irrationalism, as if these were the only alternatives. In fact a Christian may not choose for either rationalism or irrationalism, for both of them are expressions of subjectivism. The irrationalistic currents, therefore, are not christian at all, in spite of well-intentioned moral philosophers.

The irrationalists' criticism of rationalism is not at all as radical as is sometimes supposed. Until very recently irrationalists did not deliver on a thorough-going analysis of the concept "ratio," and those that have tried have not been able to come up with a viable alternative. Irrationalism is still subjectivism, and accepts uncritically the existence of the *ratio*. In effect, the big difference is that now the significance of "reason" is relegated to a rather small area. Reason is dethroned, yes, but not put out of commission altogether. You see, then, the criticism of rationalism is only superficial: the *ratio* stays.

Proto-Postmodernists

Already in the nineteenth century we find some precursors of irrationalism. Søren Kierkegaard (1813-1855) is often regarded as the "father of existentialism." This keen Dane fulminated against Hegelianism and the watered-down condition of the state church. He sought to understand what Christianity really meant. Looking around at the hypocrisy and worldliness of Christendom, he called for all true Christians to quit going to church. He died a ridiculed and lonely man.

Kierkegaard's philosophy is driven by two motives: the desire to serve the Lord and the ideal of autonomy. Rather than a disinterested grasp of the grand scheme of things, his question was, "How do I become myself?" At best, endless understanding ends in endless knowledge and, at worst, in endless alienation. For Kierkegaard *life* meant to exist authentically, that is, to become one's self by means of a series of free choices. The greatest choice such existence can make is the choice for faith.

Kierkegaard is an individualist. Everyone is alone, alone with oneself and with God. True community can be found only in heaven. Three stages of existence are possible, according to Kierkegaard. There is the aesthetic phase, in which one lives irresponsibly for pure enjoyment. Then there is the ethical stage, characterized by more responsible living, for example, when one has a family. The greatest of all, however, is the religious stage, in which one accepts God as the absolute paradox. In choosing the religious life, man chooses himself as sinner and yet Christ as the sinless, producing the paradoxical combination of sinful existence and eternal sinless blessedness.

It took almost half a century for Kierkegaard's ideas to find inroads. Then two groups of followers claimed him as their "father." On the one hand there is dialectical theology, represented by Karl Barth. This branch orients itself to the christian aspect of Kierkegaard's thought. On the other hand, there are the existentialists who lay claim to Kierkegaard's philosophy of existence.

Another early voice of irrationalism was Friedrich Nietzsche (1844-1900), who of late has been heralded as the "patron saint" of postmodernism. Like Kierkegaard, he was a lonely man. Everywhere his ideas conflicted with current traditions. He proclaimed "the death of God," meaning that Western civilization was no longer influenced by the Christian tradition as it once had been. Belief in God and in divine rewards and punishments for human behavior had lost the power they once exercised and there was nothing to take their place. To most the transcendent realm simply didn't matter any more.

Nietzsche wished to be the voice of the antichrist, preaching a gospel of nihilism. To him life meant the acceptance of one's instincts, the setting of one's own norms, and the ruthless destruction of the enemies, especially "reason," traditional morality, and Christianity. He proclaimed an active, aesthetic nihilism, that is, that we have no access to reality whatsoever. There is no "true world" anywhere. Everything is a perspectival appearance, seen from a perspective we ourselves have constructed. Language may be an expression of an innate human desire for aesthetic creation, but our grand ideas turn out to be metaphors in disguise, fictions that we author. All the values and norms of Western civilization are worthless: there are no ideals, no hopes, no purposes in life at all.

The only thing remaining in the vacuum left by the death of God was a body of primitive instincts aimed at self-preservation and self-promotion, the most important of which he called "the will to power": the desire to perfect and transcend the self through the exercise of personal creative power rather than dependence on anything external. Nothing undergirds human values except the will of the person who holds them. So, as for the pragmatic use of language, values, and moral systems for personal and social advancement—get used to it! Things have value only to the extent that we give them value. (The desire is explicitly to be creative, rather than merely to be creaturely.) Through the process of accepting one's own instincts, however, he was confident that a new kind of man would arise, an "Übermensch," a superman. It should come as no surprise that Nietzsche's ideas also contributed to the rise of the German national-socialist mentality.

Moving to the twentieth century, we can distinguish three movements within the camp of irrationalism, namely, pragmatism, *Lebensphilosophie*, and existentialism. After an abbreviated account of these movements, we will conclude with a brief survey of postmodernism.

Pragmatism

Pragmatism is typically an American phenomenon. It arose in the United States, and its fullest effects were, until recently, pretty well confined to North America. The father of pragmatism is William James (1842-1910), professor at Harvard University, and famed psychologist and philosopher. According to James, truth cannot be expressed merely in theoretic concepts. Theory is meaningful only when it promotes practical usefulness. In fact, truth *is* simply usefulness. A concept or idea is not true until it becomes true in a practical situation.

James is very much an individualist. Only individual things exist. Reality consists of parts. That is why a totality vision is not possible, according to James, for if you speak of a totality, then you no longer have your eye on the parts: you have lost hold of reality and simply added your own view of things to the things themselves. James therefore urges us to forget about totality vision, and instead to concentrate on the individual facts.

A second famous and influential American pragmatist was John Dewey (1859-1952). Dewey was influenced by Comte's positivism, evident, for example, in his belief that reality consists only of what can be experienced. Religion and metaphysics, for instance, are pure phantasy, according to Dewey. Philosophy and the sciences should have only one goal in mind, namely the increase of human control over nature. Knowledge is simply an instrument for practical living, and so he called his epistemological position "instrumentalism." Like James, Dewey framed questions about what is *right* in terms of what is *useful*. Truth is what works. The criterion applicable to truth is practical utility.

Dewey's theory of "progressive education" is well known. The purpose of education is to prepare the child for a society geared to control nature. Therefore education must be broad and must include the acquisition of practical knowledge. With respect to ethics, here again good and bad are measured in terms of usefulness. If an act promotes the welfare of the general public, it is good.

Pragmatism has thoroughly infected political processes, but has also successfully penetrated technological and educational theories. This pragmatistic context has, for example, subtly undermined the effectiveness of the christian community in North America. Pragmatism rejects the principled approach of those who believe that truth should lead actions. Very often what Christians take to be a "normal situation" is in reality nothing but a product of the pragmatistic mind. For example, it is often asserted that a christian political party should not be considered by the christian community because it is "impractical" and unAmerican: the two-party system has worked best for America, therefore it is a good thing and we should keep it that way. This kind of reasoning, as you can see, reflects the context of American pragmatism. The criterion of usefulness, of what works, is the determining factor.

This attitude has unfortunately become as common around the world as CNN. Christians, wherever they live, do well to remember that pragmatism is a subjectivistic, irrationalistic, unchristian movement that continues to sway many, but now often in a neo-pragmatic postmodern context. They do well to remember that a right-principled approach may yield unpleasant short-term results ("no pain, no gain"), but will eventually produce long-term beneficial outcomes.

Vitalism

In German, vitalism is often called *Lebensphilosophie*, the "philosophy of life." Vitalism is averse to both pragmatism and rationalism. The focus falls on the fleeting, the unique, the individual, the irrational, the experiential, as opposed to the static, logical, universal, and schematic.

The father of this type of irrationalism is Henri Bergson (1859-1941). According to Bergson, reason is limited to the sphere of mathematical science. Real life comes into view when the mathematical and physical sciences are left behind. Then one enters the area where instinct and intuition hold sway.

Intuition grasps human existence as pure duration (*durée*), in which one continuously unfolds to reach for and actualize new possibilities. This unfolding force within us is part of a bigger all-reality-encompassing creative power that Bergson calls the *élan vital* (vital impulse). Society, morality, and religion are all products of this vital force.

Being is life and life, says Bergson, is superior to matter. Hence, if being is life and life is soul and consciousness, then being is consciousness. Being is a self-awareness that is experience, impulse, duration, freedom, inventiveness. Nothing simply *is*, everything *becomes*: creative evolution, he called it.

Existentialism

Existentialism as a movement is about as optimistic as vitalism is pessimistic. It took hold especially in continental Europe. It too represents a retort to rationalism. Rejecting the elaborate rationalistic systems, existentialism focuses the attention on human existence. Existentialism radicalized Dilthey's historicism by taking the finitude of the human race to extremes. The desperate human condition, especially in postwar Europe, provided ready soil for the existentialist movement.

Existentialism comes in many varieties. Most are driven by a desire to somehow become one's own authentic self. They are all subjectivists and irrationalists, however. Many existentialists are pronounced atheists. On the other hand, some Christians, weary of rationalism, sought their philosophic salvation in existentialism and eagerly embraced it, producing a synthesis called "christian existentialism."

Karl Jaspers (1883-1968) was one of the best known representatives of existentialism. Philosophy, he believed, is concerned with existence. Existence is more than merely data, such as the sciences investigate. Existence, Jaspers tells us, "is something that can never become a mere object; it is the 'Source' whence spring my thinking and acting." In view of this, philosophy is more than a scientific theory. Existential thinking, he declared, is "the philosophic practice of life." Jaspers is a dualist who speaks of a transcendent existence, a "wholly other" of which people must become aware. Meanwhile, we exist in freedom and must strive to fulfill our genuine selves by a series of free choices. Only then will we live authentically when we affirm our awareness of transcendent existence.

Martin Heidegger (1889-1976) adopted Husserl's method of phenomenology. Heidegger believes that the task of philosophy consists of the study of *Being*. Answers must be looked for in the concrete human "*Dasein*," the "being-there" of life. Instead of the thinking self confronting its object, "being-in-the-world" must open the way for a more holistic understanding of reality. Truth, for Heidegger, does not consist in a correspondence between our statements and a fully formed reality that exists outside us. The correspondence theory of truth leads us in the wrong direction. He argues that truth is not absolute and autonomous, but relational. Truth does not come to us in our quest for the certainty of propositions, but requires an "openness to the mystery," allowing the presence of Being to shine through. Heidegger argued that Descartes and Kant had led modern philosophy down an illegitimate path: the human being is not primarily a thinking self, a subject that engages in cognitive acts. We are above all else beings-in-the-world, practically engaged and enmeshed in social networks.

With Nietzsche, Heidegger turns his hopes to art, not only as a vehicle for the revelation of truth/Being, but also as a means for the creation of truth. He nonetheless rejected the notion of the self attaining in any way to some transcendent essence. He knows of no such essence lying beyond life in the world. Heidegger's project of self-discovery soon becomes a nostalgic, world-weary, last ditch attempt to find the self as a unified totality. He was convinced that while we can be truly one with the past and the future only in the hour of death, this ultimate unity can at least be anticipated in the present.

Heidegger exerted a strong influence on Jean-Paul Sartre (1905-1980). Sartre's novels and plays contributed greatly to the popularization of existentialism. He is a thorough-going atheist, as well as an individualist. His theory of existence focuses upon man becoming himself. Man never is, he is always becoming. Hence his famous maxim: *existence precedes essence*. Man is not first of all an expression of a defined human nature, for then one would not be able to become. Man is not bound to the static condition of being an essence. Everyone is first of all dynamic existence, in freedom continuously transcending oneself.

There are obvious conflicts between the existentialist's conviction and the aims of science. For Sartre the very thought of
psychology as a science of human beings is a manifestation of
"bad faith." Once anyone starts calculating behavior, you can no
longer ascribe it to someone. The summations and predictions
of science rob us of our moral responsibility. If conduct is just a
collection of variables that, as initial conditions and eventual
effects, are tied together by general laws, where does that leave
human freedom?

It will be clear from these brief descriptions that existentialism is not easy to understand. In many respects it represents a
way of life, rather than a philosophic system, as Sartre's novels
and plays show. Many American attempts to popularize existentialism have failed because the authors—often oriented to a
positivistic mentality—have utterly failed to understand what
existentialism really tries to say.

Confessed Postmodernists

Postmodernism is hardly a unified movement and still very
much in process. On the one hand, as a reactionary presence, it
does depend on and even have some things in common with
modernity: some ideals of the Enlightenment (e.g., human
autonomy, freedom, the power of critique, and emancipation)
are still present in subtle and obscure ways. But its voices also
very clearly demonstrate the thrust to be POSTmodern. They
reject up front that there is a domain of objective truths that hold
universally for all. The focus is sooner on language as a flexible
medium of intersubjective communication and embodied understanding. Second, there is a pervasive critique of the subject-
centeredness of the modern era. The assumption that the human
subject can simply stand separate from or objectively over
against the object is exposed as fallacious. And third, postmodern thinkers consider very practical, socio-political dimensions of everyday life as crucial to the task of the philosopher.
Ahistorical abstractions are, as of late, accursed.

Because it is next to impossible to take distance from
something so close at hand, we can best be served by a number
of approaches to this contemporary mind-set. The first is a sec-
ond-hand joke about three umpires having a beer after a baseball
game and the second a glimpse at a postmodern classroom

where knowledge is nothing more than a human construct rooted in negotiated consensus. Then we will make the move to Gadamer and the "hermeneutical circle" and conclude with brief mention of three outspoken postmodernists.

Walsh and Middleton, in their book *Truth is Stranger Than It Used to Be*, retell an illustration credited to Walter Truett Anderson and then comment on it. The one umpire, we are told, says to the others, "There's balls and there's strikes and I call'em the way they are." Another ump responds, "There's balls and there's strikes and I call'em the way I see'em." The third says, "There's balls and strikes, and they ain't *nothin'* 'til I call'em." Who of these three has it by the right end of the stick? The fundamental question here is, "What is reality?" Are those balls and strikes in fact objectively out there? Or is the second ump the honest one? Postmodernists will side with the third. Walsh and Middleton explain:

> The first ump and the third ump may agree that the pitch should be called a strike, but the belief functions differently for each (with the second ump occupying a position in the middle). The first ump is a *naive realist*, believing that human knowing is a matter of seeking direct correspondence between the external world and epistemological judgments. The second ump knows that access to the external world is always mediated by the perspective of the knower. He might be called a *perspectival realist* (or perhaps a critical realist), since he recognizes that the way he sees the world invariably affects his epistemological judgments. The third ump pushes this perspectivalism to its extreme. His perspective is all there is, or at least all that matters. This *radical perspectivalism* epitomizes the postmodern shift. It is, if you will, perspectivalism gone to seed! (31)

Now, the hellenistic age is further than right field from baseball, and certainly different, but there is a striking similarity between the transition from Greek to hellenistic philosophy and the transition from modern to postmodern thought. Back then, people were beginning to call into question Plato's world of Ideas and Aristotle's Unmoved Mover, the absolutes of their day; they also had begun to ask basic questions about the nature of knowing, and their focus became increasingly practical. And of course, the question, "Are those balls and strikes really out there, or are they just in my head?" should remind us of Descartes' fear of solipsism. He reverted to a medieval proof for the existence of God to assure himself that he could trust what was clear and distinct to his mind's eye (which God, after all, created for us to trust). But to whom or to what will the postmodern turn for assurance?

One increasingly popular security blanket is "socially justified belief." I'm thinking here of Kenneth Bruffee, an educational theorist who has bought heavily into a nonfoundational view of knowledge. By being "nonfoundational" he wants to *deny* that the "authority of knowledge" lodges in any of the following: "the mind of God, touchstones of truth and value, genius, or the grounds of thought, the human mind and reality" (130). As he sees it, knowledge's authority lodges in "the conversation of mankind," because all knowledge is primarily a local, collaborative artifact whereby one's beliefs are justified by testing them against those of others. In bringing this notion of knowledge as social occurrence into the educational process, Bruffee has the classroom teacher set appropriately limited issues before the students who must discuss each of them with an eye to reaching consensus "by their own authority," first within a small group and then in increasingly larger ones. He explains:

> The knowledge constructed by each small consensus group has only the authority of a group of five students [but]… is greater than the authority of any individual student…. Small groups increase the authority of their knowledge when they compare their results with the consensus that other groups have arrived at and negotiate a consensus of the class as a whole….The final step…occurs when the class as a whole compares its consensus on the limited issue addressed in the task with the consensus on that issue of the immeasurably larger and more complex disciplinary or linguistic community (such as chemists, historians, or writers of standard English) that the teacher represents….[This] process models the collaborative process by which the authority of all knowledge increases [a conversation in which]… community members socially justify their beliefs to one another. (50-1)

Learning, then, means that one leaves a "community" that justifies certain beliefs in one way and joins another community that justifies other beliefs in other ways. That "x is y" is knowledge here; that "x is z" counts as knowledge there. The fundamental assumption is that the only reality that counts is social reality: "we construct and maintain knowledge not by examining the world, but by negotiating with one another…. [Similarly,] learning occurs among people, not between persons and things" (202).

The second umpire, above, recognized that the way he sees the world invariably affects his judgments, that it influences what he experiences and how he sizes up that "reality." In a similar vein, the academic discipline called "hermeneutics" deals with interpreting and sizing up texts (such as the Bible, a medieval poem, or more recently any meaning-laden activity or product). Already back in the nineteenth century guidelines dictated that right understanding required one to attend to the grammatical, historical, individual, and generic aspects (genre) of the text; whether that be individual texts, the text that a culture is, or the books of Scripture and creation. One of the oldest questions in this regard has to do with the fact that complex wholes and their parts are always inseparably intertwined. One comprehends a whole by understanding its parts, but the parts acquire their meaning only within the whole. Baseball is a game of balls and bats, balls and strikes, foul balls and home runs. But what the bat and these "balls" are for (their meaning) only becomes evident in the context of the whole game. So also, one can understand the sense of the voiced suggestion, "Let's go to the *Subway* for a submarine sandwich!" only when one understands what each of these words means. But one is unable to select the appropriate meaning of words like "subway," "submarine," and "/'san-(,)(d)wich/" until one realizes what the entire sentence (in this context) means. This inductive, to-and-fro movement between sense of the parts and sense of the whole is called the "hermeneutical circle."

Hans-Georg Gadamer is one of many who have struggled with these kinds of questions. What are the implications, he asks, when one realizes that studying history is never more than a dialogue with the past conducted from one's own historically defined time and place. History is an ongoing process that embraces us as well; no one can step out of it to study it. So also the notion of a single timeless objective truth existing independently "out there," just waiting to be discovered, must be abandoned. Everything about us is in the world, human existence is altogether historical, and to escape one's context is simply out of the question. But can one understand the other? People naturally develop different perspectives on the world. How could

we not? Different interpretations are inevitable. However, relativism need not be our fate, according to Gadamer: Behind the
conflict of interpretations is a shared world, language, and an
effective tradition, which he is certain legitimates the anticipation of someday knowing, of experiencing a "fusion of horizons"
for those willing to engage methodically in that dialogue.

Not everyone is convinced however. The loose label "post-
structuralists" refers to a number of influential thinkers who
have left quandaries connected to the hermeneutical circle in the
dust by flat out rejecting the pretense to knowledge. In many
ways, the only thing they will claim to know is the impossibility
of knowing. The names of Jacques Derrida, Michel Foucault,
both Frenchmen, and Richard Rorty, an American, come to mind
here. Derrida has worked hard at subverting the classical theory
of meaning that moves from thought to speech to the written
word. Foucault pursued the postmodern "language game" to its
ultimate conclusion in the dissolution of the self. And the neo-
pragmatist Rorty came to the conclusion that the best we can do
is keep our "ethnocentric" conversations going "for the hell of it"
—lest life as we know it desist.

Deconstruction arose as an extension of and reaction to the
claim that language is a social construct that possesses a common, invariant structure found among all societies and cultures.
The structuralist movement, following Saussure, had argued, on
the one hand, that people develop "texts" to provide structures of
meaning that help them make sense out of the meaninglessness
of their experience. But, on the other hand, they also embraced
the hope, in a way similar to Gadamer, that an objective, universal cultural system was or should be evident behind each such
attempt.

Jacques Derrida (1930-) and his students, however, denied
that any one meaning is inherent to any text, let alone that all
texts evidence some kind of common invariant structure. These
de-constructionists claim that meaning is never given once-for-
all and emerges only as the interpreter enters into dialogue with
the text. This claim implies that the meaning of a text (be it a
pauline epistle or a pipe) is always dependent on the perspective
of the interpreter and that any one text has as many meanings as
it has had or will have readers. The same holds for the text we
call reality: there is no one meaning or center to the world, only

differing and shifting viewpoints and perspectives. As a result, they conclude that we must continually defer or postpone the tendency to attribute meaning to texts, events, and even history. Derrida's mandate to "deconstruct" belongs really to scholars. If language constructs meaning, then their task is to take this meaning making process apart and possibly break its control over our thoughts and actions. One repercussion for the classroom has been that teaching is no longer just the transmission of a discipline or of knowledge had by those more experienced before entering the lecture hall; teaching, to be legitimate, should also include the active production (as well as deconstruction) of meaning.

Michel Foucault (1926-1984), too, is often described as a "poststructuralist." Many of his investigations dealt with a microview of concrete problems in society, history, politics, and culture. Their common focus, however, was "power," and he increasingly identified the will to knowledge with the will to power. He was trying to document the "dark side of Francis Bacon's vision," that every interpretation of reality, every assertion of knowledge, is an assertion of power, an act of violence.

In addition to Nietzsche's "will to power," Foucault also underscores Nietzsche's emphasis on the richness and variety of reality. One problem with reason and rational discourse is that they squeeze the variety out of reality into an artificial homogeneity that accommodates conceptual exchange. The result is that difference and "otherness" suffer for the sake of sameness and universality. One reason his writings were focused on the specific and the special was to advance this "otherness" and to deny the universality and timelessness so often attributed to our categories by bringing them back to the historical flux.

Structuralists claimed that one's language and subjective experience are constituted by socio-historical factors that one unconsciously internalizes. Foucault will agree, but then demands that that "order" be exposed for the power structure it is. The ground rules people unknowingly "play" by must be laid bare because they "enforce" what and how they think and live and speak. The scholar's task, then, is to bring to light the authorless, subjectless, actually anonymous system of thought present within the language of an era. He was not moving to replace it with another order, however, but to challenge the very notion of order. Apparently, on the one hand, Foucault was hoping to gain freedom from the faith of rationality and, on the other, hoping somehow to embrace or see realized the ultimate existential ideal of individual self-determination, beyond which history has no meaning.

The neopragmatism of Richard Rorty, to which Bruffee boldly appeals, leaves room for truth of sorts, but only within the environment of a cultural relativism. He maintains that it is impossible to find a starting point for human discourse that lies beyond the contingencies of one's own temporal context. Any sort of transcendent ("god's eye") view of things is out of the question. Everything one says, including what is said about truth and rationality, is embedded in one's understanding and the concepts peculiar to the culture and society that one inhabits. The most we can aim for is making our communal beliefs and desires more coherent or consistent. Coherence is the penultimate goal next to survival, and our inheritance from and our conversation with fellow human beings is our only source of guidance.

Rorty agrees that in one sense he is an irrationalist. He has resigned himself to the conclusion that most means and ends are without promise: finding contentment through subjecting oneself to seeds of reason or religion, discovering certainty by emptying one's mind of the dubitable, or placing hope in the search for some foundational structure of inquiry, of language, or of social life. All of these are chasing after the wind. On the other hand, he wholeheartedly embraces the pursuit of making his web of belief as coherent and as transparently structured as possible. This, he confides, will only happen when we together are committed to engaging an ongoing conversation and to conforming ourselves to the constraints that arise through our conversations with fellow inquirers. Any universe of discourse that falls silent will also fall away. In like manner, our task in the West is to make our culture—the human rights culture—more self-conscious and more powerful. To demonstrate to other cultures that the West's is better or superior by an appeal to something transcendent or transcultural can never be an option. The only viable foundation is and will have to remain the give and take of the conversation among competing interpretations.

In summary: The postmodern project is a bold quest to chart the waters beyond modernism without the pretense of conquest. As Rorty puts it in *Philosophy and the Mirror of Nature*: "[Postmodern philosophy must] decry the notion of having a view while avoiding having a view about having views" (371). Postmodernism embodies a resolute desire to dethrone rationalism by celebrating other valid routes to knowledge, while at the same time not giving up altogether on reason. It seldom rallies the prospect of progress, and to the extent the world's great problems can still be addressed, it seems that the best one can hope for is survival through cooperation.

The world is no longer simply an objective—given "out there." A common source of authority is not to be had. Reality is contingent, ambiguous, and participatory; and our knowledge of it—our *narrative*—is always historically and culturally conditioned and, per definition, incomplete and fragmented. There is no "meta-narrative," no grand narrative, no one puzzle into which all the pieces fit. Every kind of totalizing narrative must be dissolved. Likewise, how we envision the truth and what we accept as true are dependent on and relative to the communities in which we participate and the *myths* that we perpetuate. Any claim to a universal, supracultural, timeless truth is out of the question. At most, the truth that stands consists in the local ground rules that facilitate the well-being of the communities of which we are a part. These myths or ground rules embody the central core of a culture's values and beliefs (and are in that sense fundamentally religious). To think that there is some overarching framework, some neutral descriptive language, some immutable standards of rationality to which anyone can appeal is to deceive oneself deeply. "Wake up and smell the coffee!" we are told—a "god's eye" view of things, grasping the world *sub specie aeternitatis*, is simply silly! What is out there is nothing more and nothing less than multiple constructed realities.

A complexity of philosophic currents and cross-currents mark our contemporary age. In addition to a lingering lingual-analytic tradition, a potent positivistic presence, and a near ancient neothomism, there are many new and revitalized theories at work: psychoanalysis, feminism, neomarxism, post-structuralism, deconstructionism, constructivism, and many more. But increasingly, in what is often described as our "postmodern" context, people are beginning to despair of any integrated outlook on life. Intellectual unity, wholeness, and a comprehensive coherence seem to be out of the question. Many are beginning to resign themselves to an attitude of "different strokes for different folks." The collapse of meaning, a loss of "center," seems to doom one to self-responsibility and creative innovation when it comes to making sense of the world.

For Christians to adopt the timepiece of postmodernism is to suggest that they too see modernity, the modernist project, as the primary benchmark. But is that indeed the case? Is our place in history marked most by where we stand with respect to modernism? Or is it defined, as we said when we began, by how we stand with respect to the Word and mighty acts of God?

Some have suggested that detective stories are the best representative of modernist fiction: the detective takes the reader on a quest to uncover the hidden truth that lies beneath the perplexing surface of reality and always solves the mystery logically and with efficiency in the end. Spy stories, in contrast, filled with multiple worlds and levels of deception and illusion, are said to characterize the postmodern condition. Christians in the light of Scripture, however, know that the story that includes us all began, turned, and will culminate with the Word of God. What tomorrow will bring Christians do not know nor do they fear. But as they test the spirits of an age that no longer opposes or even ridicules the Good resurrection News of Jesus Christ and that tolerates faith in a risen Lord, along with all the other myths sincere people perpetuate, Christians will soon realize that they are witnessing the dawning of a postchristian era.

Reason enthroned or dethroned will not save us. The choice is not between modernism and postmodernism, between rationalism and irrationalism. Just as Christians must radically reject the modernist move toward the self-reflective, self-determining, autonomous subject who stands outside any tradition or community and is subject to no one or no thing, so also they must reject the postmodernist celebration of construction, collage, and juxtaposed practice. The multiplicity and discordant polyphony of ultimately decontextualized voices that it calls into being is no more an option than modernism's commitment to ahistorical truth and scientific method. As we will want to articulate in the next unit, there is, in spite of angry and desperate claims to the contrary, a trustworthy foundation and unifying center for the world as well as a grand narrative that witnesses to the promise of hope and the reality of just judgment.

II. D. 3.
Guide Questions

106. What is the difference between rationalism and irrationalism?

107. Why should Christians not join irrationalism?

108. What is the importance of Kierkegaard?

109. What news did Nietzsche have for the modern world?

110. What is pragmatism and how has it undermined the effectiveness of the christian community in North America?

111. What has Henri Bergson become known for?

112. Where does Heidegger go looking for truth?

113. Relate Sarte's credo "existence precedes essence" with his insistence on moral responsibility.

114. What is the story about the three umpires meant to illustrate?

115. Summarize Bruffee's constructivist epistemology.

116. How are the whole and its parts related to the hermeneutical circle?

117. What does deconstructionism want to deconstruct?

118. Is there a dark side to Francis Bacon's vision?

119. Why does Rorty want to keep the conversation going?

120. Explain what it is about modernism and postmodernism that the Christian must reject.

II. E.
Conclusion

We have come to the end of our survey of the history of Western thought. What does it mean? And where do we go from here? These legitimate questions require a brief discussion by way of some concluding remarks.

The history of Western thought unfolds for us a plethora of architectonic responses to the human condition. The ordered diversity, dimensions, and interrelatedness of God's creation impinges upon all human experience and demands response. Each person acknowledges that givenness and answers God's creation mandate, in one way or another. Only a few do so with articulate and methodic precision, but what they grasp often sets the pace and pattern for others. We have seen that a poorly put question will usually result in a mistaken response. So too, in formulating some of the basic problems, people—rejecting the Word of God—distort the true state of affairs, with the result that both the questions and their solutions bear an apostate stamp. Consequently, the panorama of Western thought generally presents a picture of apostasy: man as a supposedly autonomous being, as self-proclaimed creator of his destiny, needs no other source than his own inherent creativity. Hence the tragic character of Western thought: the solutions are not solutions, the promises made have not materialized, nor is there rest anywhere.

Studying this history also enables one to see and to understand the role of the Word-revelation in Western civilization. The Word is before all things, in the Word all things hold together, and in the Word incarnate we find the central event in history. This prompts the question, "How did an apostate humanity receive the Light?" The story we have told supplies the answer. We have attempted to describe the history of Western thought from a christian perspective. Such a task clearly presupposes a christian grasp of things, what we can call a christian systematic philosophy. The contours of such a scriptural philosophy will be the topic of discussion in the final unit.

Studying the history of human thought is not merely an interesting alternative hobby. It is instead a matter of utmost urgency. Living without memory leaves one lost, lonely, and dysfunctional. To carry out the christian task in our complex world requires an understanding of the spirits through the ages. More often than not, these spirits then and now turn out to be of a foundational, even religious nature. In addition, ignorance of formative processes in the past, even within the last fifty years, often binds Christians to blind traditionalism or a superficial savvy that prevents them from carrying out their task in a truly reformational way. Not that we all must become historians or philosophers. Nevertheless it would be irresponsible, if not perilous, to acquire an education, to appear to be prepared for the challenge of life, and to assume one's task and calling oblivious of the spirits that have determined the nature of civilization at the dawn of the twenty-first century. This unit on the history of Western thought has sought to make a contribution toward an understanding of those spirits.

Before bringing this chapter to a close, I once again want to address a few questions concerning a biblically sensitive, historical account of Western thought.

Much of the material in this second unit is based on the work of Dirk Vollenhoven. Throughout the world there is a small group of Christians continuing the work of Vollenhoven and his cohort Herman Dooyeweerd in an effort to promote communal christian scholarship, particularly in the area of philosophy. They are convinced that the insights of Vollenhoven have prepared the possibility of a fully systematic account of the history of philosophy from a christian perspective. The method employed in the formulation of such an account—originated by Vollenhoven—is the *problem-historic method*. This method provides an overview of philosophic conceptions based on types of ontology and successive historical currents. Not only is this method rooted in a systematically formulated christian philosophy and consequently presents the history of Western thought in biblical perspective, but it also clears the immense confusion that secular historians have managed to create. It is to be hoped that the "problem-historic method" may find an enthusiastic reception among an increasing number of christian scholars and students of philosophy.

In his writings Herman Dooyeweerd has drawn attention to another aspect of the history of Western thought. Rather than painstakingly analyze philosophic conceptions in terms of a rigorous method such as Vollenhoven uses, Dooyeweerd focused more on the transcendental conditions for theoretical thought. In his *New Critique of Theoretical Thought* he laid bare the basic religious commitments of the philosophers as well as the limits of theoretic thought. Dooyeweerd followed Calvin in expressing the commitment that "religion defines man." All philosophic activity, indeed all of human life, is prompted by a religious *ground-motive*. Dooyeweerd has found four such religious ground-motives, all of which identify the religious nature

and thrust of theoretic activity in the Western world. Three of
the four ground-motives are apostate in character and exhibit an
inner tension which no amount of theory can resolve.

The first of the four ground-motives Dooyeweerd calls the
religious motive of form and matter. The form/matter dialectic
characterizes all of pagan Greek philosophy and must not be
immediately identified with the concepts matter and form in
aristotelian philosophy. To understand what Dooyeweerd
means, we must for a moment consider the mythological background of Greek civilization.

During the early period of Greek history, worship centered
essentially around natural powers. Greek religion was a "nature
religion." These early Greeks worshiped a formless stream of life
out of which periodically generations of beings—all subject to
death and fate and decay—emerged. It seemed to them that
things came into being from this ever-on-going stream of life and
are swallowed up by it again. There is a continuous process of
coming-into-being and passing-away. The stream of life can
only continue if individuals at the end of their allotted time are
absorbed again. Hence individuals and things are doomed to
die and decay in order that the cycle may continue. What rules
the   process   are   blind   unpredictable   forces   such   as
anangke—necessity, and *moira*—fate, one's allotted portion.

At a later stage of development a new type of religion arose,
namely, a "culture religion," represented by the Homeric gods
dwelling on Mount Olympus. These gods had left "mother
earth" with her eternal cycle of life and death, and acquired a
personal and immortal form of splendid beauty. Gods they
became, of abiding form, measure, and harmony.

These two religions combined to give rise to the inner dialectic of the Greek form/matter motive. The nature religion contributed the principle of "matter," that is, mortality and change,
the elements of unpredictable mystery and the formless dark.
From the culture religion, the Greek ground-motive inherited
"form," that is, abiding being, light and heavenly splendor, as
well as reason. Dooyeweerd says that these two mutually exclusive principles controlled all of Greek thought. For example,
Heraclitus's "all is flux" is clearly oriented to the "matter" motive,
whereas Pythagoras's abiding forms of mathematics reflect the
principle of "form." Plato postulated the abiding Ideas (form)

over against the changing world of the foreground (matter). Aristotle attempted to bridge the gulf between matter and form by inventing the relation between potency and act.

Into the Greek world of form and matter, the Gospel injected a radically new, biblical ground-motive: creation, fall into sin, and redemption by Jesus Christ in the communion of the Holy Spirit. This central theme of the Scriptures constitutes for Dooyeweerd "the Archimedean point" and radical unity of meaning, in which is rooted the heart-commitment determining all christian activity. It is the controlling power that governs a Holy Spirit-directed life. It is the christian religious ground-motive, beyond the reach of theoretical investigation or exegesis: "It effects the true knowledge of God and ourselves, if our heart is really opened by the Holy Spirit so that it finds itself in the grip of God's Word and has become the prisoner of Jesus Christ." This ground-motive is a religious presupposition for any theory or science that rightly claims a biblical foundation.

Medieval synthesis philosophy is characterized by a third ground-motive: grace and nature. We have already addressed a number of the implications of this motive. In essence the nature/grace motive is the product of a synthesis mentality that adopted the tension-ridden form/matter motive of the Greeks and incorporated it as "nature." The dialectical character of the nature/grace motive is therefore compounded. It is instructive to observe, for example, how Dooyeweerd's insight into the nature of the ground-motive clarifies traditional problems. The proofs of God postulated by Thomas Aquinas, for example, have been subjected to a variety of criticisms, mostly of a logical nature. Dooyeweerd, however, demonstrates the religious character of these proofs, by pointing out that Thomas's natural theology is oriented to the Greek form/matter ground motive.

Already in our discussion of Kant we became acquainted with the fourth motive, namely, that of nature/freedom, which still today, now among postmodernists, represents the controlling power. As soon as "grace" had been eliminated, "nature" came into conflict with "freedom." If "nature" is a mechanically determined universe, as the Renaissance and early rationalists claimed, then what room is there for autonomous human freedom? The rationalists were strongly oriented to "nature," sometimes even to the exclusion of "freedom" (e.g., Hobbes). Contemporary irrationalism has gone to the other extreme. "Freedom" is emphasized to the extent that there is practically no "nature" left (e.g., existentialism).

Dooyeweerd sees the history of philosophy as a swinging back and forth between two antithetical poles within the various apostate ground-motives. This revealing insight has contributed immensely to our understanding of what christian philosophy ought to be. It furthermore clarifies the problems and antinomies that result when one philosophizes outside of the light of God's Word or in an unholy synthesis with apostate thought.

With this challenge in mind, we turn our attention now to the articulation of some basic contours of a theoretical perspective, a philosophy if you will, that is in line with Scripture and moved by the power of God's Holy Spirit and the reality of creation, fall, and redemption.

CONTOURS OF
THOUGHT PATTERNS
IN LINE WITH SCRIPTURE

III. A.
Background

Philosophy, as we have defined it, is "the theoretical investigation and account of the diversity, dimensions, and inter-relatedness of the cosmos." This is a bold statement in the sense that there are about as many different definitions of "philosophy" as there are different philosophies (philosophic conceptions). But the diversity of definitions is not exclusive to philosophy. The same holds for psychology, sociology, theology, as well as for biology and mathematics, and on and on. As we will see, these differences in defining the place and task of the various sciences and disciplines are ultimately rooted in the different worldviews of the people who take the time to define what they are doing.

Usually people are busy in their discipline for some time before they take a break to reflect on and consider exactly what they are doing. What is the nature of my discipline? How is my field different from and/or similar to other disciplines? Is there any relationship between what I am doing in my major and what she is doing in hers? Often, without thinking, we straight-forwardly accept in trust the descriptions given concerning the place and task of the science or discipline we are busy with. That adoption is not necessarily bad. You have to start some-place. But the least one may expect is that those who provide these definitions give some account of the assumptions that their definitions presuppose.

Anyone who wants to help others understand a particular discipline should be able to shed some light on the nature and task of that discipline. But doing so does present some prob-

lems: Where, for example, do you begin? With the "chicken" or
with the "egg"? With the "forest" or with the individual "trees"?
For example, a definition of "psychology" presupposes a more or
less well-defined conception or theory of this discipline in which
a stand is taken with respect to other (e.g., Freudian, behavioristic, Gestalt) theories about psychology, each of which have their
own definition of "psychology." Where does one begin? With
the psychologies (and definitions) of others, and move in the
direction of one's own view (and definition) of psychology? Or
the other way around? Not to mention the fact that someone's
psychology presupposes, among many other things, a view of
humankind, an anthropology. The same pedagogical queries
confront anyone teaching an introductory course in philosophy
whose purpose is to provide more than a survey of what is "for
sale" in the philosophic "marketplace." Anyone who naively
talks about "philosophy" as though it were the greatest common
denominator of present-day philosophies, introduces an obstacle
to systematic insight before he even begins. And the same holds
for recreation, sociology, and theology, to mention just a few disciplines.

Our definition of philosophy, for example, with which we
began, is not accepted by everyone. In fact, many would disagree with this definition.
It is, however, not an arbitrary one. This definition
is grounded in a basic conception of reality, of being
human, and of knowledge
whose roots go back to
people such as Abraham
Kuyper (1837-1920), Groen
van Prinsterer (1801-1876),
John Calvin (1509-1564),
and Augustine (354-430)
—all of whom sought to
reckon with and rely on
Scripture in their lives and
thinking. We have met
with some already and can

GROEN VAN PRINSTERER

now touch base with the others.

Groen van Prinsterer was a lawyer, a statesman, a historian, a confessor of Christ in science and politics. He fought against the unbelief and spirit of revolution that defined the day in nineteenth century Europe. In his book *Unbelief and Revolution* (1847), Groen typifies revolution as a reversal in thinking and conviction. He had a good sense of what was going on in the world and was not surprised to hear that the Word of God was labeled as diddly, as mythology, as a time-bound text. He knew too that theoretic work done in the light of that Word would be laughed at; after all, the nature of unbelief demands that people talk and act the way they do. Their response he could understand. He had more difficulty understanding Christians. Why did they so often expend so little resistance? Was it laziness? The desire to be in on what was *in*? The "need" to be accepted by others? Or did they think that apologizing for the fact that they believed through grace was enough? Groen saw around him idolatry, decay, and a way of thinking that was ultimately infertile. But in his day he also discovered an affirmation of the Bible's words: "The Lord knows the way of the righteous, but the way of the wicked will perish" (Psalm 1).

According to Groen, all of history is embedded in a divine order. Not even revolutions can do without the structure of/for creation. He sees this order that defines history especially in connection with the church, religion, and morality, but also as tied to governing, administrating, and doing justice. The biblical principles, the "ordinances of creation," that lie at the root of these institutions are, in history, either unfolded or denied. For Groen, in addition to researching "the facts," the christian historian *must* approach history in light of the truths and principles that Scripture talks about. The human responses to God and to his word that constitute history are not primarily evident in the objective form of events and milestones, but must be seen in connection with their religious direction and intent, as rooted in the choice and conviction of the heart. Groen was convinced that Scripture and history were tied to each other; "it is written!" is made manifest in "it has happened!" Scripture and history both have to be read—but always in that order!

Following in Groen's shoes was Abraham Kuyper. Kuyper was trained as a pastor but soon moved on to affect his world in other ways: to found and edit a daily christian newspaper, *The Standard*; to help get a christian political party off the ground (called the "Anti-Revolutionary Party"); to initiate the establishment of a christian university—the Free University in Amsterdam; to pilot a church reform movement; and, later in life, to become Prime Minister of The Netherlands from 1901-1905. Kuyper, more than any other one person, mobilized Dutch Calvinists in the forty years around the turn of the century to forthrightly claim every area of life for obedient christian service to God. His own career reflected the breadth he attributed to the Kingdom of God.

Kuyper talked much about two kinds of music and of politics and of science; in each field the "normal" and the "abnormal" were at odds with the other. For example, at Princeton University in the United States in 1899 he spoke these words:

> Calvinism offered the ready solution for the conflict to which the free exercise of science must inevitably lead. You understand which conflict I have in mind: the powerful conflict between those who cling to the confession of the triune God and his Word and those who seek the solution of the world-problem in deism, pantheism, or Naturalism. Note that I do not speak of a conflict between faith and science. There is no such thing. All science proceeds out of faith. All science presupposes that we ourselves believe; presupposes a belief that the laws for thinking are correct; presupposes beliefs about life; and presupposes above all faith in the principles from which we proceed. No, the conflict is not between faith and science, but between the claim that the present state of the cosmos is normal or abnormal. If it is normal, then it is moving in an everlasting process toward its ideal. But if the present cosmos is abnormal, then a disturbance has taken place and only a regenerating

ABRAHAM KUYPER

power can guarantee that it meet its destination. So, it is not faith and science, but two scientific systems that stand, each with their own faith, over against each other. Nor may it be said that it is science that stands over against theology, for we are dealing here with two absolute forms of science, both of which lay claim to the entire field of human knowledge. They are both in earnest, disputing with each other across the entire domain of life and cannot desist from the attempt to pull to the ground the entire edifice of each other's contradictory claims. (*Calvinism*, 1898)

Fighters are vulnerable. Kuyper's program was bold, at times also brazen. One might also question whether the object is really to break the back of the scientific unbeliever. But any Christian must certainly agree with Kuyper's conviction that there is not one square inch of our lives in particular and of creation in general that God Almighty does not claim as his own.

Groen and Kuyper, of course, were not alone in their reliance on Scripture. What distinguishes their thinking from that of many other Christians is what we can refer to as "reformational": Creation, sin, and redemption are for them biblical realities that are cosmic in scope. God's grace is not added on to creation or our lives, but is meant to restore both. Adam was named after the earth (*adamah*), heaven is not our home, and God through Jesus Christ seeks to reconcile all things to himself, now already. So also, we are not called to be parents or students or bankers and *also* Christians, but called to be christian parents, christian students, and christian bankers—in that sense, compared to the world, *abnormal*. Sanctification is then not a theological concept but the reality of being made holy to the Lord through progressive renewal, from the inside out, in the

D. H. Th. VOLLENHOVEN

lives and works of Christians, by the power of the Holy Spirit. God is sovereign in every area of life. He requires obedience to his word and divine will and promises increase to those who build on principles that are rooted in Scripture and are intrinsic to the Reformed tradition.

For a variety of reasons, many of which are good, people today often refer to the tradition in which they stand as their *worldview*. Albert Wolters, for example, has written a very helpful introduction to and review of the reformed tradition in *Creation Regained*. (For those wishing to review the topics discussed in Wolters' book, there is a comprehensive list of "guide questions" included in Appendix I.) There he defines "worldview" as one's comprehensive framework of basic beliefs about things and makes the claim that everyone (Christian or not) has one. Everyone lives according to basic presuppositions, and everyone's worldview rests on a faith commitment. In their book, *The Transforming Vision*, Walsh and Middleton agree and explain this "faith commitment" as the way one answers four recurring basic questions: Who am I? Where am I? What's wrong? and What is the remedy? Today, it is widely acknowledged that one's worldview has impact upon life in a variety of ways.

In the pages that follow, we will want to focus on the difference reformational thinking makes in doing and defining philosophy—or if you will, in articulating a biblical view of reality, of being human, and of human knowledge. In proceeding, I again lean heavily on the work and writings of Dirk Vollenhoven (1892-1978), but also on Herman Dooyeweerd (1894-1977) and others who have banded a-

HERMAN DOOYEWEERD

round what today is referred to as "reformational philosophy."
It is to their credit that what many today are just coming to realize, namely, that worldview and religion make a difference even
when it comes to theoretical and scientific reflection, Groen and
Kuyper and some of their students were advocating already a
century ago.

III. B.
The Place of Thinking and Knowing
in the Cosmos and Their Task

At first glance, trying to think about thinking might strike
some as a chore about as meaningful as picking oneself up by
the bootstraps. Needless to say, there have been those who were
convinced that they could grasp in thought everything it meant
for them to be and that in doing so they would be able to make
themselves into whatever it was that they wanted to become.
Human thinking, however, is not a self-contained power. Nor
can it fully grasp or understand or explain or make everything it
wishes. But it is possible for us to think about what is involved
in the human activity and results of thinking.

1. THINKING ABOUT KNOWING AND WHAT IS KNOWABLE

Let's focus for the moment on the activity of thinking and
what that activity must presuppose if it is to be meaningful.
When we talk about thinking, our first thoughts are about
humans thinking. Whether or not animals think might be cause
for discussion. But if we tentatively define thinking, particularly
in its analytic aspect, as *distinguishing that which is different in its
context*, then my dog's being able to tell the difference between
some quality brand of dog food (which she doesn't like) and a
discount store's *Ol'Boy* brand is certainly an instance of distinguishing, but not of thinking. She has no sense of price, profit,
and the value of generic brands—no sense of the economic context. She has no sense of dietary fiber, vitamins, and the
soy/meat content—no sense of the bio-physical context. In what
follows we will limit ourselves to general characteristics that are
true for persons thinking.

But what of "dog" spelled backwards? Is God's thinking similar to or different from human thinking? Will what we have to say about humans thinking hold for God's thoughts as well? To answer that question presupposes that we know how God thinks, that is, that this divine activity of his is *knowable* to us. So maybe we should turn to that question first: What is knowable and what is not? What can human beings know and think about and what is simply beyond their ken?

Not everyone agrees on what is knowable and what is not. But most Christians would agree that God, his law for creation, and the cosmos (= creation) are knowable, at least in part.

God is certainly knowable, for he not only has revealed himself in Jesus Christ, the Word made flesh, but also has told us about himself in so many words, some of which are recorded in the Bible, his inscripturated word. All of creation, too, with its creatures, is confessed to be a most important means of God's self-revelation. Yes, God is knowable, on the basis of incarnation, Scripture, and creation. But he is not completely knowable. God is knowable for us humans only to the extent that he has revealed himself in his Word and in his works. And even then few people see God acting. Indeed, the divine revealing *activity* of God's creating, speaking, and leading are beyond our analytic eye. More often than not, it is the *results* of his actions that we come to know. And it is in knowing them that we come to know him better.

God's law is also knowable. Taking God at his word, we know that obedience means to love God above all and to love our neighbor as ourselves. But God's law taken in the sense of the totality of his ordaining acts with respect to the cosmos is also knowable. Here too, as with God, his law is knowable to the extent that it is revealed in his Word and in his works.

The things and relations that make up the *cosmos*, namely, creation as we know it, are also knowable. The cosmos, of course, includes both heavenly creatures and earthly creatures. Heaven—the world of angels—is knowable to the extent we are told about these things in the word of God. The earth, or universe, is knowable to the extent that we read about it in the Bible or can investigate its past, present, and future.

Hence, in the light of Scripture, Christians boldly claim that God, his law, and the cosmos can *all* be known—though not completely or in their entirety. But God, his law, and the cosmos are knowable to the extent that these things are made known to us in scriptural and creational revelation.

But then: there is knowledge and there is knowledge. Most mathematicians know what complete induction is and how it can be applied to prove various theorems. Most children know what mud is and how it can be applied to various and sundry surfaces. Not only is the knowledge in each case different—the first is knowledge of something one can only see with the mind's eye, while the second is knowledge of something most people, at least once in their lives, actually get in their eyes. The kind of knowing is in each case different. A mathematician's mathematical knowledge is a *scientific kind of knowing*, whereas a mathematician's knowing to avoid getting mud in her eye is an *everyday kind of knowing*.

People's knowledge of parents, siblings, relatives, and neighbors, also of those animals, plants, and physical things with which they have had contact, to mention just a few examples, is an everyday kind of knowing. This nonscientific kind of knowing is the concrete ordinary knowledge had by everyone. It is foundational for all other kinds of knowing. Like all knowledge, everyday knowledge is not something had instantly or from the start. It always comes as the result of human activity: through experiencing, listening, trusting, watching, thinking, learning —through coming to know. Perceiving, recollecting, and expecting are important contributing factors to this process.

Coming to know in an everyday sense can occur in the context of knowledge communicated by others or through personal investigation and discovery. It is true, however, that the truths we receive from those we trust do establish the "home base" from which we proceed when initiating the investigation of some point or problem.

Scientific knowing differs from nonscientific knowing in that the human activity that precedes scientific knowing proceeds methodically and is not primarily directed to concrete things or specific relations, but to a defined (limited) field or domain. It is important to note that however prominent scientific knowing has become, it never stands alone but is continually undergirded and propelled by the nonscientific knowing that chronologically and logically precedes it. Time and place are givens and were givens in the beginning. Human knowing presupposes and builds on more than it will ever know completely.

Nonscientific knowledge of oneself (one's needs and wants), of other people, of parents, of spouse and children and of what they may expect of us, of what one takes to be important in life constitutes what we may call the factual or existential starting point for all scientific activity. This point of departure, that we leave unquestioned, at least for the moment, does not dissipate and remains presumed when one turns to theoretical matters and scientific questions.

Science, then, is one way of coming to know. It presupposes, builds on, and is borne by many kinds of nonscientific knowing. Science helps us to see what otherwise might be impossible to see, and it helps us to articulate what could be said on no other basis. Scientific knowledge, however, is not necessarily a better kind of knowing. Those who think that it is tend to put their hope and trust in science. But even then that faith, as all faith, is a matter of the heart, of commitment and conviction, not of scientific proof.

Christians know, not scientifically, but in that concrete everyday kind of way, whom they are to believe, and they are persuaded that only he—the King of kings and Lord of lords—has the key to life. But knowing that does not mean that science is out-of-bounds for Christians. Believing in God, they know that he demands obedience to his ordinances in all of life, also when it comes to academics, from art to zoology.

Likewise, science involves *someone* (a person moved by love or rebellion, that is, with an obedient or disobedient heart direction) *thinking methodically about* (that is, investigating and analyzing correctly or incorrectly; distinguishing that which is different, or failing to do so; and keeping in mind or forgetting the context in which these differences occur) similarities, differences, and relationships, at least some of which are normed, within *some limited field of investigation*. As we noted early on, these fields of investigation are different for the various sciences. Philosophy and pedagogy are *general sciences*, looking at the whole of things. Other sciences deal with a facet or aspect of the whole. These we call *special sciences*. Among these special sciences there are modal sciences, like biology, physics, sociology, or theology, which attend to general patterns of lawfulness and normed behavior. Individuality sciences, such as geography, zoology, anatomy, botany, and many forms of history, focus on particular configurations—in the physical, organic, and formative dimension of things.

In summary, we can say that human *thinking* always involves *(a)* someone *(b)* thinking *(c)* about something, such that when one thinks correctly, that is to say, when someone successfully analyzes things—distinguishing that which is different in its context—the result will be *knowledge* about that something, whatever it be. Whereas, when one thinks poorly the result will not be knowledge but *error*. In this process what the person knows already remains foundational, particularly what she knows in her heart (or thinks she knows) to be the case. Scientific or theoretical thinking and knowledge are different from, but not better than, nonscientific knowledge, upon which they are built. In addition, whether or not our thinking results in knowledge or error, we can say that the things we are thinking about were either knowable or unknowable before we thought about them. There are, after all, some things about which we can know nothing—at least not on this side of the grave. For example, we have no way of knowing whether or not Adam had a navel.

When two things are different, we can ask a question as to the relationship between the two. In this case there is a difference between philosophical and nonphilosophical knowing. Without being exhaustive, a few things can be said at this point, not only in negative terms, but also in a positive sense. On the negative side, we can say that philosophic knowing, although it is of a different nature, may ignore neither everyday knowing nor special scientific knowing. On the positive side, the relationship between the two is a double one: (1) philosophy presupposes both kinds of knowing and builds on both, and (2) philosophy must reflect on the place and the task of both everyday knowing and special scientific knowing and must treat these points at greater length in its epistemological inquiries.

2. SCIENCE AND BELIEF

When we take "belief" in the active sense of "believing," it may be understood as the acceptance of God's word-revelation or of whatever else one takes to have the last word in life. In other words, faith or belief is not always christian; usually it is the opposite. This opposition—of belief and unbelief—is of course very important, and christian thinking can only gain by doing full justice to it. For the moment, however, it is enough to note that as long as this belief has not been undermined by certain influences, every human being believes something, indeed, believes *in* something or someone. Believing, taken in that last sense—giving one's heart to some one or some thing—comes with being human. In other words, there are thousands of believers, even more unbelievers; but there are no healthy mature human beings who are nonbelievers.

To take God at his word, or to reject that word, is ultimately what believing is all about. This believing is not simply cognitive, but it does comprise an element of knowing (or erring). This knowing, that comes with believing in someone or something, is never a scientific kind of knowing, certainly not in the first place. It is a nonscientific kind of knowing that lays the foundation, that defines the home base, the context, within which we live and move and have our being before the face of God (*coram deo*).

Science may study these matters, realizing, of course, that it will at most only gain some limited insight into these things. Science can also reflect on the place and task of heartfelt believing and the resultant beliefs. But you don't need an expert to tell you what "heart" refers to: your innermost being, the gut of your self, the deepest center of your existence, the source of your thoughts, feelings, and actions. And, as even Marxists and Capitalists are well aware, what lives in your heart is going to make a difference in what you say and do and don't do. Basic beliefs that are not just confessed, but are also operative, will influence everything you do.

Knowledge of fundamental realities, commonly received through the nurture of parents and schooling, delineates the horizon of a person's life. As we noted earlier, the basic realities of creation, sin, wrath and grace, and re-creation, once grasped and understood by the Bible-believer as major issues, exhibit an all-inclusive character. Concepts of these realities do so as well. These nonscientific, circumscriptive concepts help to define the framework within which the Christian lives and moves and understands his being there. What we are talking about here, in other words, is *worldview*.

Worldview, of course, is more than a collection of concepts that rests on a gradually widening horizon, on repeatedly coming into contact with other people, on expanding the extent of one's sense perception. Worldview is the vision that you get from home or from the public square that you've assimilated for yourself with difficulty or have grown up with, so much that you almost take it for granted. It's not a scientific or theoretic conception, but a view, a sense, of God, the world, life, being human, your neighbor, yourself, that has become second nature to you, as obvious as the nose on your face and as ready to hand as an instinctual reaction. And, of course, it marks you for life (or death).

The vision that worldview is, as well as the beliefs and circumscriptive concepts it includes, are all *nonscientific* in character. They are also prescientific, both in the sense of had *prior to* (and not dissipating during) theoretic investigation, but also in the sense of determining the basic contours of the *presupposed* foundation from which the scientist proceeds and to which she returns. What one finds through scientific research fits in there sooner or later.

A christian (philosophic) conception then will not only contain thoughts concerning the nature and the task of belief, but must also completely agree with what we know to be the case in the light of Scripture. In other words, a Christian's (philosophic) conception ought to be scriptural, or if you prefer, in line with Scripture.

3. THINKING WITHIN THE BOUNDS OF RELIGION

Scriptural belief adheres to Holy Scripture, which speaks in words that people are able to understand. These words have a meaning by which they denote something and direct the attention of the hearer or reader to that which is denoted. But Scripture is different in that its words point to the Creator as well as to created things. It is Scripture then that provides an answer to the following three questions: "Who is the Creator?" "What is the creature in relation to him?" and "Where does the boundary between them lie?"

To the question, "Who is the Creator?" Scripture unambiguously answers "God." At the same time, Scripture never takes God to be a regulative idea or equivalent to the course of nature, but always the living God with his all-predestining Council, creating activity, and all-dominating will; in short, the Sovereign in the absolute sense of the term.

The answer to the second question, "What is the creature in relation to him?" is determined by what was said above: That which is created is completely dependent on the Creator, that is to say, wholly subjected to his sovereign law, word-revelation, and guidance.

The third question that we as Bible-believers ask Scripture is, "Where does creation stop and the Creator begin? How can we tell the creature from the Creator?" Or as it was put above: "What is the line that marks off that which is created from the Creator?" This demarcation is God's law. The law of God, the totality of God's ordaining acts with respect to the cosmos, is continuously laid down and maintained by God for all that which is created, in heaven and on earth. As Sovereign he set laws for the cosmos and maintains them. All that which is created is subjected to his laws. Accordingly, it is impossible to mention anything divine that stands under the law or anything that is created that stands above the law. Everything that stands on that side of this boundary is God and everything that lies on this side is creature.

By putting things in this way we can talk about the relationship between Creator and creature without pretending to be able to compare and contrast similarities and differences between God and cosmos. For example, some try to understand the basic relationship between God and cosmos purely in terms of their similarity. This happens when God and cosmos are seen as manifestations or phases of "being" or "process." When that's the case, God as well as cosmos are subordinated to something that stands above both, and Creator and creature end up as coordinates to a more fundamental reality. Others try to understand the basic relationship between God and cosmos purely in terms of their difference. This error happens when people set God and cosmos over against each other as the divine and the nondivine and end up like Karl Barth, calling God "the wholly Other."

Note also that this boundary, the law, does mark off that which is created from God, but not God from that which is created. To say that something limits God would be incompatible with the acknowledgement of the infinity of our God who is always and everywhere acting in and upon—and certainly not only from within—the cosmos.

Along the same lines, this "boundary" should not be conceived of in spatial terms, for spatiality itself belongs to that which is created. A spatial boundary is always a boundary within the created order and never one between Creator and creation.

The law does not hold for God. Although he is bound by virtue of his steadfast love and faithfulness to maintain his law once put to the creature, God is not subjected to the law. We find the combination of these thoughts already in Calvin: "*Deus legibus solutus est*" (God is not subject to laws) and "*Deus non ex lex est*" (God is not arbitrary).

The law's mode of being is that of "holding for." The law, therefore, always stands above or "transcends" that for which it holds. This is the biblical alternative to objectivism (where the criterion is found in the object) and subjectivism (where the standard is found in the subject). So, when we speak of God's thinking, we must realize that his thinking is not subject to law and is hence not in a class with creaturely thinking. The law is the boundary between creation and God. Therefore it is pointless to philosophize about God's thinking or about how God knows what he knows. Our own thinking *is* bound to the cosmic law-order and can only function meaningfully within this context.

The law of God holds for everything and therefore allows no exceptions at all. In the first place it includes the Love Command and also his structuring law for the cosmos. This structural law, God's will for creaturely structures, includes what we usually refer to as the laws *of* nature, but which are actually God-given laws *for* nature, as well as God-given norms. With the laws of nature, which are impossible to disobey, we see God's will being done immediately. In the case of norms, like Do justice! Love kindness! Walk humbly!, when these laws are obeyed, even though they often are not, we see God's will being done mediately, that is, through the agency of human beings.

The fact that these norms can be transgressed does not mean at all that they are thereby abolished.

To acknowledge the law as boundary between God and cosmos is a requirement of the fear of the Lord. That is significant for more than thinking and science, but certainly may not be lacking in our thoughts if we are going to avoid error and to gain genuine knowledge.

The answers to these three questions, then, are of great importance, also for philosophy in particular and theorizing in general. Both in the sense of activity and in the sense of result, philosophizing and philosophic conceptions, theorizing and the theories that follow, belong to the realm of creation. They are not elevated above the law of God but subjected to it, to the word-revelation, and to the guidance of the sovereign God.

"*Arché*" is Greek for "origin," for the dominating beginning of everything. Christians know that the *arché* of everything, including our thinking and philosophizing, is God and that the boundary beyond which our thinking cannot go is the law of God (more specifically, the law of God for thinking and for theoretic knowing). The inability to transcend God's law holds even if it is not acknowledged. Philosophers who declare that humankind or scientific thought is autonomous (that is, a law unto itself), who reject the word-revelation, and do not mention the guidance of God in no way attain what they want. As is evident from the present state of current philosophy, what pretended autonomy attains is nothing but anarchy in its thinking as well as in its terminology.

4. OUR FIELD OF INVESTIGATION

The answers above also imply a distinctive conception of the task of philosophy in particular and theorizing in general. In the first place they limit this task. Philosophy may never deny or seek to push aside that which exists, not even to the smallest degree: to do so would be to deny God or his work, or fail to do justice to their nature. That is also why philosophy may not take the place of believing the word-revelation of God: all of our knowledge about God rests directly or indirectly on believing the word-revelation, and what a philosopher who rejects the word of God claims to know about him turns out upon closer investigation to be pure speculation.

But even though the task of philosophy and theorizing is limited, those who keep the boundary between God and cosmos in mind are not going to run out of work. Those who believe that God created the cosmos proceed every time from the presupposition that the wealth of creation is much greater than was ascertained heretofore. For that reason a christian thinker can never say, "Look here, I've got it. I put the lid on a closed system." On the contrary: his theoretic conception, though acquired systematically, is always a provisional, tentative one. He remains filled with expectation and attuned to new surprises. These will no doubt complement the main conception that agrees with belief, yet will time and again enhance and often alter earlier findings.

Philosophy, nonscientific knowledge, and the knowing peculiar to the special sciences are similar in that they are all instances of human knowing. Philosophy is different from the other two in that it is a nonspecial (or general) scientific kind of knowing. Philosophy remains related to everyday knowing and scientific knowing in that it presupposes, relies on, and builds on both. They are not to be rejected by, reduced to, or amalgamated into philosophical knowing. Though always open to inquiry and review, nonscientific and scientific knowing compose the basis or foundation for philosophical knowing with which it must be in line as well.

Systematic philosophy's field of investigation is, one could say, the entire domain of the cosmos. More specifically, it investigates the diversity, dimensions, and interrelatedness of the cosmos. This study includes the general structure of creatures and their ontic genesis. Philosophy reflects on the meaning of that which is created in its synchronic and diachronic dimensions, that is, in its structure and in history.

Philosophers, as all scientists, depend upon a community of people with a common mind at the level of basic beliefs. In addition to articulating this group's intuitive answers to "ultimate why questions," philosophers seek to systematize or conceptualize the whole of what that community has come to know. They reflect on the combination of the results of scientific and nonscientific thinking.

In that sense philosophy's task is also an integrative and contextual one—at the conceptual level. With respect to the other sciences, for example, it is not as though philosophy has to put back together what science has taken apart. But philosophy takes the results of science, not the realities which this knowledge is about, and situates them with respect to the rest of what one knows. For example, philosophers remind the specialists (when necessary) that their field is a limited one and is connected to many others. Philosophy, you could say, works at keeping things in perspective.

5. THE POINT OF ORIENTATION

But how can people keep things in perspective when they themselves are part of the field being investigated? Not even philosophers can transcend (stand outside of or somewhere beyond) the cosmos in order to get a view of the whole. A helicopter might aid one in getting a bird's eye view of a forest, but how is a creature going to get the cosmos in view? Or how does a person (with emotions) take stock of human emotions? What in the world is going to provide us with a reliable landmark, a point of orientation? How can we say that scriptural thinking, at least in principle, oversees the whole of the cosmos?

On the basis of what they know (nonscientifically) from Scripture, Christians may claim without flinching to oversee the entire domain of the cosmos. Only from God's word can one come to know about the transcosmic certainty of the covenant between God and human beings, between God and creation, initiated and maintained by the ever-faithful Creator and Sustainer of life. What we see there is the cosmos in relation to God as under his law and therefore subject to him. (Not even Christians can see the cosmos from God's point of view.) It is the word-revealed reality of the covenant and of (true) religion—to be right with God through Christ—that makes it possible for Christians to see that which is cosmic as it is. Without Scripture the most anyone can have is an intra-cosmic perspective.

Because the whole cosmos is subjected to God's law and therefore to God, we will take BEING-SUBJECT as our point of orientation. Being-subject to God is a reality that cannot be denied of anything in the cosmos. It is and will remain true of everything that we can investigate. All further dimensions and differences are oriented to this "being-subject."

Our point of orientation is also decisive for the route that we follow. Beginning with subjectivity in this sense of the word, we look for further specifics within that which is subject to God and his law and discern a great and diverse field. As was noted previously, the cosmos knows two decidedly different kinds of creatures. So there is first of all a twofold specification: that which is subject to God is either subject in a heavenly way or in an earthly manner. Both of these creaturely realms contain what we are initially unable to survey completely. The diversity and dimensions of the earth, however, are what we all know best.

No theoretic account of reality can be exhaustive. My intention in what follows is only to point to the most important differences and distinctions that reformational thinkers have discerned within the cosmos, so that others may see them as well.

III. A. and B.
Guide Questions

121. Do you agree with Groen Van Prinsterer's description of nineteenth century Europe?

122. Abraham Kuyper denies that there is a conflict between faith and science. The conflict that he sees is a different one. Do you agree?

123. What difference does sanctification make when it comes to articulating a view of reality, of being human, and of human knowledge?

124. Is God knowable? If so, to what extent?

125. Describe the knowing of everyday. How is scientific knowing different? How are these two kinds of knowing related?

126. What is the difference between believers and unbelievers? Where do nonbelievers fit in?

127. Walking the talk does not always come out on top. Are all confessed beliefs also operative beliefs?

128. What should we keep in mind when we think about how God knows what he knows?

129. Distinguish, within God's will for creaturely structures, between norms and laws of nature.

130. Given what we can investigate, why do we *need* a point of reference or orientation?

III. C.

The Diversity and Connection Among
That Which is Subject to God in a Heavenly Way

Heaven and earth belong to that which is created. They are both similar in their being subject to God. In other words, that which cannot be denied of both heaven and earth is their "being-subject." Nevertheless, with the words "heaven" and "earth" we are saying more than that they are created. Each refers to a different diversity within that which is subject to God; "heaven" and "earth" articulate "being-created" more specifically.

Comparing them, we observe that heaven and earth are similar in that they are both created. "In the beginning God created the heavens and the earth." Likewise, they both are subjected to God's will and, therefore, to him.

Besides similarity there is, however, also a difference between heaven and earth.

1. DIFFERENCES IN HEAVEN
THAT EXIST BY VIRTUE OF CREATION

"Heaven" here refers to the world of angels. Angels are heavenly creatures. Heaven is to be clearly distinguished from the starry heavens and firmament (or sky) that belong to the earth (Genesis 1:7,14ff). We know nothing about the nature and ministry of angels except by way of word-revelation, and therefore on the basis of belief.

Now, while it is true that God's word-revelation about heaven is rather sketchy, it nevertheless casts a light on this part of the cosmos that is completely different from what philosophers, to the extent they are interested in these matters, have thought as well as from what Hallmark sympathy cards and Hollywood's movies would have us believe.

In brief, the givens of Holy Scripture can be summarized as follows:

a. Heaven and its dwellers, including seraphs and cherubs, belong to that which is created (Genesis 1:1).

b. By virtue of creation, heaven is correlated with earth.

c. In heaven there exist spirits, angels, and messengers who differ, by virtue of creation, in individuality, task, and rank. There are many of them and they play significant roles: they are God's messengers, they praise God, they exercise God's providential care, they encourage christian obedience, and they represent and carry out God's justice. In one passage (but not Luke 2) we are told that angels sing as well.

What we are told in Scripture concerning these matters is, however, exceedingly sparce. It is often silent on questions we would like to have answered. Sometimes all we are told is what is not true for angels.

Heavenly creatures and earthly creatures are very different: for example, Scripture not only does not speak of female angels, but also explicitly denies the existence of wedlock between angels (Matt. 22:30).

Nevertheless, the givens that Scripture offers us about angels are important because we then possess information about creatures that have that mere-being-creature in common with us, even though they differ from earthly creatures.

Consequently, acknowledging the existence of angels should keep us from equating earthly-being with created-being; earthly creation is only a part of that which is created.

2. THE ANTITHESIS AND THE WORLD OF ANGELS

The difference in the world of angels between good and evil angels is a different kind of difference than the diversities mentioned above.

Scripture (Jude 6 and 2 Peter 2:4) tells us that the antithesis arose through the fact that one of the most important angels did not remain standing in the truth—in the constancy, safety, and faithfulness of God. In his irreparable fall Satan was followed by many other angels, and they came to stand in radical, thoroughgoing opposition to the faithful good angels. Christians do not believe *in* the devil; that would imply a confidence in Satan. They do *believe that* the devil exists and that Christ came to destroy this prince of darkness grim.

Correlated with the resulting difference between good and evil angels, the difference between heaven and hell arose. This difference does not exist by virtue of creation; instead, it exists by virtue of the judgment of God on account of the sin of the angels. It is important to make a clear distinction between these two so as not to end up in an antithetical dualism or in a view that sees the lowest as demonic, the highest as heavenly, and the nature of the earth as defined by their combination.

III. D.
The Diversity and Connection Among
That Which is Subject to God in an Earthly Way

1. TWO ROUTES: FROM CONCRETE TO ABSTRACT AND BACK AGAIN

The word "earth" refers here to the world in which human beings live, locally, but also stretching to the far reaches of the universe. It refers only implicitly to the wealth of diversity created in the earth by God. Scripture refers to the relationship of "earth" to this rich diversity in a number of ways: sometimes as a relationship of that which was initially encompassing to that which was initially encompassed: "Now the earth was formless and empty, darkness was over the surface of the deep, and the Spirit of God was hovering over the waters" (Genesis 1:2); or as the unfolding of this diversity out of the earth as the work of the Spirit of God, who guides all of this, reciprocally connected, to development: "How many are your works, O Lord! In wisdom you made them all; the earth is full of your creatures" (Psalm 104:24).

The diversity that manifests itself in this process of unfolding is much too great for us to survey well without further analysis. And so, moving from this rich diversity within earthly creation toward a number of analytically irreducible differences, we can discern a number of these differences and make a number of corresponding distinctions. God made the diversity and covenants with the earth (Genesis 9:13); analytically, we are responsible for distinguishing correctly as we work the earth and care for it (Genesis 2:15).

In the first place, looking for basic differences within the earth, Christians must not forget to reckon with the unique relation between the earth and God that we call the *covenant*—a relationship in which humankind is required to be a steward on earth as image bearer of the Creator God who thrones in heaven. With this distinction, the difference between humankind and that which is subject to its care is given. Apart from this commonality, however, there exists a great diversity of kingdoms (such as animals, plants, and nonliving things) and kinds within those kingdoms.

Within these kinds we finally come upon individually different things. For example, some animals are chordates (spinal), some of whom are mammals (nursing), not all of which are carnivores (meat eating), only some of which are Canidae (wolf/fox-like), and of these only some are hounds (dog-like), and some of these are border collies, one of whom my children call "Max" and another my neighbor calls "Stanley." This dog is not that dog, nor is this stone that one. We will call this basic difference of irreducible individuality—remember, even "identical twins" are different—the *this-that difference* or also the individual difference. But things do not exist separately and unrelatedly next to each other. They are connected with or related to one another in various ways: economically, socially, organically, or whatever. Individually different things often demonstrate a clear similarity in the make-up and diversity of their ways or modes of being. This book has a cover, takes up space, and is printed on paper, but so is your dictionary and your Bible. The diversity among these modes of being is different in kind from the this-that difference. Taking up space and being filled with words are not one and the same, but taking up space is not a "this" and being filled with words not a "that." We will call this second basic kind of difference the *modal difference*. And then there is the difference between good and evil—obedience and disobedience—a third kind of difference that cannot be reduced to either of the previous differences.

The sequence humankind, kingdoms, kinds, things, modes of being, and good and evil can be arrived at through analysis: when analyzing that which is concrete, further and further, one finally arrives at diversities that cannot be further analyzed. We could call this inquiry—from the fullness of concrete everyday reality to abstract, irreducible differences—the "first route."

But it is also possible to follow the reverse route—the "second route," if you will—from these abstract differences and move toward the concrete coherence and interwoven complexity of everyday. In this case one begins where analysis ended, with the analytically irreducible diversities, and proceeds in the direction of ever greater involvement. It should, however, be noted that the analytically irreducible diversities, our three different kinds of differences, are not elemental in nature, like some sort of atomic facts with which one might want to try and reconstruct reality. To analyze is not the same as finding component parts. Rather, to analyze is to distinguish that which is different in its context.

As it stands, we could confine ourselves to analyzing concrete everyday reality further and further, for the first route indeed has an important advantage over the second. That advantage is simply the fact that the whole, in its breadth and depth, comes to the fore via the methodic investigation of its diverse components. We are reminded that every thing, each displaying a variety of modal dimensions, belongs to a kind, and every kind to a kingdom, and that all of the kingdoms are included, via humankind and religion, in the covenant of God with the earth. It's all there. Everything is included! And all of it is subject to God and his law.

Because we cannot do without this glimpse of the whole, we may not just attend to the second route apart from the first. For one can only have a clear view of the determinants or specifics of "that which is subject to God in an earthly way" when their connection with that whole is kept in mind: the earth, after all, is not just a collection of kingdoms; a kingdom is not simply a bunch of kinds; a kind is not an aggregate of things; and a thing is not the sum of any number of analytically irreducible properties or characteristics.

There are, however, great advantages to be had when the second route follows the first. First of all you eliminate the danger of never getting beyond vague generalities and speaking holistically, for example, about "the big picture" without ever seeing the abundance that they contain. And second, you clearly get to see that the "whole" that was seen first cannot be constructed or re-constructed from the "parts" obtained through resolution. What is lacking is precisely the context and connection that was kept in mind when following the first route.

The breadth of this study does not permit us to give equal time to both routes of this two-fold investigation.   So, after a brief review of the first route, we now turn our full attention to the second.

The this-that diversity and the modal diversity, which we will deal with first, both exist by virtue of creation: they are part and parcel of what God wanted for his earthly creatures and to this day continues to uphold and maintain.   The good-evil dif-

ference, as was the case in the world of angels, does not exist by
virtue of creation. In the beginning, when God created the earth,
disobedience was not a factor; evil could only come once the ball
was rolling. After surveying the structural diversity of individuality and modality first, we will pick up this third dimension of
earthly creatures, because the good-evil difference gets at how
our response to what God wants for his creatures is directed:
our way or his. After discussing these basics we can then proceed ever further in the direction of the concrete complexity and
diversity of everyday life.

In doing so, we need to discuss many things right off the
bat that are of primary importance. At the same time, keep in
mind that none of the important things that we will be addressing later are excluded in the knowing activity that is going on
right now. For example, following the route we have chosen,
religion will be discussed last, but that does not mean that we
are eliminating religion from our investigating activity right
now. On the contrary, it is religion that defines our very being
and also distinguishes a Christian's knowing from that of nonchristian thinkers. So much relies on the word-revelation of
God, accepted by faith as a faithful witness: our conception concerning the origin and extent of creation; our expectation, always
attuned to new surprises, with which we do our investigating;
and the definition of the fields we can explore and of our point
of orientation that dominates the entire route. We also owe to
the word of God the insight that what we here examine first is
not the fullness of concrete everyday life. The same holds with
respect to everything else that is not discussed right away: it is
tabled because it is simply impossible to deal with everything at
once.

2. THE STRUCTURE OF THINGS AND PEOPLE

Say we were studying what all is implied in being a bachelor. Trying to say everything at once about remaining single for
the rest of your life is one thing, but it's another to get stuck simply repeating generalities such as "All bachelors are unmarried
men." In fact, once we learn that "bachelor" *means* "unmarried
man," to say so is to state a "tautology," to repeat the obvious, to
claim nothing new. If our knowledge and understanding of
what it means to be a bachelor is going to grow, we will proba-

bly want to know more, some specifics, to discover other similarities or differences among bachelors. For example, we might
investigate whether bachelors live active or secluded lives, or
study how their golden years compare to men who married.
Knowing what marks bachelors off from others is only the
beginning.

Something similar is true of the earth. Christians know that
there exists nothing more than Creator and creature, that all
creatures are subject to God and his law, and that his creatures
are either heavenly creatures or earthly creatures. That almost
everything around us, whatever it is, whether great or small,
acknowledged or not, is subject to God in an earthly way is obvious (to the Christian). Atoms, bachelors, criminals, and
dromedaries are all earthly creatures and, obedient or not, are
subject to the Creator in an earthly way. And the list could go on
and on, right down to xebecs, yams, and Zoroastrians. But however true, however biblical, however trustworthy might be the
knowledge that everything we can investigate is subject to God
in an earthly way, we should be able to say more than that, to
articulate various ways and means that these creatures can avail
themselves of being God's subjects.

In this and the following section we hope to do just that:
given the fact that what we have to investigate is subject to God
in an earthly manner, what are some of the specifics? Can we
open this up? In what ways is this true? How does saying so
help us to grow in the knowledge and understanding of the
earth—our home—and the calling and tasks that God gives us
here? We will look first at the diversity, dimensions, and inter-
relatedness of individual things and then move on to integrate
the reality that, after the original beginning, every thing comes
from some thing else.

Two Most Simple Determinants and Their Basic Relations

Two of the most simple determinants of "that which is subject to God in an earthly way" are found in and among things,
namely, modal differences and the this-that difference. The
order in which we deal with these two kinds of diversity is
immaterial since they never *occur* separately. The one we will
come to call "functions" and the other "functors" in a way that
parallels "actions" and "actors." As actions require actors, and

there are no actors minus actions, so also "functions" require "functors," and there are no functors minus functions. Though the one never occurs without the other, they can be discussed separately. That is what we will do first. Later we will deal with their combined occurrence.

The First (Modal) Determinant and its Diversity
When a person uses the word "social," he is referring to something that is earthly (created). Being social does not exclude being earthly created, but simply presupposes it. Being social is one way (or mode) of being an earthly creature. Being social is one way in which some earthly creatures are. It's a matter of being-earthly-created in a determinate or specific way. If every earthly creature were social it would be impossible to speak of a diversity in the determination of being-earthly-subject. Then "being social" would mean the same thing as "being created," which it does not.

Not all earthly creation is social in character. Other modes of being-earthly occur besides this one. What this means can be illustrated by examining any ordinary event. Let's use the following newspaper report. It is an illustration in revised format borrowed from L. Kalsbeek's *Contours of a Christian Philosophy.*

> Last night an arsonist torched two local farms. Only a few of the cattle in the barns were saved. Fire fighters were hampered by the farms' distance from the rural water main and the fact that the water in the sand pit between the two farms was frozen over. The homeless families were taken in by their neighbors. The damage to both farms was covered by insurance. (36-7)

When we look a bit more closely, various facets of this event become apparent. Some are obvious, others might take a trained eye. The fire marshall's arrival on the scene tells the onlookers that the officials suspect arson; their immediate indignation suggests the *trothic* aspect of this event: "You can't trust anyone nowadays!" The expressions of kindness by the neighbors in providing shelter, clothing, and comfort for the victims also point to the trothic dimension. The *jural* side is present too. State law dictates that arsonists be prosecuted. So also other legislation sets strict standards affecting the payment of fire insurance and the efforts of relief agencies.

Despite the human misery, there is a certain *aesthetic* dimension to the sight of flames blazing up high against the dark evening sky. The firefighters and neighbors fighting the fire together suggests the *social* side of the event. The losses may be covered by insurance or absorbed by the farmer and his family; in any case, the *economic* aspect becomes evident when the sun rises on the charred remains of the family home. The conversation of the onlookers and the gestures of the firefighters on the ladders suggest a *semantic* aspect. The farmer himself becomes more aware of this aspect when he attempts to settle his insurance claim and must make sense out of the legal jargon of his policy statement. Likewise, the journalist's shorthand notes, his taped interviews, and his final copy for the newspaper involve meaningful symbols to describe real human events.

When we realize that there is no running water on the farm, that the farm house was built around the turn of the century with few fire retardant materials, and that the firefighters will have to depend for water on the latest tank-truck technology, we begin to sense the *formative* aspect of the situation. The threat of the fire's spreading to the nearby garage and toolshed points to the *spatial* aspect of the event. As the newspaper account points out, two farms were involved in the fire; this event affects a certain number of people, both those living in the house and those on the fire crew. The morning after, the count of the dead animals and the calculations of damages further highlight the *numeric* or arithmetic aspect.

The ice that hinders the hosemen in their work, the billowing smoke, and the hiss of the water as it strikes the flames point to the physical or *energetic* aspect. The ivy covering the walls of the farmhouse did characterize the *organic* or biotic aspect, until it died because of the intense heat of the fire. Its death, however, is totally devoid of emotion or grief, whereas the cows low in pain and panic at the threat to their lives, indicating a *psychic* aspect to their experience. Because they cannot make analytic distinctions, it does not occur to the trapped animals to loosen the ropes that bind them. The farmer and the firefighters who try to save the houses and their contents are able to do their work only because they do possess this capacity. Their carefully planned efforts and the fact that the authorities can sit down the next morning to reconstruct the entire event show us that the fire also has an *analytic* aspect.

But there is also the dimension of faith present. We will call it the *pistic* aspect (from the Greek word for faith). One of the farmers who has suffered this blow is a Christian. Precisely because he is a farmer, dependent upon uncertainties of weather, fluctuating markets, and the like, he has learned to experience the comfort of Christ's words that "not one of these sparrows will fall to the ground without your Father." Perhaps another sees the event as the result of chance or bad luck. Furthermore, each person at the scene, whether victim, neighbor, or firefighters, discovers some kind of meaning—or its absence—in the event.

The various aspects of this event were mentioned in a rather haphazard fashion. They can also be listed in a specific order that will be explained in a few pages. In this regard, we distinguish the following irreducible modal aspects (listing them "from top to bottom," or as we will see below, in their order of decreasing complexity). (Unless noted otherwise, quotations are from Henk Hart's *Understanding Our World*.)

PISTIC The pistic dimension of earthly creation, and human creatures in particular, has to do with certitudinal belief and faith life. Key here is "our acceptance of or surrender to a trusting relation to something, its truth, its reliability, its certainty" (182). Certitudinal belief (faith) relates reality to its ultimate foundation but is not the same as religion, which is "the ultimate basis for all our actions as it determines our priorities and shapes our fundamental loyalties" (183). So also, belief (faith) is not identical with faith in Christ. All people believe. All are guided by and committed to their ultimate beliefs about things. But not everyone believes *in* Jesus Christ. (Faith *in* progress, *in* Karl Marx, *in* science, *in* economic growth, *in* the rights of the individual, *in* the autonomy of human reason, *in*... whatever people have religiously surrendered and subjected their lives to, you name it: all of these (un)beliefs, alone and together, have also shaped the course of history.)

TROTHIC The trothic facet of earthly creation has to do with bonds of fidelity, loyalty, and faithfulness in friendship, marriage, family, and even in husbandry. "Keeping troth is standing in permanent relations of trust, keeping one's promise" (191).

JURAL   The jural or juridical mode of being is characterized by the call to justice and covers the domain of the legal code, public justice, and retribution.

ECONOMIC   The economic is the domain of value-weighing thrift and of frugality in managing scarce goods: a wealth of possibilites, only a few of which we can realize. In today's world the "optimal use of resources, talents, and the fruit of our labor (raw materials, services, and goods) requires a network of relationships providing for the exchange and distribution and optimal use of these fruits, talents, and resources such that excess and waste and exhaustion are avoided." But from the beginning, all "human beings have an economic task insofar as all of them must responsibly manage their own affairs" (192).

SOCIAL   "'*Intercourse*' is the word that best characterizes this mode of functioning, even though this word has been strongly reduced in meaning by many people." "Social" has reference to community and interhuman, collective action. "A social relationship is a specific kind or mode of functional interrelation. It is intended to convey the consciously practiced development of relationships between people in which the fostering of relationships is an 'end in itself,' as it were" (193). Hospitality and etiquette are also examples of social phenomena. "Social stratification, the neighborhood social center, the club, the reception to meet people, the church picnic, the fellowship hour, and many more phenomena point to the irreducible specificity of this mode of functioning" (194).

ANALYTIC   The analytic dimension has to do with "the irreducible modal nature of those functions which are typically found in analyzing, thinking, conceptualizing, arguing, reasoning, inferring" (194). Key here is the human ability to distinguish differences in their context and the distinguishability of other things. While it may be that the "university is the organized community of people professionally busy with analysis in a predominantly occupational way," every healthy human being is busy analytically every day.

SEMANTIC By "semantic" we understand everything that is language, not only the spoken but also the unspoken part of it. Language conveys information and is the carrier of conceptual meaning. "Almost all words are conceptual vehicles or names for concepts. They are grammatically related in the way in which we find the structure of reality relating to the concepts themselves" (195).

AESTHETIC The aesthetic mode is the field of humor, play, imaginativity, and nuance. The aesthetic aspect of things is not always its beauty, but some things are especially suggestion-rich and laden with hints. "Aesthetic life," writes Seerveld somewhere, "is as integral to being human as building sandcastles at the beach and giving your children names."

FORMATIVE The "formative" has to do with making, crafting, creating, forming, building, producing things; it is "the functional area of tools, instruments, skills, methods, and techniques" (195). We recognize this kind of activity "in our methodically controlled relations with our environment, that is, the instrumental and purposive relationships between conscious creatures, the design of action, the moment of choice and decision, and the means-end relationship" (176). Making is present in almost all human activity and some animals do *make* nests, but plants, in this sense, do not make sugar.

PSYCHIC By "psychic" we understand the mode of behavior, in animals and humans, that is primarily a sensitive (feeling, emotional) kind, including drives, instinct, stimulus-response, and perception.

ORGANIC By the organic or biotic aspect we understand primarily dynamic functions such as growth, reproduction, metabolism, restoration, birth, genesis, and maturation; all require the "interdependent integration of all functions of the entity such that they become parts of a coherent and singular whole which functions to generate growth, that is, which continually generates and regenerates all of its parts for its own continued development and existence" (196).

ENERGETIC This aspect of earthly creation is familiar to us in the phenomena of mass, force, matter, atomic and molecular structure, energy levels, and the like.

KINEMATIC This mode has to do with movement. It is a dimension we can get at in terms of what we call "inertia": the tendency of matter to remain at rest, or, if moving, to keep moving in the same direction, unless affected by some outside force.

SPATIAL With reference to the spatial dimension of earthly creation, the following observations are in order: (a) The spatial is not a form of intuition (Kant), but a property of all things—continuous extension. (b) The spatial does not, as we might suppose on the basis of tradition, have a Euclidian (3D) structure: Euclidian space is one way of conceiving the spatial dimension of earthly creatures—one that most closely approximates the manner in which we sense the spatial mode of the things around us.

NUMERIC The numeric aspect is the domain of magnitude and discrete quantity. In other words, that of more and less.

There is obviously a rich diversity to this modal dimension, perhaps even greater than we have seen so far.

For the sake of brevity we call the diversity discussed above "modal diversity"; it is a diversity that includes many "modal differences," which when arranged in a systematic order can be referred to as the "modal scale." As we will see below, problems arise when one or more of these irreducible differences are absolutized or eradicated.

These matters are admittedly somewhat abstract. And so another example is in order lest some lose heart that all of the above has little to do with the everyday reality of earthly creation. Once again leaning heavily on Kalsbeek (38-39), let us take a look at an ordinary hybrid tulip blooming in your garden. You hold a single tulip in your hand and immediately discover its numeric aspect without even having to count; but should you wish to examine the flower more closely, you will discover a number of leaves on the stem, of petals on the flower, or of stamens within it.

If you planted your tulip bulbs too close together last fall, you now realize that each needs a certain amount of room in order to grow well. Of course, already when planting them next to each other, you noticed their spatial character.

And the fact that your bulbs "stayed put" when you spread them out on the ground before you planted them has to do with the kinematic aspect of your tulips.

Your basic knowledge of botany tells you that your plant feeds and breathes. These processes are at bottom phenomena rooted in the exchange and flow of energy.

The slow death of the flower in the garden or its rapid demise in your living room displays the organic phenomena of biotic life.

You can see the flower and touch it. (Note, however, that while you can see it, it cannot see you or anything else for that matter; while you can touch it, it cannot feel.) This is only possible because of its psychic aspect.

If you are interested enough to do a little research, you can discover the formative aspect of your tulip in the lengthy cultivation of this hybrid from its ancestor, the wild tulip.

Some claim that beauty is in the eye of the beholder, but even if you find some tulips ugly, what all beholders are struck by, whether it is the tulips' graceful line or homely color, is the aesthetic aspect of those flowers.

Furthermore, because of their semantic aspect, you can talk about your tulips—they are name-able—whether you are Dutch or not.

Again, the tulip can be analyzed; it exits for us in an analyze-able way in the analytic mode.

And assuming you are like most people, you have planted your tulips where people can see and take note of them. That has to do with the social aspect of those tulips—even though it's never crossed your tulips' minds to socialize themselves!

Although the people who raise bulbs with an eye to selling them are more conscious of a tulip bulb's economic aspect than you are, you will remember that aspect soon enough when you go to buy some more bulbs next time.

The jural aspect of your tulips comes to the fore in that they are yours now. You can decide their fate and may call for legal protection against people who steal or damage your tulips.

Being yours, they "demand" (but do not always receive) the tender loving care that a faithful gardener will give them without a moan (in days gone by, referred to as the task of "husbandry"). This is the dimension of troth!

And even though the dirt under your nails and the pulled muscle in your back provide proof that a great deal of human intervention has gone into your tulips' growth and being-there in your garden, you still see them, in faith, as the creation of God (while your neighbor considers them a refined product of an evolutionary process).

As we proceed the significance of modal diversity will grow. But we can state now already that since it does not make sense to speak of "being-subject" without accepting a law that holds for that which is subject, we can also say that there is a determinant (or further specification) of God's law that corresponds to each determinant of being-earthly-subject. Therefore, if it makes sense to speak of "being-subject to God in a social way," then it makes just as much sense to speak of a God-given law that holds for the social dimension of creation. The same holds for each mode of earthly being.

In other words, we can say that a diversity in law determination is parallel to the diversity in the determination of "being-earthly-subject." Consequently, a numeric law holds for that which is numeric, a spatial law for that which is spatial, a social law (a norm actually) holds for that which is social, and so forth. Each of these laws holds from the foundations of the world, for they were dictated by the Creator. These laws for earthly creatures together contribute to the structure of earthly creation. But there is more.

The Second (This-That) Determinant and its Diversity

To say "this number" is to say something other than simply "number." And in this case, too, the difference in words corresponds to a difference in what they denote. Let's take a closer look at this difference.

We can take the words "this number" to refer, for example, to the number *three*. The number three is a number. And being a number it is something subject to the numeric law. But we do not find this property only in the case of everything that is number or numeric. The point here is that the determinant denoted by the word "this" does not conflict with the similarity between the number three and all other numbers. Neither does it do away with this modal similarity: it presupposes it. *This* is simply an other, a different, determinant.

This determinant—the *this-that difference*—is a second, analytically irreducible determinant. It is a different kind of difference. In other words, the this-that difference is different from, and cannot be reduced to, the modal difference.

In order to check this out, we could ask the question whether the this-determinant might not possibly be one more modal difference, which could then be added to the modal diversity elaborated above. For example, we can ask, "Is the difference between *number* and *this* similar to the modal difference between, for example, the numeric and spatial aspect?" To ask the question is to answer it "No," for it is plain that that which causes the number to be "the number three" is something other than another modal dimension.

But how about this question: Is the determinant "this" possibly a further specification of the numeric mode? This, too, is not the case. To support this negation it is sufficient to place the term "this number" and the term "rational number" side by side. A rational number is a number that can be expressed as an integer (e.g., 2, 3, 4, etc.) or as a quotient of integers (e.g., 1/4). Irrational numbers cannot be so expressed (e.g., π). In the case of "rational number," we further specify numbers as numeric; however, though there are many rational numbers, there is only one number three. Consequently, the determinant being-this does not further specify the numeracy of three, but is a determination that retains its significance even when all further specifications of its numeracy have been added up.

Needless to say, the this-that difference—we will also call it the difference of individuality—is difficult to circumscribe or pin down in a definition. But that, of course, is the point: the this-that difference is different from any other difference and therefore hardly can be defined in terms of something else.

If no other number existed besides three, then it would be impossible to speak of diversity in the this-determination of numbers. But obviously there are many many more numbers than three. So while we can distinguish only fifteen irreducible modal differences in earthly creation, the diversity in this-determination is infinitely larger. There are certainly many more individually different this's and that's than there are numbers.

The this-that difference does not only occur in the case of the numeric law sphere—it occurs in all law spheres: one stone is not the other, and a distinction can be made between this falling apple and that falling apple, between this and that analytic activity, between this marriage and that marriage.

One final point before moving on. Given "this number (three)" and "that number (four)," or "this tulip" and "that tulip," we can see that in the this-that difference it is possible that *this* and *that* are alike in that the same law holds for both. Following through, we can say that all the this's and that's for which the same law holds together constitute the *domain* or the sphere of this law; they are its *law sphere*. Since there are many laws, in the sense of divine ordinances, there are therefore many law spheres.

Mutual Irreducibility and Combined Occurrence

We have seen above that the this-that difference (the individuality of things) is different and distinct from the modal difference (the how of things). In that connection, we say that these two differences are mutually irreducible. You cannot reduce the one to the other, or vice versa.

Using vertical and horizontal lines, we can diagram these two mutually irreducible differences as follows. If we picture the difference between a this and a that as vertical lines, then the difference between one modal aspect and another can be pictured most adequately by means of horizontal lines.

a. The diagram for the difference of this and that: ‖   ‖

b. The diagram for modal differences: ────────

Being-individual and being-modal are different from one another. That is why they had to be dealt with and named separately. But their being-different does not involve being-separate. In fact, neither of these determinants occurs alone. For example, a specific number is both numeric (modally different from space, for example) and also this number (something that is individually other than every other number).

Therefore, the diagram for this occur-   ──────╫──────
rence in combination becomes the following:

But we can say more. Every stone is subject to God's law for the numeric, spatial, kinematic, and energetic modes. In the case of a plant, besides the four subject modes just mentioned, we distinguish an organic mode. In the case of an animal, besides the five that we came across in the plant, also the psychic, and in higher vertebrates also some formative functions. Besides these seven we have mentioned, a human being possesses all the others that were distinguished above.

And yet, what we have said so far is still incomplete. For in all these cases, the modal aspects that are not mentioned with the stone, plant, and animal are nevertheless present, but in a different sense. I hope to return to this point later (remember: you could sense/feel your tulip—it was sense-able—even though it could not sense/feel you). Be that as it may, the examples mentioned above are sufficient evidence of the fact that in any individual there exists together different modes of being.

The diagram for this more complicated combination is shown here:

Taking account of what has just been said, such an individual this, whatever it be, in its diverse ways of being an earthly subject, is of "one piece" and can properly be called an individual subject-unit or *functor*. Atoms, organisms, animals, and humans are all examples of functors, acting entities that are relatively complete and independent units.

These functors or "things" are much more involved or complex than we have discerned up to this point. Included in that "much more" is *time*, at least insofar as it is modal and therefore can already be discussed at this point.

I have not discussed time up until now, because only now is it possible to suggest that time is neither an individual nor a modal difference. Nevertheless, we do find time in all the modes of every functor's being. Time comes to expression in each mode in a different way: everyone is familiar with kinematic "clock" time, but time is also in the energetic as half-life, in the organic as development, in the psychic as tension, in the formative as period, in the aesthetic as aesthetic duration, in the semantic as adverbs of time and the tense of verbs, in the analytic as first the premises and then the conclusion, in the social in the giving of priority (for example, "ladies first"), in the economic in the giving and receiving of interest, in the jural as length of validity (think of the retroactive force of a positive law), in the trothic in the choice of the "right" time (to tell her you love her), in the pistic in the alternation of liturgically festive and ordinary times.

It becomes evident, now that we are also taking time into account, that we have so far conceived the different modalities of an individual functor as though they were timeless. We can now dispense with this abstraction. The modalities of an individual functor never exist outside of time. Now it is possible to introduce a shorter term for this being-subject of the individual functor to laws of differing modality. That term is "the *functioning* of the functor." Consequently, we can say concisely: a functor has more than one function.

The functions of any one functor differ from each other, of course, modally. As we proceed we will also want to distinguish between those modes of being that a functor must necessarily, and therefore always does, exhibit—these we will call *subject functions*—and those modes of being that are creational possibilities that need to be opened up by other more complicated functors—these we call *object functions*. If we take our tulips as a case in point, then their numeric, spatial, kinematic, energetic, and organic modes of being are subject functions. You simply will not find a tulip that does not function in these ways. That tulips can be felt or raised or can be analyzed or sold and bought or worshipped, etc., are examples of their functioning as objects. They are felt but cannot feel; they are raised and sold but cannot do likewise. Nor do they have to be felt or raised or be bought in order to be what they are. And yet all of these possibilities have been laid within the creature. Human beings can see the colors of a tulip and make tulip hybrids only because God has placed these psychic and formative object functions within creation. They are there already, waiting to be discovered!

Connections Between Individually Different Entities

Individually different things are always connected in some way to other individually different things. Likewise, a dandelion or the wind, a pet or my neighbor, is never known disconnectedly as a completely separate, singular entity. We can begin with the simplest case, namely, where two individually differing entities are similar in their modal functions and therefore subjected to the same laws. Yet, similarity is not the same as connection. I might have been born on the same day as Prince Charles, but that does not mean that there is any connection between him and me. Nevertheless, such connections do exist.

Examples of inter-individual connections are not hard to come by. In the numeric law sphere the numbers three and four stand in a certain relationship to one another. Spatially, two circles can intersect. In the kinematic law sphere the one force can be changed into another. Two dissimilar organisms can live together closely linked with each other (symbiosis). My dog's emotional state can put my nerves on edge. Lego pieces don't build themselves; they are usually put together according to an imagined plan, something a child can do even without knowing the word "Lego." In the analytic domain, two propositions can stand in the relationship of premise to conclusion. All of these illustrate "connections."

So far, we have talked only about "connection" in general. We now need a term that denotes specifically the-connection-between-that-which-differs-individually. In other words, there are also connections between the social and economic aspects of a society or the bio-chemical dimensions of one's health. These would be inter-modal connections, which we will come to straightaway. For the-connection-between-that-which-differs-individually we will use the term "interrelation."

We can say that different numbers stand in a certain relationship to one another. But we cannot say that numbers do or do not intersect, that they are or are not of equal force, that one number is cause and the other effect, or that numbers live in symbiosis with each other. For numbers are something other than lines or forms of energy; they are different from billiard balls and organisms. The interrelation between two or more numbers therefore turns out to be different in kind from the connection between that which differs individually in the non-arithmetic law spheres. The interrelation between worms and roots, between vinegar and your tongue, between a tune and your skipping is simply different in kind from the numeric connectedness of two or more numbers. In other words, the modality of an interrelation is the same as the law sphere in which the interrelation occurs. Terms such as "intersecting," or "being of equal force," are therefore more specific and concrete than the generic wording "interrelation."

A thing is more than its relationships to other things. In other words, a functor is not taken up in its interrelations. At the same time, a functor without interrelations does not exist. Because the emphasis falls in this way on the interrelations in which a thing stands, we will want to further investigate the notion of "interrelation."

One point is the following. Up until now we only spoke of "the" interrelation between two things, let's say between the relatum X and the relatum Y. That, however, is an abstraction; it leaves something out. Actually, there are *two* interrelations between the relata X and Y, namely, the interrelation of X to Y and the interrelation of Y to X. For example, the relationship of the circumference of a circle to its radius $= 2\pi$, that of the radius to the circumference $= 1/2\ \pi$; likewise, the route from Chicago to Paris is an other than that from Paris to Chicago (try it some time!). So also the interrelation (A) between mother and daughter is different from the interrelation (B) between daughter and mother. It is already evident from these few examples that both interrelations are not equal but differ according to the direction of the relation. What is it that determines direction in this context? Direction is determined by the answer to the question, "Which one of the relata is the starting point for the relation? Which of the relata has priority?" The same holds for the interrelation between a previous and a following moment, between yesterday and today; or between buyer and seller, speaker and listener, warden and prisoner, professor and student.

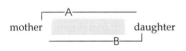

With direction present in every interrelation, two words of caution. Both have to do with *irreversibility*. First of all, when the relata remain the same, the one direction cannot be replaced by the other. In the illustration above, the "mothership" interrelation A cannot be replaced by the "daughtership" interrelation B; a mother cannot become the daughter of her daughter. Second, when the direction remains the same, the relata are not interchangeable. If mother and daughter would "change places," then we would have the disorderly situation of parents submitting to the authority of their children.

So connections between things are not always so simple. There are, however, always at least two sides, two interrelations, to a relationship. And these relationships are of a different kind. There are always at least two stories to be told in the broken trothic relationship we call divorce. There has to be a give and take to talking, but then also a take and give to our being social. When buyers are looking at high prices or sellers face a flooded market, economic connections stagnate. A parent needs the child (without a child you are not a parent) and the child needs the parent; not necessarily in the same way, and yet both sides, both needs, are primarily trothic in kind, not organic or semantic or social or jural.

The Connection Between Subject Functions

The fact that two entities are part of a single law sphere was not enough to establish the existence of a connection between them. Similarly, in the case of modes of being, we miss the grounds we need for using the term "connection" if we simply refer to the fact that some subject functions often occur together.

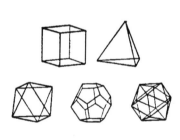 Talk of socio-economic forces, bio-physical factors, and psycho-somatic imbalances may be common enough, but are these pairs randomly lumped together or really connected? It is one thing to observe that a plant is subject to laws holding for the numeric, spatial, kinematic, energetic, and organic modes, but it is another thing if I am able to answer the questions, "Is the organic-being of a plant *connected* with its energetic aspect, or is the spatial-being of the plant *connected* with its property of being-numeric? And, if so, what evidence is there of a connection between these subject functions?"

When we attempt to answer these questions, it appears that there is something presupposed, namely, a natural order of subject functions. Let's begin by examining whether any order exists between the numeric and the spatial modes and, if so, what that order is. A polyhedron, a solid figure with several plane surfaces, for example, is subject both to spatial and to numeric laws. It both takes up space and its sides can be counted. But at the same time, there is more here than a "both-and" relationship. The fact is that spatial properties presuppose numeric ones, but not vice versa. For it is possible to express the magnitude of a line with the help of numbers, but not possible to distinguish the relationship of numbers by only using the relationship between radius and circumference. Therefore, when calculating the length of a line, interrelations between numbers are helpful, but interrelations between lines are of little use when working with numbers. That is one reason why students first learn to master arithmetic and then move on to geometry.

That the spatial aspect presupposes the numeric indicates a certain (irreversible) order between these two least complex modes of being. There is number everywhere where there are lines. But space need not be a factor when speaking exclusively about numbers. Therefore, numbers are presupposed in the case of lines, but lines are not presupposed in the case of numbers. In the order of the subject functions—those modes of being that a functor must display in order to be what it is—we say that the numeric *precedes* the spatial.

Similarly, every movement presupposes spatiality; energy is never present without movement; and every organic activity presupposes the conversion of energy. Moving on up the modal scale: a psychic state presupposes organic life. Formative activity is only found among sentient creatures; design requires awareness. And it is only when you have mastered the skills and technique in-line skates require that you can get them out really just for the aesthetic fun of it. Language, whether it comes to expression or not, presupposes formative, symbolic activity; it presupposes, for example, that we with others form symbols to refer to other things. Without words and propositions to lay down what we have grasped, no human thought would be possible. Social intercourse presupposes language, discourse, and inferring. Conversely, a line's being tangential to another does not presuppose conversion of energy: I can no more explain a tangential line in terms of motion than I can explain the relationship of numbers in terms of lines.

For the sake of brevity I have only indicated that every function presupposes that which is just under it. Actually, a higher, more complex function rests upon *all* the other lower functions. Organic health gives psychic life stability in the clutch, and good psychic integration will certainly strengthen analytic development. So, too, a measure of technical competence is prerequisite for all forms of art, language, science, and societal leadership. That the more complex modes presuppose the less complex ones becomes evident, for example, when there is something wrong in those lower functions. Then the higher functions do not function well either. An inflamed appendix can easily affect the more complex modes of my being human, and certain kinds of brain damage can disturb emotions, undo learned skills, surpress creativity, and close down thinking processes. If psychic life is disturbed, it quickly shows up in malfunctioning social intercourse. So also, mental illness, understanding the world poorly, economic instability, or living unjustly are singularly or together going to have impact upon family and confessional life.

Thus, there appears to be a natural order of subject functions in which the more complicated always presuppose the less complicated, but in which the lower, less complex mode of being does not presuppose the occurrence of the higher functions. More specifically, the subject functions occur in the order in which they were given on pages 207-210. Moreover, on the basis of this "being-presupposed," it is also clear why we will repeatedly list the numeric mode of earthly being on the "bottom." It is the least complex.

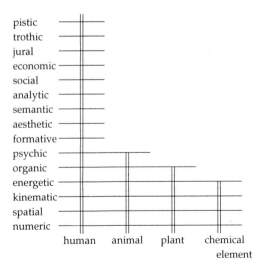

pistic
trothic
jural
economic
social
analytic
semantic
aesthetic
formative
psychic
organic
energetic
kinematic
spatial
numeric

human   animal   plant   chemical
                          element

We are, of course, talking here about connections between subject functions and these are always functions of functors. The basic differences between kinds of functors can be represented by the different lengths of the vertical lines in the diagram on page 221.

Not every individual this is a functor. We are using the term "functor" to denote an individual this that possesses four or more subject functions. Hence, numbers, circles, causes, and electrical charges are not functors; neither are my fingers or my ears. Functors are relatively complete and independent unities that always have at least four subject functions. These subject functions, however, are not like layers of a birthday cake or a sheet of plywood. We have already made the point that the "higher" ones presuppose the "lower" ones, but much more can be said about their connection. When we look more closely we see that they are intricately interwoven.

Now I must admit that the contents of my fishing tacklebox are both intricate and interwoven. You go for one lure and inevitably half of the mess comes along with it. But that is not what is meant by intricately interwoven. A better analogy here would be a piece of homespun fabric: its warp and woof of quantity, extension, forces, energy, growth, sensibility, formativity, style, significance, conceptualing, use, and still more totally enmesh its threads.

Most healthy people experience this cohering web of human functionality at least once in a while. We know that *power* is not only in fist action, but reverberates within a person's desires and speech and loyalty. Feelings are not thinkings, and yet there is often if not always emotional content inside thought, and there is a creational pressure to have emotions be thoughtful. There are semblances of vitality to be found in activity beyond one's muscles, for example, in our conversation, occupational routines, or family life. To articulate the nature and intricacy of the interwoven fabric of earthly creatures functioning every day is not easy and requires a good deal of patient analysis. As long as we are not inclined to substitute our theorizing about this fabric for the fabric itself, however, a deeper understanding of these connections between functions does hold the promise of better equipping us to restore a coherence to life when that has been broken.

Further evidence of the interwoven connection between a functor's subject functions is found in the *analogy* of one function within other functions. Analogies "spin" one of two ways. A subject function can bear a striking resemblance (= analogy) to a less complex subject function, if it has one, but also to a more complex mode, if such are present. Analogies within one subject function that "refer back" to lower functions we are going to call *retrocipations*.

Examples of this connection—that does not occur in the numeric because it is the least complex of the modes—can be found everywhere in the cosmos. For example, the "dimensions" we refer to with "3-D" are definitely spatial in character. Nevertheless, space here refers back, because of the multiplicity of dimensions, to number. Actually, all the functions above the numeric retrocipate on the numeric. Every nonarithmetic mode possesses a multiplicity that is inherent to that nonarithmetic mode—a multiplicity of dimensions, of forces, of elements, of organs, of sensations. And those multiplicities are, respectively, spatial, kinematic, energetic, organic, and psychic in character, but still refer back to the numeric aspect. The same is true for all subject functions above the spatial: they retrocipate on the spatial. Supra-spatial functioning, whether it is kinematic, energetic, social, or jural, traverses a course on the basis of which it is possible to describe this occurrence, as far as this analogy is concerned, in a curve—"see," for example, the tone of a b-flat trumpet. Furthermore, all the functions above the kinematic indirectly refer back to the kinematic. They all bear a dynamic character, for example: electromagnetism in the energetic, growth in the organic, emotion in the psychic, the rhythm of music and poetry. Further examples of retrocipation are the development found in modal functions more complex than the organic; the "feel" of things in supra-psychic modes; the role played by the means-ends framework in the supra-forma-tive; the imagina-tivity and flair in functions more complex than the aesthetic; the langu-age of the sciences, of social interaction, of commerce in the supra-semantic; the nonscientific conceptual element of both thinking and knowing in every mode of being above the analytic; commerce in the suprasocial; the thrift principle in the supra-economic; the harmonization of interests in the supra-jural; and the assurance of belief in the pistic. In each case, higher, more complex modes of being exhibit moments that are analogous to the characteristics of less complex modes and yet obviously belong to the more complex function.

The higher a subject function is situated in the order of functions, the more retrocipations it possesses. Whereas the spatial has only one retrocipation, we find no fewer than fourteen retrocipations in the pistic. It is noteworthy that of the retrocipations in the pistic aspect, two have been prominent in history: the retrocipation to the analytic (belief) and to the trothic (commitment) have received special attention. However, these two are not the only retrocipations. Other examples are justification(jural), sacrifice(economic), fellowship(social), regeneration(organic), and integration(energetic). These and other retrocipations are traits present in all faith-life—christian or not.

Since a function's retrocipations always are inherent to it, we indirectly can include all of a functor's functions simply by referring to that functor's highest subject function. Thus a river is an energetic functor. A plant is an organic one. Animals, likewise, are psychic functors, although some of the higher vertebrates are formative functors. And, for the time being, given the totality of human functions, he can be called a pistic functor. This highest subject function, the one that characterizes a functor, also can be called its *leading function*.

Moving on then, the connection between subject functions is seen not only in functions referring back to less complex aspects. Less complex subject functions also refer forward —"reach" ahead, so to speak—to that functor's more complex subject functions. We call these analogies within a subject function *anticipations*.

Everyone, for example, in going through the series of positive whole numbers for the first time, will mention only rational-natural numbers and count: one, two, three, four, and on. But by only mentioning "natural numbers" they fail to take into account the connection of these numbers to more complex functions. However, if they take the retrocipation of space to number seriously, they will discover by way of this detour that the enumeration "one, two, three..." is far from complete. For instance, the length of every line can be divided in all kinds of ways into a number of parts, including the length of the hypotenuse of an isosceles right-angled triangle. If the lengths of the equal sides of the triangle are one, then the length of the hypotenuse is $\sqrt{2}$. The $\sqrt{2}$ is a number as well; even though it is an "irrational" number, it fits into the series of positive numbers without any difficulty. The same holds for $\sqrt{3}$, as well as all the rest of the irrational numbers. The numeric, as the domain of discrete quantity, refers forward in the irrational numbers to the continuity of space. If we take this into consideration, then we no longer count 1, 2, 3, 4, but $1(=\sqrt{1})$, $\sqrt{2}$, $\sqrt{3}$, $2(=\sqrt{4})$, $\sqrt{5}$, $\sqrt{6}$, $\sqrt{7}$, $\sqrt{8}$, $3(=\sqrt{9})$. It is this forward reference of a function to more complex subject functions that may be designated with the term "anticipation."

Anticipation occurs, of course, only where there are more complex subject functions present. The organic subject functioning of a plant, then, does not include any anticipations because the organic is a plant's highest subject function. It is what we called its leading function. So too, the pistic functioning of human beings anticipates no other function.

Within this framework we discover a rich diversity of anticipations. The numeric, for example, anticipates spatial continuity in the irrational numbers and kinematic and energetic subject functions in differential and integral numbers. So too, the spatial anticipates the kinematic: Archimedes already (287-212 B.C.) spoke of a gravitational "line" and a "center of gravity" in mathematical figures.

In the case of organisms such as plants, animals, and human beings, the energetic function anticipates higher subject functions. Water, sap, and blood are themselves energetically qualified physical fluids. The water in a stream is just that and anticipates nothing in particular. Sap in plants is also physical but more complicated than water in that its composition anticipates the organic subject function of the plant. With animals we are looking at the fluid we call blood: it too is a nonliving physical stuff, more complicated than sap, also in that it anticipates the animal's organic and psychic functioning, as with its faster circulation in anxious circumstances. Human blood is no more alive than sap or animal blood, but it anticipates even more complex subject functions: increased blood pressure when our conscience is bothering us or our blushing (the widening of blood vessels near the surface of the skin) when embarassed.

We find the same to be the case in the organic aspect. Humans and more highly developed animals possess a brain that is clearly organic in character. Brains do not occur in plants. All the same, there is a difference between animal and human beings. In animals the brain anticipates only the psycho-formative functions (feeling pain, for example, and behavioral instincts). In human beings, it also anticipates subject functions more complex than the formative—think of the significance of the brain for thinking, speaking, and investing. This difference, of course, implies that we should avoid equating human and animal brain functioning. The organic functioning of human beings and animals is similar in modality, but different because of the unity woven by the anticipations (and retrocipations) of each. Something similar is true of their psychic functioning. Human suffering (a psychic function) is different from animal suffering—not only, for example, because one's feeling for justice (that is lacking in an animal) has been offended, but partially due to the fact that the primary pain in a case of encephalitis (inflammation of the brain) differs because that inflammation, too, is not the same in humans and animals.

There are anticipations to be observed in more complex modes as well, although they are only seen in human beings. To list examples for each domain of anticipations would soon become cumbersome, so a few must suffice. Feelings and emotions are psychic in character; so too is having a feel for colors or cadence(aesthetic), perceiving the identity of things(analytic) in their continuity, a sense of justice(jural), or feeling insecure when we are unable to surrender in faith(pistic). These are human psychic functions that anticipate the modes indicated. The semantic anticipates the economic in the norm that requires not too few and not too many words, just as analytic functioning anticipates in the economy of thought the economic function (avoiding superfluous argumentation). So too the analytic process of verification anticipates, but never achieves, pistic certainty. Jural functioning anticipates the trothic in the consideration of extenuating circumstances in the making of a verdict and anticipates certitude when we act in good faith.

The highest subject function of a functor possesses only retrocipations and the lowest possesses only anticipations. A functor's other subject functions have both. Patient attention to these details will contribute to deeper insight into the unity of functors.

The character or modality of the subject function does remain the same in retrocipation and anticipation. Length remains spatial, that is, it is only subjected to the law for that which is spatial; a gesture remains organic, that is to say, it is only subjected to the law for that which is organic. The joy of faith is not pistic, but psychic (emotions, feelings); and an association or union that has the advancement of its members' economic well-being as its goal (e.g., labor organizations and management associations) is not itself a business enterprise: its president is not related to the other members as employer to employees. In other words, the analogies—the analogous moments, the anticipations and retrocipations, within a subject function—are inherent to that subject function.

Subject Functions and Object Functions

Plants do not feel, but they can be felt. We defined those modes of a functor's being that are creational possibilities that need to be opened up by other more complicated functors *object functions*. We are now in a position to talk about object functions in a more systematic fashion.

Statues, sequoia, or sheep can be felt or exchanged for goods or analyzed or held as property or worshipped. In these cases they are functioning as objects. Similarly, neither coins, paper money, nor stock certificates have economic subject functions. They have just four subject functions: numeric, spatial, kinematic, and energetic. Only human beings have an economic subject function; only people are directly subject to God's norms for economic activity. Money and stock certificates are not; they are subject to these norms only indirectly, as objects, via human activity. The highest subject function (= leading function) of metal coin or paper money is the energetic, but as media of exchange they also have an economic object function. In the economic law sphere, then, we find both subjects (functors

—people—actively functioning economically) and objects (functors without economic subject functions, such as statues, sequoia, sheep, or money, that through human involvement are brought to function economically anyway). We can likewise talk here about a subject-object relationship between people buying and selling and the sheep or statues bought and sold.

Not all subject-object relations are between human and nonhuman things. A bird's nest, for example, of dead twigs, string, and mud, because it is not alive, has just four subject functions. The bird(s) that made the nest had two or three more subject functions: organic, psychic, and formative. Once made, there is a very real relationship between the bird and this instinctually (psychic object function) fashioned (formative object function) nursery (organic object function). These three are the nest's object functions. In analyzing it, however, we are also opening up its analytic object function.

So also a plant, which does not possess subject functions in the supra-organic spheres, does possess potential *object functions* in all of the other spheres. As we saw some time ago, a flower, such as our tulip, has no feelings, yet it can be felt, seen, and tasted. It is not formatively busy but in a nursery does prove to be formable. It is also aesthetically pleasing or not; can be given a meaningful/semantic name; and, though it does not think, is analyzable. It has social usefulness, for example, for highlighting the center of a college campus. And although it is not itself economically busy, for lilies of the field do not toil or spin, it does have an economic value; it can, jurally, be a possession or an exhibit in a criminal court case. It can be a symbol of troth in friendship and marriage ("Say it with flowers!") and can be a pistic object of belief or unbelief.

Take one more example. This analysis casts some light on the elements of the sacraments of baptism and holy communion. As far as their leading function is concerned, they are nothing but water or bread and wine. In other words, these things are energetic and organic functors, and not the body of the Lord as Luther believed. But they lend themselves as pistic objects to be the sign and seal of God's covenant faithfulness.

In summary, every functor possesses a possible object function in all those spheres more complex than its leading function. If we proceed from the functors rather than from the subject functions, then it is correct to say that all functors, including those that do not possess all the subject functions that occur in the cosmos, do have functions in all spheres. Conversely, every functor occurs functioning either as a subject or as an object in any given law sphere. This is sometimes called "the universality of the law sphere."

It is important to note that this reality of sphere universality, combined with that of retrocipations and anticipations, not only makes "-isms" possible, but also plausible. The various "-isms" in the course of human history arise from the absolutizing of one or more aspects, each of which cuts across all created reality. "Isms" are convincing, of course, only to the extent that they have a leg to stand on. Advocates of -isms *have* seen something; but the problem is that they take that something that is true in part—something that is relatively true—and make it into an absolute. Then all they see is that one aspect, or process, or pattern, and push all the other dimensions of reality to the side. But in so doing they level and reduce the diversity given in creation. Marx said that everything is tied to the socio-economic, vitalists say that everything that's anything is intimately related to the organic; fideists easily reduce everything that counts to the pistical. Given the universality of the law spheres, however, we can see that in principle everything earthly is related in one way or another to the socio-economic and the organic and the pistic dimensions. Only by remembering and believing that all of these creational diversities are subject to God and his law can we ever hope to keep things in proper perspective.

But, now, getting back to subject and object functions, let's take another look at the relationship of these two.

Concerning the relationship between subject functions and object functions, we can say positively that those functors with only four, five, six, or seven subject functions owe their presence as objects in the higher law spheres to the fact that another functor's higher subject functions retrocipate to these same lower subject functions. Negatively we can say that it is not possible to derive subject functions from object functions or vice versa. For example, there is nothing inherent to the physical-chemical character of gold such that we could ever conclude its significance as an object in the economic sphere. Also, a living organ(ism) can not be built up out of the physical-chemical elements that make it up. Life will never be created in a petri dish. Attempts to do this always rest on a failure to recognize the difference between subject functions and object functions. Carbon, hydrogen, and oxygen atoms all have four subject functions. They function as objects in the organic mode of being. Here too, we need to recognize the wealth of the cosmos and are bound to acknowledge each of these functions as existing next to each other.

In the human cultivation of plants and animals, subject and object belong to different functors. But that need not be the case. There are also subject-object relations in which subject and object belong to the same functor, as for example when you painstakingly remove a little sliver from your thumb.

We can try to picture the object functions in a schematic diagram. Proceeding from the diagram of functors found on page 221 we can use hyphenated lines to indicate object functions. The vertical lines group the subject and/or object functions with their less complex subject functions into kinds of functors.

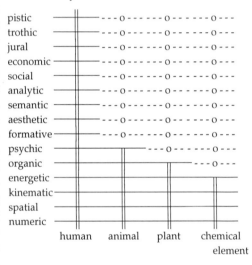

In this way, the classes of objects are indicated by the intersecting points of the horizontal and vertical lines.

Objects can be classified modally, just as retrocipations can be within a subject function. That is, they can be grouped as organic objects, sense-able objects, formable objects, imaginable objects. The number of classes within the different groups is not equal, however. The organic law sphere has only one class of objects, namely, energeticly qualified functors now functioning as objects for entities with an organic subject function. The psychic law sphere possesses two, and the aesthetic and subsequent law spheres each possess three classes of objects.

The Combined Occurrence of Both Connections

Just as modal diversity cannot be reduced to individual diversity, so the connection between modally different functions cannot be reduced to the connection between individually differing "this's." In other words, retrocipations and anticipations and opened up object functions cannot be reduced to interrelations. The opposite is also true. An interrelation between functors is a connection between two or more in the same law sphere, whereas vertical connections are connections between functions in different law spheres. In other words: interrelation is not to be reduced to vertical connection. However, here as elsewhere, irreducibility does not mean they are unconnected. On the contrary, vertical connections occur only in combination with horizontal ones.

The Divisive Difference: Good and Evil

Besides the two most simple determinants we have been discussing, namely, that of individuality and modality, a third basic determinant occurs in that which is subject to God in an earthly way. It is the difference of *good and evil.*

As in the case of that which is subject to God in a heavenly way, here too the good/evil difference is not an original determinant. That is to say, its presence in the earth is not by virtue of creation. God is not the author of evil. Nevertheless, since the Fall, this fundamental difference plays an extremely important role in the earth, especially in human existence.

We have seen above that it is impossible to reduce a modal difference to an individual difference or vice versa. The same holds with respect to the good/evil difference.

The good/evil difference is first of all a purely dual difference. When it comes right down to it, things and relations are present and functioning either obediently or disobediently. In other words, in the light of Scripture, there is no in-between when it comes to good and evil. On that score, it's like being pregnant. You can't get just a little bit or sort-of part-way pregnant. You either are or you aren't. So also with good and evil.

The character of the good/evil diversity not only is a purely dual one; it is also antithetic. Evil (wrong) stands over against good (right) as disobedience stands over against obedience.

There is a radical thorough-going opposition between good and evil—an antithesis.

We tentatively distinguished not two, but fifteen modal differences. Likewise, no one aspect stands over against another, but each is related to the others in terms of anticipations and retrocipations. In other words, the modal difference is neither dual nor antithetical. It cannot be reduced to the difference between good and evil. In like manner, the good/evil (right/ wrong) difference cannot be reduced to a modal difference. The differences between belief/unbelief (both are pistic), between being faithful/unfaithful (both are trothic), between justice/ injustice (both are jural) are not modal differences.

The same can be shown with respect to the irreducibility of the "this/that" difference and the good/evil difference. As Augustine pointed out, you may not say that the church (a this) is good and the state (a that) is bad.

But here too, irreducibility does not exclude a combined occurrence. For obedience, just like disobedience, is neither a thing nor a function. In the case of human beings it is ultimately a direction toward God or away from him in their hearts and in their functioning.

This irreducibility, then, requires that a "third dimension" be distinguished in our diagram. We can use the difference between left and right to portray the basic antithetical difference between disobedience and obedience. If we limit ourselves to drawing this difference in the case of one function, we can represent the third determinant's two directions with horizontal arrows pointing in opposite directions. In $\longleftarrow\!\!\Vert\!\!\longrightarrow$ point of fact, however, the good-evil difference is present at all functional levels of experience and most prominently in those modal aspects that are subject not to "laws of nature" God lays down, but to God's norms. In the formative, imaginative, lingual, analytic, social, economic, jural, trothic, pistical aspects of human life and society, the antithetical battle between good and evil, between obedience and disobedience, between the Kingdom of God and the powers of darkness are most evident.

On earth we meet the good-evil opposition *between* people, among people in their use and abuse of things, but even more importantly *within* people. Because good and evil, in spite of the sharp opposition between them, are both included under the direction of human life and because the difference in direction does not really originate in the functions that are determined by this difference in antithetical direction, we must look for some indication of what it is that directs these functions for good and for evil, for better or for worse. Whatever it is, it must lie before —or if you prefer, behind—all human functions.

Here, too, Scripture points the way. Think of Proverbs 4:23: "Out of the heart are the issues of life." (NIV: "guard your heart for it is the wellspring of life.") Note that the "issues of life" does not refer here to the functions as such, for then every "thing" would have a heart. The issues of life and death are two: obedience and disobedience, the two religious directions in which the functions work in human beings.

Although the structure of a human being, if we leave the heart out of the picture for the moment, corresponds as we saw to other earthly things in that it too is functional, we now understand how it can be that a human being is *more* than other things, different from other kinds of functors. What makes a human's structure different from that of other things is the heart in the sense of that which is *pre-functional*. The heart, as we know from Scripture, is the seat of religion.

Any functor is more than its functions. And yet with human beings something different is going on, a depth dimension missing with any other earthly creature. A human creature indeed is of a piece whose single existence manifests itself in all sorts of ways: a human being is so big, has such a shape, moves, has weighted mass, breathes, feels, forms, can play imaginatively, talks, thinks, socializes, saves possessions and spends them, fights, loves, prays. All these ways constitute the person's corporality. Human discourse, innuendos, and penetrating critique are all corporeal acts (and can kill as surely as rocks and bullets). They all are manifestations of the one same individual—who that individual is "at heart." It is here that people are different from penguins, poplars, and plastic. Human existence is thrusted, inwardly focusing, and intrinsically referential, in all one does and means, toward the true, or some pretended, Absolute. What defines human beings as human beings is not some little man or soul or thing inside us, but the structured thrust of the whole rooted as it is in the human heart.

These things also throw scriptural light on the relationship between soul and body. The difference between these two, at least to the extent that it can be discussed here, lies in the fact that the soul is prefunctional, while the body is functional. It follows from the above that soul and body are not related to each other as a higher group of functions and a lower group of functions, but as that which determines the direction and that which in the same person is determined in its direction. Hence the connection between them is found *within* the person—it is an intra-individual connection. Yet it is not an intra-individual connection between functions or between "parts" of the person: for while the connections discussed previously all lay in the area of the functions, this connection is one by which the entire mantle of the functions (2 Cor. 5:1-8) is nothing more than one of the relata.

Though meaning well, Christians, for reasons going back to Plato, the Orphics, or Descartes, are often mixed up on matters concerning body and soul. Many are convinced, for example, that they *have* a soul, and an *immortal* one at that. But God, in Genesis 2, did not *give* Adam a soul; by the power of God's spirit he *became* a soul, a living being. Dualisms in anthropology are not acceptable. Hart makes a similar point concerning human spirituality:

> A person is not a body *and* a spirit. The human body is a spiritual body and the human spirit is a bodily spirit. The entire person is a body; the entire person is a spirit. Spirit is not a separate entity dwelling within a body. The human body is not simply a physical corpus or an organism. A person is referred to as a spirit simply as an indication of the specific and peculiar centeredness of all human action. It is not centered by any of the human functions. Rather, in humanity the concentrated integrality of all functional diversity is found in the openness of the person to the origin and destiny of the universe. And a person is able to be an integral and centered being in conscious concentration on this origin and destiny. (279)

Human beings are of one piece, called in every phase and facet of their lives to glory in their Maker. The human being in its totality is directed by the living habits of the heart. On that score, human beings *are* souls, earthlings, human earthly creatures of God. Their home is not in heaven, nor were they ever meant to be or become heavenly creatures.

CONTOURS OF SCRIPTURAL THOUGHT PATTERNS

Given these anthropological ponderings, there is no need to deny the separability of the soul from the body at death—that is the miracle of life after death. At death, because of sin, the whole person is rent in two in a way similar to the infamous guillotine: the head rolls and the trunk drops. Soul and body, like the rolling head and falling trunk, simply never have existed separately before then. Nor did God ever intend that they ought to be separate. To then confess the resurrection of the body is to know that in Jesus Christ we will be made *whole* again.

God does not put souls into bodies. As we saw in our survey of history, the question, "When does the soul get put in the body?" is a pseudo-problem. The Bible tells us that God created Adam out of the dust of the earth and breathed into him the breath of life, and he became a living *nephesh*, a living being. And yet, still in line with Scripture, it can be said that the direction setting heart, the inside, the soul, the inner man, is primary, is the person's central core. Out of it are the issues, the wellspring of life, for good or for evil, in love or in hate, obeying or disobeying. What lives in one's heart directs the bodily cloak of integrated and modally irreducible functions. The spiritual core—our living obediently or disobediently—permeates in, under, and through everything we are about; from the way we spend our money to what we do in bed, to the kinds of groceries we buy, to whether we recycle, to how and why and what we adore during our lifetime. All of those things and more are moved by and rooted in what lives in our hearts. There too, the antithesis of good and evil rages.

Before moving on, a misguided assumption found among some Christians should be addressed having to do with a "faculty psychology." In the Augustinian tradition, for example, is a long-standing tendency to see memory, mind, and will as three separate but related "faculties" of the soul (Greek: *psyche*) that image the Trinity in human beings. Others distinguish other "faculties." But I would agree with Calvin Seerveld (1981) that such talk should be avoided. He suggests that

> a human's energy, metabolic processes, desires, ability to control things, attempts to imagine things, communicate verbally, think, and other distinct functions are not to be understood as "faculties," some sort of autonomous powers which she or he has corralled and tries to keep in subjugated order. No, all the discernible ways

humans can act are the very defining, cosmic, operating order of reality which each then as an individuality-structured entity enjoys. These ways of being-there in God's world which a woman or man bodies forth are facets of God's ordinances for all kinds of things, their existential reality. And the full-bodying tin-can human breathes, feels, opens a door, thinks, and does all the rest, not as if these were ontologically separate compartments one "participates" in; but all the many mutually irreducible ways in which a woman or man functions are interpenetrating, intra-related moments of his or her concrete existence. (77)

God's command to his children, "Love the Lord your God with all your heart [and with all your mind] and with all your soul and with all your strength [or might, means, and wealth]" (Deuteronomy 6:5) does not suggest that we have separate faculties, but that we are to love and humbly serve him boldly in and with the fullness of our being.

Other functors are defined by a leading function, and we did use the term "pistic functor" once to circumscribe human beings. We have just seen, however, that no function (or "faculty") can fully define who the total human being is and that good and evil ultimately depend on the obedient or disobedient direction of the human heart. However, the pistic function is not simply one among many human subject functions. On the one hand, human pistic functioning very clearly guides all of experience and helps keep it open. On the other hand, as Hart puts it,

[Pistical functioning] structurally qualifies, that is functionally determines and defines the nature of only a certain number of specific human acts and relationships. These are acts of faith, and phenomena such as prayer and worship. Moreover, the specifically qualified faith relations are found in institutional relationships such as the church. In all other human functioning, the faith functions only guide human life and keep experience open. Since there is no higher function to which this opening up can be directed, it is directed to the origin and unity of all of reality. This source, we will recall, is also the origin of unity for human existence. (276-7)

Pistical functioning remains unique in that all human functions anticipate this most complex of subject functions. It in turn provides for or disallows the openness of human experience to what lies beyond the limits of our subjective existence. A person's life is not functionally closed off. Human *pistis* always involves committed acceptance of the ultimate, or a pretender, in an act of submission to true revelation, or to what people mistakenly embrace as a trustworthy revelation. In this way all of one's human being is open to (what people in faith take to be) the ordering principle and origin of reality.

All of earthly life was intended to be an appealing, colorful, diverse, and stimulating single interwoven fabric. If all people shared the same assurance we have in Jesus Christ by the power of his Holy Spirit, there would be no rifts, no antithesis, no religious division—only functional diversity.

3. THE STRUCTURE OF THE KINGDOMS AND OF HUMANKIND

In the previous section we dealt with the structure of things and persons. In so doing the concrete existence and interwoven complexity of that which is subject in an earthly way was approached in a variety of ways. Nevertheless, our meandering reflections still are a far cry from actual concrete existence. Any functor, be it thing or person, is, after all, an individual creature, but one that also always stands in genetic connection with other things of its kind. This idea is nothing new. Everybody knows that each functor within animalkind falls into a subgrouping dependent upon a common genetic or internal morphological structuration. Something similar can be said about atoms and minerals as well as about peonies and people. All of these also take their own place in religion. Consequently, if we want to see that which is subject in an earthly way to God and his law, these two traits, at least, have to be discussed.

The Structure of the Realms

That which is subject in an earthly way, be it human or not, does not stand by itself but is included genetically in one or another realm. Consequently we have to discuss the variety of these realms, or functoral communities, and then their mutual connection.

The Variety of the Realms

Earthly subjects, creatures, entities, call them what you will, exhibit a variety of genetic connections or kingdoms: at the very least, the realm of physical things, the realm of plants, the realm of animals, and the realm of human beings. Biologists may want to be more precise when it comes to fungi and algae, but these four are sufficient for our purposes. As Hart points out, "[If] an entity is truly to exist in our space-time world, then it must either be a physical thing, an organism, an animal, or a person. Whatever is not one of these four will have to be accounted for in terms of functions of these four, or relations of or among them" (269).

To the extent these genetic connections are all "realms," there is a similarity. To the extent a variety exists, there is also a diversity. On the basis of previous discussions, we can also state concerning the similarity of things belonging to one realm that all have leading functions in the same modality. So too there will be a similarity in the number of subject functions and object functions and a similarity in the structure of each of these functions in connection with the number and the nature of the anticipations and retrocipations. There is also a similarity in the modal determination of the intra-individual and inter-individual interrelations. Concerning the diversity, we can say that the things belonging to different realms differ in the modality of the leading function.

But we note another point of similarity and difference between the realms. As of yet we have said little about *genesis*, that is, about the process of becoming, about the movement from earlier to later. When we take the genetic connection into account we find, first of all, that all things, except for the ones God created first in the beginning, came and come from previous ones. The rule *nihil ex nihilo*—nothing comes from nothing—holds for later things without exception. Second, the genesis of these things, taken in the sense of the way in which something comes to be, takes place *within* the realm to which the functor in question belongs. The things of one realm are not genetically interrelated with the things of another realm.

What is unique about genetic connections is the evolving of the younger thing out of one or more previously existing older things. This evolving, therefore, is completely different from the evolving that supporters of the functionalistic theory of evolution teach, that is, evolutionism. According to them, more complex subject functions come forth from, evolve from, less complex subject functions. Were that the case, for example, that physical-chemical factors contributed to generate organic life where there was none before, we could no longer speak of modal irreducibility.

All genetic connections follow a rather simple scheme. One thing a genetic connection always includes is the transition of one or more things from an intra-individual relationship to an inter-individual relationship: one (or more) becomes two (or more). For example, an atom becomes an ion and an electron; one mushroom reproduces asexually via spores and so becomes many; one amoeba multiples by fission forming two amoebae; a pregnant woman gives birth to one or more children. An apple tree can produce tens of genetically identical apples, each of which is individually unique. Water molecules divide into hydrogen and oxygen atoms. But never does a separated part ever maintain the identity of the one from which it comes.

When two or more entities are involved in the genesis of a younger entity, then an additional transition takes place prior to the one mentioned above. In that case the constituent parts that were originally related inter-individually (and will later become the younger entity) together enter into an intra-individual relationship: two (or more) become one (or more). For example, two (or more) atoms or molecules become one (or more) molecule(s); or two become one in bisexual (egg + sperm) reproduction, e.g., in the case of poppies, pandas, and people. An apple is the result of sexual reproduction, of two things coming together to become indistinguishably single. A child also is the fruit of a husband and a wife; it is constituted from two components that become indissolubly one. It is incomprehensible that anything or anyone could separate out these two components, let alone that once divided, one or both would be self-identically the same person as that child.

It is interesting to note that in the case of chemical combinations, the change is apparent in all of the subject functions. Not only the energetic function changes (an oxygen atom "behaves" differently than an oxygen molecule), but also the spatial (change in constellation) and the arithmetic (unit) functions change. It can also be noted that these transitions do not involve or imply an increase in the number of subject functions. And as for human reproduction, it has to do with the human being as a whole person, including the soul in the sense of heart. Every person after Adam and Eve came from two others, except for Jesus Christ.

The Connection Between the Different Realms

Although there is no genetic connection between the realms, they do not exist completely separate from each other either. This is obvious from the many relationships between things belonging to the different kingdoms. These relationships are of two basic kinds. In one case, there is an affinity between subjects belonging to different realms. In the other case, the subject-object relationship predominates.

As for the *affinity* between subjects from different realms, we can say that there are many kinds of inter-regnal connections (connections between realms). Involuntary cooperation is one kind: the sun generating warmth on the earth, the roots of plants preventing erosion, bees pollinating flowers while gathering honey. These can be said to all "work together," to the extent that this cooperation is in some ways like human activity. But one should be careful not to anthropomorphize the activity of nonhuman things involved in this inter-regnal cooperation.

Inter-regnal connections of affinity are also evident when the relationship between subject functions of functors from different realms is paired with the correlation active-passive, as when the growth of plants and animals is intentionally promoted by human beings. A 4-H champion and its owner don't part ways easily. The affinity is even stronger when the inter-relation shifts from an inter-individual to an intra-individual one. For example, inorganic salts are a basic requirement for plants and animals as well as human beings. These two are combined in other ways when we look at the biospheric environmental nexus of which all are a part.

Inter-regnal connections are also very evident in *subject-object relations*. Here the activity of a member of the higher realm directs itself to or unfolds one or more things of another realm in their object functioning. This subject-object interrelation exists between all of the realms. A plant will use a stone to support or protect itself. Animals use plants for food and nests, but they also fertilize flowers, spread seeds, and provide manure. This connection plays an even more important role in the relationship of people to things in the nonhuman realms. Hart highlights how crucial humankind's dependence on other creatures is and suggests that subjects making things from objects is quite natural:

We need air to breathe, water to drink, seeds or meat to eat, the earth to walk on, and the rivers in which to swim. Without trees to burn or to make shelters, animals to ride or to pull our burdens, and the natural resources to make our utensils and instruments, human existence would not only be impoverished, but we would be unable to exist. We not only have functions on levels shared with others, but we also depend on other realms for our existence. By our existing in communal continuity, the environment is objectively developed in farmland, raw materials, domestic animals, dams, canals, planted forests, and now even in attempts to harness the energy of the sun. All of these objective cultural realities have a great impact on the "natural" environments. Insofar as humanity is one with the rest of nature, however, these impacts are human, though not unnatural. (275-6)

In the organic law sphere people, animals, and plants function as subjects, while physical things function as objects. In the psychic law sphere people and animals function as subjects, while plants and physical things function as objects. With respect to functioning as subjects, we find then, a parallel in the organic mode of being between people and plants and animals; in the psychic, and in some cases in the formative, between people and animals. In the more complex modes of being this parallel does not hold true. Here humans alone function as normed subjects, and functors from other realms are present only as objects.

Human knowing depends on much more than the subject-object relation. Think, for example, of your understanding of yourself and others. Nonetheless, the subject-object relation plays a crucial role: if physical things, plants, and animals did not function as objects in the analytic law sphere, even nonscientific knowledge about these realms would be out of the question.

Likewise, in the formative law sphere the subject-object relation is not the only one. Note that cooperation is primarily a subject-subject relationship. But here too, the subject-object relation is very important. Obviously the formative law sphere has a different character than the analytical. It is not after a knowing, but rather a controlling or mastering of the object by the subject. Turned to the past, our interest is in reconstruction. When in this mode of functioning we turn our eye to the future, our interest touches the field of construction and, ultimately, technology.

The Structure of Humankind

Integrally interwoven with being a human is one's being a fellow-creature, bound together with other selves in society and neighborhoods. Taken more broadly, the human race is also connected with other realms. People are not bound to any particular environment, but we all do live in some environment. Humans adapt, more or less well, to their environment and use its elements to adapt that environment to their habitation. Partially on the basis of these connections, people build societal relationships and institutions. These sometimes compete for time and attention, but all are included in the task that humankind is called to complete: "Till the garden and care for it." This task is given to humankind by God. Hence, even more important than these connections is the relation in which the human race stands religiously, that is, in relation to God. Consequently, we now have to deal with these connections and with religion.

The Societal Connections

Societal connections occur only in human life: clubs, corporations, school boards, associations, cooperatives and businesses, guilds, states, families, marriages, education, ecclesiastical denominations. All these connections display the following traits. They are *formed* connections by virtue of their formative basis. Their semantic character comes out in the fact that *consultation*, conviction, and convincing are everywhere present as constitutive factors. These societal connections derive the common trait of the presence of *the authority-respect correlation* from the social function. Furthermore, the leading function of such a connection determines its destination, its purpose, its primary focus. Finally, those in authority have to *positivize* the norm and maintain the subsequent positive laws that hold for that particular connection (doing so, of course, not without contact with those who owe respect).

In every societal relationship, authority and those who bear authority (we also say, "who are in authority") should be clearly distinguished. Don't confuse your parents with the office of being parents. The way the present president fulfills his responsibility may not be equated with the office he fills. So also, the authority and respect these people have hinges on more than their popularity. Undoubtedly, those who bear authority in freely formed associations are people selected and acknowledged by others. But the presence of the correlation authority-respect rests not on custom or whim, but on the structure of the cosmos and, hence, goes back to a creation ordinance. It is worth remembering that just because the office exists and is filled "by the grace of God" in no way implies that office bearers have something divine or infallible within or about themselves.

Part of the task of those who are called to give leadership and bear authority is to maintain the positivized laws. Positivized law, in this context, refers to specific translations, defined applications for a particular people, or time, or place, of what general laws (norms) of God require of us. We know Micah 6:8 instructs us to act justly, to love mercy, and to walk humbly with our God; "positivized law" in church, family, government, and business tries to answer the question as to specifically what does *doing* Micah 6:8 mean in our day. Maintaining these particular rules and regulations for church, family, government, business, and association includes two facets. First, if the positivized laws no longer fit the changed constellation or if they display gaps or loop-holes, then they ought to be replaced or amended. Maintaining rules and regulations that are out of date brings injustice with it. Second, office bearers have to maintain the connection against those who, though belonging to that connection, try to withdraw themselves from requirements that the cooperation in this connection sets. For example, the government that requires military duty for all its citizens cannot limit itself to simply making a list of those who refuse to serve in the armed forces. Whoever refuses, whatever the motive, must also bear the consequences. The same goes for councils who call members to congregate, for parents who set curfews, clubs that require dues.

The interhuman (subject-subject) relationship is predominant in these connections where living together and orderly cooperation are basic requirements. All the same, the subject-object relation is also present. As rehearsed earlier, the number of classes of object functions is even greater in these spheres than in the organic and psychic spheres. The subject-object relation in a societal context is also different in nature. The subject-side of this relation has priority and exihits a dominating character. An example may clarify this relationship.

Business is one kind of societal connection. Subject-subject relationships between employer and employee, between shop owner and customer, between baker and farmer are primary in this regard. But it is not only people that have a part to play here: physical things, plants, and animals all possess an object function in the economic mode of being by virtue of their created structure. Hence, they are all potential economic goods, independent of all human activity. Were this not the case, there could be no talk of price. Yet the price of these goods is something other than the goods themselves. The "price" is determined by the need of the human subjects, who can intentionally raise and lower it. To open up this aspect of creation is part of our calling as human beings. The point to remember is, of course, that we have been commanded to do so obediently, to do so with a healthy sense of economic responsibility.

There is a variety of kinds of societal connections. Their diversity can be attributed to differences in their leading functions. For clubs and associations the leading function is the social; for business and factory, the economic; for the state, the jural; for marriage, friendship, and the family, the trothic; and for the institutional church, the pistic function.

Societal connections, like those just mentioned, are not functors, properly defined. A marriage does not have a physical subject function nor does a business have mass or weight. State and labor unions are not independent action units, but modally qualified associational forms of interhuman relationships. Each connection includes all of the human functions between the formative and its leading function. That means, for example, that the institutional church has a trothic side ("brothers and sisters" in Christ), a jural side (church discipline), an economic side (annual budget), in addition to a social (fellowship), analytic (belief), semantic (symbols), aesthetic (liturgy), and formative dimension. Likewise the family has its own rules, decorum, and financial side—so also with the state, and right on down the line. Nevertheless, similar modal dimensions in different societal connections differ from each other due to the fact that all of these functions are also defined differently given the variance in leading function. That is why, for example, church, family, and governmental finances, and discipline for that matter, are different in character, the one from the other.

In a similar vein, the task of the office bearers in each societal connection is unique. That is what Abraham Kuyper was getting at when he spoke of *sphere sovereignty*. Each societal connection (= sphere) has a God-given task and competence that are defined by the intrinsic nature of that sphere. On the one hand, those in authority in each life connection have to positivize the norms holding for that connection (and not others) in consultation with those who pay respect. General norms dictated by God from the foundations of the world need to be applied to the here and now, and that is the God-given responsibility of those in authority. On the other hand, his point was that one sphere should not lord it over another. Big business, the state, or even the institutional church may not usurp the responsibilities and decision-making powers of another sphere. Each is directly responsible to God. Kuyper's insight has lost nothing of its power. One can sooner say that its significance and influence have increased. It is considered by many as a hallmark of Calvinism.

To avoid misunderstanding, however, one ought to distinguish, more explicitly than Kuyper did, between sovereignty and relative autonomy. The first has to do with modal differences, the second with individual differences. Kuyper insisted that all of life falls under the sovereignty of God, but also that within society family and factory are each sovereign for their own life connection; the first is trothically qualified, the second is qualified economically. Within the circle of both kinds of connections, however, exists a great diversity. There are many families and many factories and businesses. Naturally, it makes no sense—in fact, it is confusing—to also call the freedom of the different families with respect to each other's internal rules "sovereignty." In any case, there is a difference here, and a distinction in terminology can only clarify things further. One finds these differences elsewhere as well. Countries have the same sovereignty, namely, jural sovereignty, which should not be violated by big businesses or churches. However, with respect to each other, countries are not sovereign but relatively autonomous, as are the provinces or states within the territory of the same country.

And while we're making distinctions, one should also sharply distinguish relative autonomy from two other matters.

First of all, relative autonomy differs from autonomy as we found it flaunted in the history of philosophy, namely, in the sense of the self-sufficiency declaration of human beings with respect to God. Autonomy in this sense stands over against heteronomy, that is to say, over against the acknowledgement that God, not we, lays down the law. Second, relative autonomy is different from autarchy—the attempt on the part of a state or a family to be completely self-sufficient. Relative autonomy realizes other legitimate societal connections, each of which must be given the respect due it.

What about the relation of societal connections to *religion*? Is there really a relationship here? Family, church, state, business, and other societal connections are all related to the human heart. Their character is functional, such that their contours may change over the course of time. But the realization of their structures, which do not change, is rooted in the obedient or disobedient human response to a task given by God and entrusted to humankind throughout the ages. It is here, in carrying out this task, that the direction of the human heart is decisive. The question is always, "In which direction is this or that societal connection headed?"

Here too, it is the law of God that is the criterion for good and evil, right and wrong. What does he require of us in our dealings with fellow human beings? As summarized by Christ (Matt. 22:39), with reference to the Torah (Lev. 19:18), we are "to love our neighbor as ourselves." But who is our neighbor? In the light of Scripture we can say that our neighbor is every person to the extent we are placed in his or her proximity during the divinely directed course of our lives.

To love our neighbor as ourselves means "in the same way." This surely implies that we also ought to love ourselves—of course, in the same way as we love our neighbor. But then—lest we begin to chase our own "tail"—"as" requires a criterion that lies beyond the one love (of self) as well as the other love (of neighbor). That criterion, too, is found in the word of God to his stewards: we are to love ourselves and our neighbor as images of God to the extent we and they, as children and servants, are like unto the Father in Heaven.

The structure of this love is antithetical. That is, the command that requires me to love my neighbor and myself to the extent that we display traits of our Father also requires that I hate my neighbor and myself to the extent that we display the opposite. The character of this love is pre-functional, defining one's very being. We are not talking here about warm fuzzies or romance, but about what moves us in everything we do and refuse to do. It does not coincide with our functional existence, because this love (or hate) defines that existence. Hart describes how this love or hate for God or idol permeates a human's whole being.

> "Being a Marxist" is likely to be characteristic of much more in a person's life than "being an economist." It has implications for life-style, educational strategies, political decisions, attitudes to organized religion, and a host of other strategic areas of action. "Being a Marxist" seems not to be confined to a single area of a person's life, but "being an economist" or "being a garden enthusiast" clearly is. A person can thus be an economist *in addition* to being a good many other things. On the other hand, a person is a Marxist *in everything* he says and does. In that latter sense he is not anything *else* (on the same level) in addition to being a Marxist. (93)

One should not equate this love with a specific functional relationship, as with trothic relationships, and certainly not with a sexual relationship, although this love permeates both of these as well. Love here is a matter and attitude of the heart with respect to our neighbor before the face of God.

Neither loving or disregarding our neighbor nor the command to love our neighbor stands alone. They are dominated by the command to love God above all. In this way one's relationship to his neighbor is also dependent on religion.

Religion

Although we continually reckoned with the Word of God in the preceding pages, the actions of God presupposed in that Word and our response to that Word have not been discussed in any detail.

The reason for this delay is primarily that not everything that can be observed in creation can be dealt with at the same time. But why postpone the discussion of religion to the very end? Certainly not because it is of little significance, but rather because it dominates the whole of human existence, and it was therefore appropriate to first analyze that which is dominated.

We now also must examine religion more closely. For however great the diversity we have found so far in the basic structure of the earthly subject, we certainly have not grasped the earthly subject in its full concreteness as long as religion has not been discussed.

In addressing ourselves to this part of our task, we must emphasize beforehand that it is impossible, in a study such as this one, to give anything approaching a complete discussion of religion. We will restrict ourselves to a summary of essentials. We must limit ourselves to the most important questions in this regard, namely: What is religion? What does it presuppose? and What is its structure?

What is religion? Religion is the relationship of humankind to the first and great commandment: "You shall love the Lord your God with all your heart, and with all your soul, and with all your mind, and with all your might." From this summary of the law, that was given by Christ (Matt. 22:37)—following in turn the Old Testament (Deut. 6:5)—it is plain that God appears here as the God of the covenant. Therefore, *religion is the relationship of humankind to the God of the covenant in obedience and disobedience* to his fundamental law of love.

God's covenant with creation presupposes first of all the existence of God and his creative ability. The activity of Logos and Spirit play a special role in this creative activity (Ps. 33:6). This creating does not of course presuppose the existence of anything apart from God, like some kind of stuff that is waiting to be formed.

The covenant also presupposes the result of this activity, the existence of heaven and earth and specifically (as far as the earth is concerned) the existence of man. This man with all his interrelated functions was formed by God out of earth. He became a living soul by God's breathing into his nostrils the breath of life. Already with respect to this structure of living functor and modal functions, he differed from all other creatures. Moreover, he was created from the beginning in the image of God. His nature was good and being created, addressed, and directed to the good of God, he could reflect in the covenant as the concrete correlate of the Triune God, his glory on earth (cf. 2 Cor. 3:18). He was made ready to satisfy the requirements of God's Law in original righteousness.

The covenant also presupposes the establishment of this covenant between God and human beings on the part of God, including the appointment of an image bearer to the prefunctional office of mediator. Filling this office was the first Adam, by whom came death, and now the second Adam, in whom is life everlasting, Jesus Christ.

As for the structure of God's covenant: As in every covenant, so in a religious covenant there are, after its establishment, two parties: God and the human race in its religion. The instituting of the covenant is consequently "unilateral"; its structure is "bilateral" (two-sided). Present in the covenant from God's side is Logos-revelation. It always involves, on the one hand, the promise of blessing in the case of covenant-faithfulness and, on the other hand, the threat of curse in the case of covenant-breaking. From the side of the human race in its religion, there is always an appointed bearer of the prefunctional office, a mediator who must act before God in the things that must be performed on behalf of those comprehended in the covenant.

These are the ever present features of the covenant. Although they are beyond the scope of this survey of biblical thought patterns, one can find other features in the history of religion that are not constant. These features have to do, on the side of the law, with the content of the Logos-revelation, and on the side of religion, with the man invested with the office, with his relationship to the Word of God, and with the relation of those comprehended in the covenant to the office-bearer.

III. C. through E.
Guide Questions

131. Is Satan subject to God in a heavenly way or in an earthly way?

132. Describe the three different kinds of differences. Which one does not exist by virtue of creation?

133. List three things in your immediate vicinity. Using the list of modal aspects, indicate how each of these functors functions or could function in at least three of these 15 modes. Do not use the same mode twice.

134. What defines a law sphere and what does such a domain include?

135. What is the difference between subject functions and object functions?

136. Any relationship has two sides. Explain and illustrate using two examples.

137. What do retrocipations refer "back" to? What do anticipations anticipate?

138. What is it about most "-isms" that makes them at least plausible?

139. Which of the three kinds of difference is dual and antithetical?

140. What defines human beings as human beings?

141. Are your heart, mind, soul, and strength "faculties"?

142. First came *creatio ex nihilo*; then came the rule *nihil ex nihilo*. Explain.

143. What are "inter-regnal connections"? Give two examples.

144. List three societal connections, each having a different leading function. Elaborate on the formative, semantic, and social dimension of each of these three societal connections.

145. How are "norms" crucial to Abraham Kuyper's point in advocating "sphere sovereignty"?

146. What follows from the command to love your neighbor *as yourself*?

147. What is religion? What does it presuppose? What is its structure?

III. E.
THE CONNECTION BETWEEN HEAVEN AND EARTH

Much more could be said about the basic structures of created earthly reality, but not much more about heavenly reality. As for the relationship between heaven and earth, we know, only on the basis of Scripture, that angels make a difference on earth, for better and for worse, but also that since being tempted Christ has gained the upper hand. All the power in heaven and on earth has been given to Christ as creature. He not only is the second Adam, but stands at the head of all the angels as well. In Jesus Christ all things hold together.

> He is the image of the invisible God, the firstborn over all creation. For by him all things were created: things in heaven and on earth, visible and invisible, whether thrones or powers or rulers or authorities; all things were created by him and for him. He is before all things, and in him all things hold together. And he is the head of the body, the church; he is the beginning and the firstborn from among the dead, so that in everything he might have the supremacy. For God is pleased to have all his fullness dwell in him, and through him to reconcile to himself all things, whether things on earth or things in heaven, by making peace through his blood, shed on the cross.
>
> Colossians 1:15-20

* * * * *

In Conclusion

In Christ Christians see reality, at least in principle, as it really is. The horizon of creation a well as the breadth and depth of sin and redemption are revealed to them in Scripture. Because they see the "whole" first, Christians can approach in confidence the situations, questions, and confrontations that every day brings.

Given the certainty that we have in Christ and the promise of his Spirit, Christians must learn to proceed with a forthright fervor by positioning themselves positively and equipping themselves better through discerning inquiry and biblical thought patterns.

The action that faith requires demands a dimension of zeal. Not that life must be lived in the "fast lane" or that despair may

never show its face. But as time and opportunity present themselves, Christians may not shy from their advantage. Rather,
they must learn to display an uninhibited and forthright fervor.
Confected clichés and slithery self-righteousness, as always, are
out of place here. Given the fact that Christians are not their
own but belong body and soul to Jesus Christ, the accent may
fall on the *difference* this belonging makes, on the *truth* and *reality*
of human creaturely life, fallen and now redeemed, in Christ
here and now.

   Soli Deo gloria.

APPENDIX ONE

Guide   Questions

for   Albert M. Wolters'

Creation Regained: Biblical Basics For A Reformational Worldview. Grand Rapids, MI: Eerdmans, 1985.

[Chapter I]
1. Define "worldview" and explain the four basic components of your definition.
2. Describe the role of worldview in life.
3. Discuss the relation between Scripture and worldview. Be familiar with Romans 12:2 and 15:4.
4. What is unique about the reformational worldview? In which ways does it differ from other worldviews advocated by Christians.

[Chapter II]
5. Explain the meaning and importance of the correlation between creating activity and created order. Be familiar with 2 Peter 3:5,7.
6. Law stands for "the totality of God's ordering acts toward the cosmos." Explain. Be familiar with Psalm 33:9.
7. Describe the distinction between "norms" and "laws of nature." Take note of Psalm 147!
8. How has the distinction referred to in question 7 been distorted in the western and eastern world?
9. Distinguish between general and particular laws, explaining what is meant by each term.
10. As regards "Word," be familiar with the relation between Genesis 1, John 1, Colossians 1, and Hebrews 1.
11. Briefly summarize what Wolters says about "the scope of creation." Why does he refer to 1 Timothy 4, Romans 13, and 1 Peter 2?
12. What is creational revelation? Be familiar with Psalm 19, Acts 14:17, Romans 1:18-20 and 2:14-15.

13. Explain the following statements or terms and passages of Scripture:
    a. conscience as intuitive attunement to creational normativity;
    b. the two meanings of wisdom; and
    c. Job 38-41 and Isaiah 28:23-29 as to "creation."
14. Explain the nature and importance of the fundamental knowability of the creation order.
15. What is meant by "spiritual discernment"? Describe what kind of dualism must be avoided.
16. Explain how creational and Scriptural revelation are incommensurate and commensurate.
17. Indicate how "spectacles" and "a miner's lamp" can be used to illustrate the relationship of God's revelation in his word and works.
18. Explain the statement: "The Scriptures are like a verbal commentary on the dimly perceived sign-language of creation." Take note of the images of blue-print and tape-recording.
19. How does the development of creation imply civilization?
20. What is meant by the creation (or cultural) mandate, especially in relation to history or the historical process?
21. Which image does Wolters use to avoid the false dilemma of cultural optimism and pessimism? Take special note of the statement: "The ravages of sin do not annihilate the normative creational development of civilization, but are rather parasitical upon it."
22. Describe the meaning and importance of 2 Peter 3:10, especially in relation to Revelation 21:24,26.
23. Describe how gnosticism and humanism deny the goodness of creation. Be familiar with 1 Timothy 4:4.

[Chapter III]

24. Describe the nature of the Fall and its effects on societal, cultural, and personal lives and on the nonhuman world. Be familiar with Romans 8:19-22.
25. Explain the importance of the following statements concerning the relation between sin and creation:
    a. Sin neither abolishes nor becomes identified with creation.
    b. The perversion of creation must never be understood as a sub-distinction within the order of creation, nor must creation ever be explained as a function of perversion and redemption.
26. Sin is alien in creation. Explain.

27. Explain the meaning of structure and direction.

28. With respect to the relationship of structure and direction, explain the following statements:
    a. Creation is like a leash which keeps the vicious dog in check.
    b. Structure is never entirely obliterated by (mis)direction.
    c. Evil is not inherent in the human condition.
    d. The law is like a spring.

29. What are the three meanings of "world" in the Bible?

30. What does Wolters say about the compartmentalizing of life into sacred and secular realms?

31. Mention and briefly explain some of the different words used to refer to the perversion and distortion of creation.

[Chapter IV]

32. In connection with redemption, be familiar with the following:
    a. restoration and re-creation;
    b. reconciliation, renewal, salvation and regeneration; and
    c. *donum superadditum.*

33. "If salvation does not bring more than creation, it does not bring less either." Explain.

34. Regarding the Kingdom of God, be familiar with:
    a. its basic meaning;
    b. its demonstration in Jesus' ministry (Matthew 11:4,5);
    c. the meaning of "already present" and "not yet reality";
    d. its call for restoration, not repristination; and
    e. its claim on all departments and stages of creation.

35. Concerning the tendency to restrict the Kingdom of God, explain the following:
    a. pietism (Luke 17:21);
    b. the view of Roman Catholics and many Protestants;
    c. dispensationalism; and
    d. liberal protestantism.

36. Explain the two-realm theory.

37. Explain the statement: "The contrast here is not between two realms but between two regimes."

38. Summarize the illustration given on pages 69-70.

39. "The horizon of creation is at the same time the horizon of sin and salvation." Explain.

[Chapter V]

40. Noting again what is meant by structure and direction (or creation and antithesis), take special note of the following two statements:
    a. "the religious conflict rages for the sake of the created structure."
    b. "they see abnormality where others see normality, and possibilities of renewal where others see inevitable distortion."

41. Concerning the first meaning of "reformation" (of persons, society and culture), explain the following:
    a. the distinction between sanctification and consecration;
    b. 1 Timothy 4:5; Romans 14:14; Zechariah 14:20-21; and
    c. cultic reduction of sanctification.

42. Concerning the second meaning of "reformation," explain the following:
    a. the distinction between progressive renewal and violent overthrow;
    b. the positive meaning of reformation, especially why it can reject both revolution and conservatism. Take note of the claim: "Conservatism leaves things internally untouched and revolution annihilates things. Reformation renews and sanctifies them."

43. Concerning societal renewal, explain the following:
    a. why the order of society is not the result of invention and convention;
    b. the distinction between structure and positivisation (give examples);
    c. the meaning and importance of "differentiated responsibility";
    d. totalitarianism; and
    e. two ways of perverting God's order for society.

44. Using the example of aggression, describe the false dilemma of ailment or cure and indicate the solution Wolters suggests.

45. Describe the false dilemma that has arisen in connection with spiritual gifts and how it can be resolved.

46. Give a succinct and clear summary of Wolters' discussion of sexuality.

47. Summarize briefly the discussion of dance. Take special note of the statement: "We are always in danger of rejecting the creational in the name of the fall, and of accepting the fallen in the name of creation."

WORKS CITED

Bruffee, Kenneth A. *Collaborative Learning: Higher education, interdependence, and the authority of knowledge.* Baltimore, MD: Johns Hopkins University Press, 1993.

Bruyn, Theodore de. "Jerusalem versus Rome: The context of Augustine's assessment of the Roman Empire in the *City of God*," in *Christianity and the Classics: The acceptance of a heritage.* Lanham, MD: University Press of America, 1990.

Descartes, René. *The Philosophical Works of Descartes.* Trans. E. Haldane and G. Ross. Vol. 1. Cambridge: University Press, 1911.

Galilei, Galileo. *Discoveries and Opinions of Galileo.* Trans. Stillman Drake. New York: Doubleday, 1957.

Guinness, Os. *The American Hour: A time of reckoning and the once and future role of faith.* New York: The Free Press, 1993.

Hart, Hendrik. *Understanding Our World: An integral ontology.* Lanham, MD: University Press of America, 1984.

Hegel, G.W.F., *Science of Logic.* Trans. A.V. Miller. New York: Humanities Press, 1969.

Helleman, Wendy. "Basil's *Ad Adolescentes*," in *Christianity and the Classics.* Lanham: University Press of America, 1990: 31-51.

Kalsbeek, L. *Contours of a Christian Philosophy: An introduction of Herman Dooyeweerd's thought.* Amsterdam: Buijten & Schipperheijn, 1975.

Kirk, G.S., J.E. Raven, and M. Schofield. *The Presocratic Philosophers: A critical history with a selection of texts.* 2nd edition. Cambridge: Univerisity Press, 1983.

Kuyper, Abraham. *Lectures on Calvinism* (1898). Grand Rapids, MI: Eerdmans, 1931.

Middleton, J. Richard and Brian J. Walsh. *Truth is Stranger Than It Used to Be: Biblical faith in a postmodern age.* Downers Grove, IL: InterVarsity Press, 1995.

Moberg, David. "The Eyes of Faith." *Faculty Dialogue* Fall 1991: 147-153.

Oates, Whitney J., ed. *The Stoic and Epicurean Philosophers: The complete extant writings of Epicurus, Epictetus, Lucretius, Marcus Aurelius.* New York: Random House, 1940.

Plantinga, Alvin. "Advice to Christian Philosophers." *Faith and Philosophy* I (1984): 253-271.

Rorty, Richard. *Philosophy and the Mirror of Nature.* Princeton, NJ: Princeton University Press, 1979.

Russell, Betrand. *A History of Western Philosophy.* New York: Simon and Schuster, 1945.

Schuurman, Egbert. *Perspectives on Technology and Culture.* Trans. John H. Kok. Sioux Center, IA: Dordt College Press, 1995.

Seerveld, Calvin. "A Christian Tin-Can Theory of Man." *Journal of the American Scientific Affiliation* June (1981): 74-81.

Seerveld, Calvin. *Rainbows for the Fallen World: Aesthetic life and artistic task.* Toronto: Tuppence Press, 1980.

Seerveld, Calvin. "The Pedagogical Strength of a Christian Methodology in Philosophical Historiography" *Koers* 40, 4-6 (1975): 269-313.

Vollenhoven, Dirk H. T. *A Vollenhoven Reader: Essays on christian philosophy.* Trans. John H. Kok (forthcoming).

Vollenhoven, Dirk H. T. *Kort overzicht van de geschiedenis der wijsbegeerte voor de cursus paedagogiek.* Amsterdam: Theja, 1956.

Vollenhoven, Dirk H. T. *Isagogè Philosophiae.* Amsterdam: Theja, 1943.

Walsh, Brian J. and J. Richard Middleton. *The Transforming Vision: Shaping a christian worldview.* Downers Grove, IL: InterVarsity Press, 1984.

Wells, David. *God in the Wasteland: The reality of truth in a world of fading dreams.* Grand Rapids, MI: Eerdmans, 1994.

Wolters, Albert. *Creation Regained: Biblical basics for a reformational worldview.* Grand Rapids, MI: Eerdmans, 1985.

INDEX